Imperium

Structures and Affects
of Political Bodies

Frédéric Lordon

Translated by Andy Bliss

VERSO

London • New York

CENTRE
NATIONAL
DU LIVRE

Cet ouvrage publié dans le cadre du programme d'aide à la publication bénéficie du soutien du Ministère des Affaires Etrangères et du Service Culturel de l'Ambassade de France représenté aux Etats-Unis. This work received support from the French Ministry of Foreign Affairs and the Cultural Services of the French Embassy in the United States through their publishing assistance programme.

This work was published with the help of the French Ministry of Culture – Centre national du livre
Ouvrage publié avec le concours du Ministère français chargé de la culture – Centre national du livre

This work received the French Voices Award for excellence in publication and translation. French Voices is a programme created and funded by the French Embassy in the United States and FACE Foundation.

French Voices logo designed by Serge Bloch

This English-language edition first published by Verso 2022
Translation © Andy Bliss 2022
Foreword © Alberto Toscano 2022
Originally published in France as *Imperium. Structures et affects des corps politiques*
© La Fabrique 2015

1 3 5 7 9 10 8 6 4 2

Verso
UK: 6 Meard Street, London W1F 0EG
US: 20 Jay Street, Suite 1010, Brooklyn, NY 11201
versobooks.com

Verso is the imprint of New Left Books

ISBN-13: 978-1-78663-642-3
ISBN-13: 978-1-78663-640-9 (UK EBK)
ISBN-13: 978-1-78663-641-6 (US EBK)

British Library Cataloguing in Publication Data
A catalogue record for this book is available from the British Library

Library of Congress Cataloging-in-Publication Data
A catalog record for this book is available
from the Library of Congress

Typeset in Minion Pro by Hewer Text UK Ltd, Edinburgh
Printed and bound by CPI Group (UK) Ltd, Croydon CR0 4YY

Contents

Part III

THE HORIZON OF HORIZONTALITY

Foreword: Passions of State

by Alberto Toscano

In a crooked nod to Thomas Hobbes's *Leviathan*, the French edition of Frédéric Lordon's Spinozist essay on the affective dynamics of our political institutions sports its own frontispiece. Instead of the 'Mortall God', comprising untold subjects and looming over the Wiltshire landscape, drawn by Abraham Bosse for the 1651 edition of that founding text of our political modernity, we have the nineteenth-century Japanese painter Hokusai's universally reproduced *The Great Wave Off Kanagawa*. This initially perplexing allegory is soon clarified, as we are reminded that Baruch Spinoza, in his unfinished *Political Treatise*, defined *imperium* as the 'right which is determined by the power of a multitude'. Lordon, following Bernard Pautrat's French translation of the *Tractatus Politicus*, has opted to keep the term in Latin, wary that other renderings – such as 'dominion' or 'sovereignty' – would diminish its scope and impact. Albeit constructed out of its alienated subjects, Hobbes's state-machine still kept its kingly head; Hokusai's wave is nothing but water, and its might is not just charged with menacing dynamism but cresting toward dissolution. The state too, Lordon will insist, is nothing but the multitude – once we understand that this multitude cannot but produce an excess or transcendence (that is, a kind of *sovereignty*), compelled as it is to collect itself into a society. Accordingly, *imperium* should not be treated as an object of adoration or aversion, fantasy or fear, 'it merely describes a necessity' (p. 1).

Imperium is at one and the same time a polemical as well as a constructive project, firmly aimed at the current French and European political conjuncture, while building on Lordon's distinctive research programme. That programme, of a 'Spinozist social science', was inaugurated in 2002 by *La Politique du capital*, an inquiry into the conflict that pitted the BNP against Société Générale and Paribas in 1999. That study employed Spinoza's notion of *conatus* – the conflictive perseverance in being that in the *Ethics* individuated any entity or 'mode' – to argue for a vision of capital as an intrinsically political and antagonistic relation. This intellectual centaur – empirical inquiry wedded to seventeenth-century philosophy – is less bizarre than it might at first seem. That a Spinozist social science should be of French coinage is no accident: from the historical scholarship of Martial Gueroult to Alexandre Matheron's pioneering study of individual and community in Spinoza, from Gilles Deleuze's radical reinterpretation of Spinoza's philosophy of immanence to the centrality of Spinoza to the Althusserian project (not to mention the rich production of Spinozist studies by contemporary scholars in the Hexagon), France has an altogether impressive tradition of Spinoza interpretation. At the heart of this retooling of a seventeenth-century metaphysics for twentieth- and twenty-first-century ideological purposes is the liquidation of that 'Cartesian' subject animating the humanist visions of politics borne by phenomenology and existentialism. While the targets may have changed, Lordon's perspective remains anchored in this affirmation of Spinoza as the thinker who can emancipate us from the delusions of free will, allowing us to approach human behaviour in a disabused materialist vein.

In *L'intérêt souverain* (2006), the edited volume *Spinoza et les sciences sociales* (2008, with Yves Citton), *Capitalisme, désir et servitude* (2010, published by Verso in translation as *Willing Slaves of Capital*), *La société des affects* (2013), *Les affects de la politique* (2016) and *La condition anarchique* (2018), Lordon has consistently advanced the claim that Spinoza's theory of human action, built on the notions of *conatus*, desire (the essence of human being) and affect (the cause and pattern of desire), is capable, when brought into dialogue with critical and heterodox strands in economics, sociology and anthropology, of undoing paralysing antinomies between individual and collective, structure and agency, while crucially resisting the growing hegemony over the social sciences of a politically loaded metaphysics of liberalism. Against liberal and neo-liberal theories of atomised *subjects* of choice, Lordon proposes we take inspiration from the author of the *Ethics* to develop a *structuralism of the passions*. This is not a combinatorial structuralism à la Lévi-Strauss, but the generic assertion – which Lordon claims can be sourced in Marx, Bourdieu, Durkheim and Mauss, inter alia – that human beings are in the first instance moved by their passions, while in the final analysis these passions are determined by social structures. Unless we jettison political and social philosophies of 'the subject', he intimates, no such structuralism can emerge, and we shall continue to treat passionate individuals and impersonal structures as incompatible terms, devolved to separate disciplines in a disabling division of intellectual labour.

In *L'intérêt souverain*, Lordon applied this approach to the critique of anti-utilitarian theories of the gift economy (linked to the MAUSS research group), chided for converging with the very liberalism they nominally opposed in thinking of interest solely in the mode of the calculative reason of *homo oeconomicus*. In *Willing Slaves of Capital*, he argued that a Spinozist theory of desire and affect was able to produce insight into the capture of the desires of the dominated in contemporary labour and wage relations, and to bid farewell to the utopian tendencies in Marx; Lordon proposed we follow Spinoza instead in recognising the place of bondage to the passions in human affairs, and therefore the at best *regulative* character of communism (contrary to the misleading title of the English translation, Lordon is adamant that there is no such thing as *voluntary* servitude, since our complicity is a matter of *desire*, not *will*). *La société des affects* explores the relevance of such a Spinozist social science to a host of different concerns, including the sociology of Pierre Bourdieu, institutions as sites of struggle and the need to revitalise the relationship between philosophy and social science – native to the French sociological tradition from Auguste Comte to Émile Durkheim and Gabriel Tarde and beyond.

Such a project may sit strangely with Lordon's disciplinary location as an economist. The notion of a Spinozist political economy is far less discordant when we realise that Lordon is steeped in Regulation Theory. His dissertation was supervised by Robert Boyer and his contribution to the aforementioned volume on Spinoza and the social sciences is a co-authored essay with André Orlean, bringing Regulation Theory and Spinoza jointly to bear on the genesis of money and the state.[1] Regulation Theory always foregrounded the place of social norms, relations and institutions in forging the 'mode of regulation' capable of containing (for a time) the contradictions inevitably bodied forth by a given regime of accumulation. Lordon's turn to Spinoza can thus be seen as supplementing the Regulationist approach, positing a regime of desires and affects which doubles and supports a given economic configuration. The concern of a Spinozist social science is thus, in his words: 'the place of the passions in the institutional configurations that support regimes of accumulation and the general conditions of their loss of stability'.[2] Like the Regulationists, then, Lordon is concerned with periodisation, with the analytical (but also prescriptive) investigation into systemic change, the historical and geographical varieties of capitalism, but also, and increasingly, the urgency, forms and potential impasses of transitions *out of* capitalism. The turn to Spinoza is also intended to supplement and surpass Regulation Theory in another, political sense, by foregrounding the formation of 'common affects', of group passions, as a *conditio sine qua non* of social transformation. It is here that *Imperium*'s concern with our collective investments in institutional and state power comes to the fore.

That *Imperium* is to be understood both as a Spinozist treatise on the passions of state and as a conjunctural polemic becomes clearer when we observe that its arguments were first sketched out in an *excursus* in Lordon's 2014 *La Malfaçon* – a book building on his participation in the anti-austerity *Manifeste des économistes atterrés* and especially his blog for *Le Monde diplomatique*: *La pompe à phynance*. *La Malfaçon* – roughly translatable as 'factory defect' – skewered the 'Europeanist' leanings of the *soi-disant* French left, above all the journalists, academics and economists close to the now-moribund Socialist Party, whose achieved

---

1 The most interesting critical review of *Imperium* was published in a Regulation Theory journal. See Bruno Amable and Stefano Palombarini, 'Imperium: quelques remarques sur la philosophie de Frédéric Lordon', *Revue de la régulation. Capitalisme, institutions, pouvoirs*, 18, 2015, pp. 1–15. For Lordon's work within the Regulationist horizon, which had already homed in on the incompatibilities between financial markets and democracy, see *Les Quadratures de la politique économique. Infortunes de la vertu*, Albin Michel, 1997..

2 Frédéric Lordon, *La societé des affects. Pour un structuralisme des passions*, Seuil, 2013, p. 13..

mutation into a '*Droite Complexée*', or neurotic Right, Lordon captures with acerbic verve. *La Malfaçon* detailed the 'constitutionally right-wing' character of the European construction and the confiscation of sovereignty at the heart of a euro at the beck and call of German elite strategies, arguing for a break with the euro and the creation of a common (rather than single) currency, if needs be in a Europe without Germany. The critical ideological component of the polemic was the imperative to reconquer the oppositional language of nation and sovereignty, sequestered by the far right and abandoned by the left. Again, common affects were at stake.

But whereas the polemical targets of *La Malfaçon* where primarily on the cynical or deluded fringes of social democracy, *Imperium*'s arguments against a post-national consensus are oriented leftwards. Lordon confronts the spectrum of contemporary theoretical proposals for emancipatory politics with the 'paralogisms' that beset their affirmation of a communism shorn of communal or national belonging, as well as of durable and appropriate political structures – in other words a 'communism' without the common affects and institutions that could hold it together. It is as though, bewitched by the vanishing horizon of the state's withering away, today's radical theorists lack the means to think that even a transition beyond the state as we know it will not translate into a termination of the state as such or of its emotional infrastructures. Among the diverse targets of Lordon's critique, sometimes explicitly addressed but rarely discussed at great length, are Alain Badiou, Jacques Rancière, Toni Negri, David Graeber, Pierre Dardot and Christian Laval, and the Invisible Committee (stablemates in the radical imprint La Fabrique, and enduring sparring partners).[3] Lordon's general theory of the state is in this respect the counterpart to a critique of the general anti-statism, and repudiation of 'sovereignty' in some of the most prominent theories on the left. It cuts across the countless differences between anti-sovereigntist communisms and radicalisms to diagnose something like a spontaneous oppositional philosophy of the present.[4]

---

3 For a more sustained critical engagement with the anti-statist political imaginary of radical Left theory, Anglophone readers will have to wait for the translation of Lordon's 2019 *Vivre sans . . .*

4 This polemical contrast between the Spinozist theory of *imperium* and contemporary anti-statism largely bypasses the question of the capitalist state, and thus

The constructive complement to Lordon's polemic against the political and anthropological wishful thinking of today's communists involves enlisting Spinoza's political theory of affects, as developed in the *Ethics* and the *Political Treatise*, to produce a general theory of the 'state' (or a *theory of the general state*) grounded in a sociologically and economically informed political anthropology. Building on his prior efforts to generate Spinozist theories of capital and the social, *Imperium* proposes that a critical anthropological realism concerning the state can instruct left-wing thought in the weakness of a 'rationalist' (Badiou) or 'vitalist' (Invisible Committee) optimism that would ignore the lessons of Spinozism in its effort to envisage a communism beyond our 'passionate servitude'. For Lordon, such a servitude to our affects, and their contingent worldly causes, is what subtends the inescapable production of state-like institutions, which are both immanent (there are no otherworldly or immaterial sources for them save for the multitude itself) *and* transcendent (they exceed, capture, and alienate the powers of that multitude). The antagonistic potential of our *conatus* and the affects that guide it also dictates that any belonging, any identity, will always comprise an exclusion. To ignore these minimal and general traits of political anthropology is to succumb to political illusion. A Spinozist materialism, on the contrary, in a definition from Louis Althusser that Lordon likes to recall, means at the very least 'not telling ourselves stories'.

This dictum is all the more important in a moment of crisis, such as our own, which for Lordon has the virtue of demanding the abandonment of congealed theoretical specialisations – whence the opportunity for a 'Spinozist social science' – but in which the price of self-delusion is all the greater. Lordon has explored the political and economic facets of financial crises and their afterlives in several interventions over the last

---

those theories of the state, especially of Marxist manufacture, which theorised its 'withering' as a complex and protracted transition, rather than an irenic escape. Lordon has since incorporated these issues far more forthrightly into his purview, namely in *Figures du communisme* (2021), which can in turn be regarded as a theoretical balance sheet of a ruptural or revolutionary turn in his own work, accelerated by his militancy at the forefront of the 2016 *Nuit debout* social movement against the El Khomri labour legislation. See, 'Frédéric Lordon: We Are Not Friends with Everyone. We Do Not Come Bearing Peace', trans. David Broder, Verso blog, 25 April 2016, versobooks.com; and 'Frédéric Lordon: "With Nuit Debout the Fire Didn't Catch Hold" ', trans. David Broder, Verso blog, 12 September 2016, versobooks.com.

decade and a half or so (*Et la vertu sauvera le monde … - Après la débâcle financière, le salut par l' «éthique»; Jusqu'à quand? Pour en finir avec les crises financières; La crise de trop. Reconstruction d'un monde failli; On achève bien les Grecs. Chroniques de l'euro 2015*; and the financial tragicomedy in alexandrines *D'un retournement l'autre*). The horizon of crisis is palpably present in the urgency with which Lordon undertakes the theoretical detour through a reconstructed Spinozism to address the ambivalent persistence of 'nation', 'state' and 'sovereignty' – not to be confused with the mere endurance of their disastrous contemporary incarnations, or indeed with their capture by the ascendant forces of the right, for whom sovereignty will only be *popular* if it is *ethnic* or indeed *racial*.

The book's preface touches, in an intentionally impressionistic manner, on some egregious instances of contemporary state violence in France, evidently intending to dispel any suspicion of the author's complacency or complicity.[5] It starts with a vignette about CRS cops serving as de facto doormen for a gathering of the elite Le Siècle club at the Hotel Crillon and being greeted by chants of 'Capital's militia' (p. vii). No doubt, but not only that. Lordon suggests, advancing the proposition that while we should strive toward 'less law, fewer police and fewer institutions' (p. 258), that the outright abolition of repressive functions is not on the horizon. *Imperium* then moves to a programmatic introduction setting out the parameters of Lordon's Spinozist research programme, especially its preoccupation with the endurance of the state's affective and anthropological sources as a problem for emancipatory theories of politics. It unfolds in three parts. The first part, 'Groupings', is divided into three chapters, dealing separately with the 'paralogisms' incurred by those left positions that repudiate (national) belonging; the social as excess and elevation (in Jean Wahl's formulation, a 'trans-ascendance'), in which the power of the multitude generates its own pole of power and alienation; and the way in which, on the basis of

---

5 The brutality of the French repressive state apparatus has experienced a notable escalation even in the few years since the book was originally published, most glaringly in response to the Gilets Jaunes mobilisations. See Mathieu Rigouste, 'The violence of the French police is not new, but more people are seeing it now', *Guardian* 13 February 2020. For Lordon's own reflections on the police, see 'Frédéric Lordon: "The Police Force We Have Is Fucked Up, Racist to the Bone and Out of Control" ', trans. David Fernbach, Verso blog, 29 July 2021, versobooks.com.

a political anthropology of division and disagreement, 'verticality' emerges as a manner of unifying and holding in check the centrifugal, and potentially violent, features of the life of the multitude. The second part, 'The Elementary Structures of Politics', sets out the core elements of Lordon's Spinozist theory of the *imperium* as the 'right that defines the power of the multitude', and as an ineluctable dimension of verticality that no anarchism, communism or insurrectionalism can ultimately circumvent. It is an 'extremely general mechanism, at work in all large finite groups, the mechanism of immanent transcendence ... the power that the multitude has to affect itself' (pp. 79–80), the matrix of all powers in the social world. The three chapters in this part are concerned with, first, the *imperium* itself, or the 'general state' (defined as the 'process of self-formation, by which members conform to the norms of the group under the generic common affect of the *obsequium* (a common affect of recognition and compliance)' (p. 80); second, the definition of a political body and 'what it can do'; and third, the affects of politics. The third and final part, 'The Horizon of Horizontality', homes in on the critique of what Lordon perceives as a dominant trend in radical thought, with its denial of the inevitable if modifiable dimensions of statehood, nationhood, belonging and exclusion, with all their affective compulsions and consequences. The first chapter in this part focuses on the question of 'capture': the process whereby the powers of the multitude find themselves absorbed and crystallized by an immanent–transcendent form (the 'state'), especially in what concerns the reaction to disruptive, centrifugal violence; the second, on the anthropology of horizontality, explores what Lordon views as the shortcomings, foreclosures and wishful cogitations of those anarchist or anarchisant anthropologies (Pierre Clastres, Marshall Sahlins, James C. Scott, David Graeber) which, rather than taking stock of the ambivalence of the human social animal, treat antagonism and malignity as a product of a parasitic and purely alien state-machine; the third chapter in this part, 'Reaching for the Universal (A Political Ethics)', explores the conceptions of universality compatible with such a Spinozist political and philosophical anthropology, surveying the necessary institutionalisations, exclusions and particularities that perforce accompany even the most expansive and self-critical of emancipatory or communist projects. The conclusion then briefly revisits the question of capital's relationship to the state in this Spinozist frame (the subject matter of *Willing Slaves of Capital*), to finally conclude on a sober but combative vision of a communism of reason not as an implementable reality (for our passionate bondage can never be eliminated *in toto*) but necessary as a regulative ideal, overseeing a Beckettian understanding of emancipation (fail again, fail better ...) which, in the spirit of a Spinozist materialist political anthropology, refuses to tell itself stories.

Lordon defines the multitude as 'the collective itself', 'the reservoir of power of the social world – one might even say the reservoir of power that *is* the social world' (pp. 68–9). This multitude necessarily composes itself in distinct (and thus at some degree exclusionary) *bodies*. It is from this ontology of political composition, Lordon suggests, that we can move beyond an idolatrous or phobic relationship to contemporary forms of political belonging, *in primis* the *nation-state* – which continues to set the parameters for what is politically thinkable in our moment (pp. 141–2). As he observes: 'the concept of a political body is both the most vulnerable to being misappropriated for essentialist ends and the most capable of radically emancipating itself from such a fate, providing of course that we have the appropriate concept of it' (p. 3). All political bodies, be they communes or empires, are, at this level of generality – the one selected by Lordon's inquiry, which plays off the counterpoint, implied or explicit, between the general state and the states we're in – 'unions of parts held together in a certain relation to one another through a common affect' (p. 4).

To understand group formation, we must therefore grasp the 'same principle [which] underlies the coherence of groups and their finitude: the servitude to the passions' (p. 4) – the fact that, as Spinoza's *Ethics* details, human life is not governed (solely) by reason, but by affects that can never be combined and pacified by any kind of spontaneous harmony. To simply assert a rationalist communism (or indeed, in what merely appears as an alternative, a communism of *life*) is to wish away the weight of common affect, as the principle of union *and* disunion. All populous collectives require, to avert affective implosion through passionate discord, the verticality of an *imperium*, a right or power which, having the multitude as its only basis, like the Hokusai wave, nevertheless rises up to overpower it. *Imperium* seeks to transport the tiresome activist opposition of verticals and horizontals (a faded echo of the historical contention between 'authoritarian' and 'libertarian' socialists) into a more sophisticated theoretical terrain.

As Lordon has it, 'The *imperium*, that right defined by the power of the multitude, is thus the only force capable of containing *over the longer term* the centrifugal tendencies which the servitude to the passions, in its divergent forms, constantly recreates' (p. 7). A prescriptive 'post-nationalism' is for Lordon the denial of this fragmentary condition of human social life, its separation in different groupings of belonging; it is the stubborn but futile disavowal of the political, anthropological, and social fact of human division, in its material necessity and emotional dimensions. Yet, in a refrain that returns throughout *Imperium*, this is no cause for despair: a general theory of *imperium* does not preclude any more emancipatory forms of verticality and allows (or perhaps demands) that we maintain the 'maximal programme of emancipation' as a 'regulative ideal'.

These are some of the grounds on which Lordon will present an acerbic catalogue of objections against those left critiques of belonging that treat it as 'progressive' when it is nostalgic or utopian (as in the case of national liberation) but reactionary in every other variant. Against them, he enjoins that we recognise, for instance, the reality of suffering caused by a lack of belonging generated in the experience of involuntary migration. To deny any validity to national affects in the metropole (or rather to feign to do so, since for Lordon such affects never actually disappear, they are simply disavowed) while allowing them, romantically or condescendingly, for the subaltern is a paralogism or indeed a hypocrisy he counsels us to leave behind – in order to critique and rethink forms of nationality, belonging and citizenship rather than to fantasise about their (impossible) overcoming.

Contrary to a Habermasian vulgate, 'the Europeanist agenda to "abolish the nation", in failing to realise that the end point of this would be a new national identity (a European identity), would have the grotesque and contradictory effect of precipitating a new form of affiliation, even as it seeks to reject affiliation' (p. 25).[6] Such a critique can even take the form of a 'paradoxical mode of national affiliation' (pp. 25–7), where 'we' are the ones who are identified by 'our' capacity not to belong. Lordon also criticises those 'impossible disaffiliations' that

---

6 Lordon has recently touched on the 'dark side' of a Europeanism that during World War II could try to come to terms with the Nazi occupation. See 'More than One Idea', trans. David Broder, Verso blog, 10 January 2018, versobooks.com.

ignore the fundamental point that bodies are not delocalisable and that the place where one lives (be it as an enemy of the nation or a secessionist in an enclave or commune) is always part of the territory of a broader if non-homogeneous community.

Central to *Imperium*'s critique of a post-national left is its dissection of the reliance on contemporary emancipatory thought on an ultimately liberal and contractual conception of horizontal associationism. The targets here seem especially to be Dardot and Laval and their impressive treatise *Common* (which could be read as a kind of rival to *Imperium*), while the argument is really brought home in the rich discussion of sixteenth- and seventeenth-century theories of sovereignty through the contrast between the French jurist and political philosopher Jean Bodin (1530–96) and his German counterpart Johannes Althusius (1557–1638), with the latter's theory of *consociatio* revealing both the strengths and limits of a federalist political imaginary which, much as it may try to maximise subsidiarity and decentralisation, can never fully forsake the moment of verticality and capture. What all varieties of horizontalist federalism or associationism cannot avoid is the incontrollable excess of the whole over the parts, the 'immanent transcendence' of a *potestas* birthed by a *potentia* that can never be simply universalised by reason but is always both united and divided by common affects and servitude to the passions. Following Durkheim, it is this excess of the whole over the parts that for Lordon marks out the sociological perspective and its abiding value. The aim of a general theory of the general state will thus be to produce the 'conceptual genesis' of this verticality. Drawing on the Spinozist mechanism of 'imitation of affects' to account for the genesis and closure of social totalities, Lordon goes on to argue that verticality is a scalar effect, an inevitable product of social formations growing past a certain threshold, beyond the 'synoptic condition' in which individuals can exist in mutual transparency.[7]

As he turns to the question of social division, Lordon presents us with a somewhat Hobbesian Spinozism (no doubt in deliberate polemical contrast with Negri's more anthropologically affirmative variant), for

---

7 Though *Imperium* does not confront those theories of socialist planning that tried to construct synoptic conditions in contexts of large-scale complexity, the relation between the politics and economics of scale is explicitly thematised in *Figures du communisme*.

which the world without the state is not a composed of horizontal associations but of bands or gangs or rackets – as though the insufficiently reflexive imaginaries of horizontality, secession and enclave of today's anti-systemic communes or *groupuscules* always took for granted the background condition of a reproductive state and its residual provisioning of public goods and infrastructures. Yet as we shift into nationalised, instituted, totalised forms of collectivity, we still must realise that all groupings involve passionate convergences (and divergences) and that capitalist desires, for instance, can never operate to deracinate and deterritorialise these into a potentially revolutionary homogeneity – but we must likewise accept that such passionate convergences are always unstable, requiring the incessant work of reproduction, and thus always liable to transformation and conversion.

In this general theory, where Spinoza's affective analysis of collective formation is completed by Bourdieu's theory of the state, we grasp that the multitude can only exist under various regimes of 'capture', which is to say only through various institutional processes that mediate the *potentia multitudinis*, the power of the multitude. Emblematic moments in which we glimpse an exception to this rule, such as the Paris Commune, may derive their qualities from their defeat, or better from not having lasted long enough for the 'endogenous force of the mechanisms of capture' (p. 173) fully to reveal itself. As a process of production of internal consistency, the state, relying on common affect, on a passionate convergent servitude, also produces its own limits (for other processes of unification necessarily develop beside it). The tension constitutive of both a general theory of the general state, and of emancipatory practice itself, is then to be located between this inevitability of the transcendent excess of the state and a social ontology 'from below' – in which the 'foundation of state authority, and of all other forms of authority within society, resides in this elementary structure of politics that is the self-affecting of the multitude' (p. 81). To evade or neutralise the tension, as both anarchist anthropologies and communist philosophies are wont to do, Lordon suggests, is to avoid a true confrontation with the problem of political emancipation.

To take this problem seriously is to think through the constitution of political bodies, in their singularity – a constitution which, as what Spinoza termed a '*certa ratio*' (p. 97), is *relational* rather than substantial. It is to reflect on the 'porous closure' of these bodies, addressing what a body can do in terms of its singular *ingenium* – the 'folds' impressed on it by its unrepeatable biography and stabilised into 'habits'. It is also to meditate on the differences between two forms of joy available to political bodies. Transposing a distinction from the *Ethics* onto the terrain of group passions, Lordon distinguishes between *titillatio*, which affects some parts of the body more than others, and *hilaritas*, which affects all parts equally (p. 114), and which receives full development in democracy as *omnio absolutum imperium* (p. 115), an *imperium* absolute in everything. There are thus 'two elementary structures of politics: the auto-affection of the multitude (*imperium*) gives to political groupings their principle of consistency; the form-relation (*certa ratio*) gives them their principle of singularity as distinct bodies'.

As Lordon unfolds the consequences of his interpretation of Spinoza's *imperium* – namely that the 'state' (generically understood) is an inevitable product of the multitude's self-constitution, a verticality that cannot but emerge, at a certain scale, from its internal 'communication' – it becomes evident that he belongs to that skein of political interpreters of Spinoza (such as Alexandre Matheron or Étienne Balibar) who refrain from the expansive communistic reading of the Dutch philosopher proposed by Negri in particular. It is also evident, especially from his references to Durkheim as a neglected if brilliant interpreter of Spinoza, that Lordon wants to assert the sociological as well as anthropological insight of the *Ethics* and the *Political Treatise*, over and against any purely political reading, but also against any approach to Spinoza that would treat his theory of action as deducible from his theory of substance. Lordon's is then a wilfully truncated Spinoza, whose starting point, the *conatus*, is but a passage in the Dutch philosopher's systematic deduction.

This retooled materialist anthropology sustains Lordon's explorations of what he calls the *affectio nationalis* (p. 123), the ways in which national loves and hatreds shape collective formations to demand we 'appreciate the clinical literalness of the Spinozan lexicon as it applies to the world' (p. 124) – something we may witness in the spurious pride taken in the achievements of our imagined communities, in sport or war, that is to say in processes whose rational foundation can be sought in a 'mechanism of confirmation by imitation … an unrivalled power of collective cohesiveness … a power that soothes the axiological anxiety through the force of the collective' (p. 128). It is through this ontology of political bodies that we will also be able to grasp the processes of insurrectionary or liberatory sedition, when a common affect of indignation reverses that of *obsequium* or reverence. As Lordon remarks, his eye on the present, 'All revolutions and all the great uprisings begin as a configuration of Spinozan sedition: the coming together of a large number of people in a common affect of indignation' (p. 136). Against dreams of communist disaffiliation, we need to recognise that 'secessions are formations based on common affects and *eo ipso* are generators of affiliation, which is to say of identity. The Commune was an identity' (p. 137).

In the final analysis, a certain kind of separation (which is also to say excess, transcendence, alienation) thus belongs to the very concept of power, as emerges even from the most pioneering political philosophy of 'symbiotic' federation, that of Althusius. This is also why it is spurious to repudiate the very idea of sovereignty, as though the phenomenon it identifies could be denied by a sheer act of theoretical will; as if even the Althusian or anarchist idea of an association of associations didn't imply sovereignty as 'the ascending effect of a system of mandates' (p. 154). It is only a restrictive obsession with Bodinian sovereignty, a sovereignty fully separate and transcendent vis-à-vis the power of the multitude, which could suggest that the abolition of sovereignty is the emancipation of the multitude – a multitude fantasised as being angelically without *imperium* (to take sovereignty beyond Bodin, and *a fortiori* beyond Schmitt, is among the contributions of this Spinozist turn).

For Lordon, to deny the excess of the *imperium* is to fantasise about a world of transparency and reconciliation; to forget that *we* are the state, albeit a state in which we are 'strangers to ourselves in the opacity of exceedance' (p. 177); that the state is an *endogenous* and not *parasitic* product of our collective history. Instead of an anarchist anthropology *against* the state, what is required for Lordon is a Spinozist political anthropology *of* the state which grasps its underdetermined and ambivalent character in terms of the human passions that shape and innervate it, and which will not take the exceptional moment of insurrection as the key to its anthropological reflection, preferring a communism of the ordinary, of the 'day after' the revolution.

Lordon advances a politics of the limitation, modification and transformation of the state, in which the question of *education* – which habits can be engendered to live the *imperium* and our common affects differently, minimising the degree of our alienation – can be properly formulated. This is an education that will not fantasise the end of self-interest but shape its compositions into forms that do not drain us of our collective power, in a Spinozist 'expanded utilitarianism of power' (p. 218), which counters the politics of imperatives that Lordon ascribes to Badiou. Since the lesson of Spinoza instructs us that it is not possible to live without the law and without obedience, it is necessary to transform them through a 'materialist ... politics of the universal' (p. 233) in the regulative horizon of a communism of reason, which may allow us to seek to 'de-mediate' the expressions of our collective power, making it possible for the collective body in which we participate, which we help to compose, to experience *hilaritas*. Lordon's final imperative is thus 'keeping our revolutionary desire alive while eschewing revolutionary illusions, and seeing things as they are without surrendering to the current order' (p. 260).

Imperium demonstrates the suggestiveness and vitality of Lordon's Spinozist inspiration when it comes to thinking about our passionate attachments and investments in the symbols and institutions of politics, in this state that, as La Boétie declared, sees with our own eyes.[8] This is a state which, *pace* Nietzsche, is the *warmest* of all monsters. The resilience of nationalist imaginaries in the present, including in progressive configurations, together with the resurgence of the aspiration for popular sovereignty against its financial confiscations, signal the urgency of rethinking the state and its relation to collective emancipation. An anthropological note of realism surely cannot go amiss in these debates, especially if it allows us to move beyond the improbable proposition that common affects could be mobilised by unalloyed universalisms. No doubt, the state conceived at such a transhistorical level of generality – as a product of social creatures of passion, projecting their power into partly alien structures to forestall conflict – cannot wither away. The abolition of *imperium* would be tantamount to the termination of the very conditions for the exercise of collective power

---

8 For some critical reflections on the thorny and vital problems raised by Lordon's 'Spinozist Jacobinism', when it comes to grasping the relation between state and capital, nation and class, see my 'A Structuralism of Feeling?', *New Left Review* 97 (2016), 89–93. While the Spinozist matrix remains firmly in place, as does his criticism of the anti-statist political imaginary of the contemporary radical Left, Lordon's explicit commitment to the ineluctability of a communist transition in more recent writings (Vivre sans ..., *Figures du communisme*) has shifted the terms of that earlier debate.

and the formation of common affects. *Imperium* will have at least partially succeeded in its own terms if some of its readers can retain their revolutionary, even their communist desires, while no longer telling themselves some old and comforting stories.

Preface

A Reminder of What the State Can Do (Aide-Mémoire)

Place de la Concorde, Paris. More precisely, in front of the Hôtel Crillon. It is the monthly meeting of the Le Siècle club, the informal gathering of the oligarchy of the day, blithely unaware of just what a caricature it is. Except that, on this particular occasion, a few hundred demonstrators have gathered to greet these leading dignitaries with mocking chants, slogans and explicit hand gestures. One by one, the great and the good run the gauntlet of this welcoming committee: politicians from the left and the right, captains of French industry, compromised intellectuals, economists for hire and sympathetic press barons. As is often the case, there are probably more CRS riot control officers than there are demonstrators. It is not clear if it is because of the unexpected number of demonstrators or because it is part of their original brief, but the CRS hold open the doors of the hotel for the arriving guests, who are surprised at the reception awaiting them and only too happy to be ushered rapidly into the safe company of their peers. Take a moment to reflect on this: the CRS – which is to say the state police – acting as *doormen* to the capitalist oligarchy, quite literally.

At the more fractious demonstrations, you regularly hear the anarchists (and others) chanting 'Police nationale, milice du capital' (the police are the militia of capitalism). One might take a more moderate stance and suggest that this analysis could be refined somewhat, and indeed it should be. But such a spectacle certainly gives food for thought . . .

Picasso and Einstein. Keen to settle in France and to become French citizens, they applied for naturalisation but were turned down. So much for bureaucratic discernment.

In truth, it reflects just how much the state administrative apparatus has been infested by the notion of essentialist identity. Even those who have managed to slip through the net have been looked at askance in the process. Edifying extracts from naturalisation files have been thrown up by research into the archives of the Ministry of Justice.[1] Georges Perec: 'Jewish, not in the public interest.' Igor Stravinsky: 'Even naturalised, he would still be a composer attached to Russian art.' Chagall: 'Russian Jew, naturalisation not in the public interest.' Brassaï: 'Judgement reserved, loyalty not proven.' They nevertheless made it through, perhaps because their official applications read like love letters to the powers that be, odes to France, oaths of allegiance and passionate declarations of their espousal of French identity. The civil service annotated these statements in the margins as if marking a school essay: 'incomplete assimilation', 'succeeds when he bothers to make the effort', 'well brought up and with a strong desire to act appropriately'.

Looking at these 'celebrity' cases makes one realise how many great men and women the nation must have passed up, or nearly passed up, and also the extent to which the notion of 'value' underpins the awarding of citizenship. In other words, being French is something that has to be earned, and only a foreign elite are deserving of this privilege. The shortcomings of the civil service thus lie not so much in its rigid application of infantilising norms, but rather in its lack of discernment. No one cares about the mass of ordinary people who were rejected – it is the thought that France might have missed out on Chagall that is disturbing.

'The reports of the Ministry of the Interior will never reveal the killing of hundreds of our brothers by the police forces or the fact that not one of the perpetrators has ever been held to account.' After this sentence appeared in the fanzine of the French hip-hop band La Rumeur, Hamé,

---

1 Doan Bui and Isabelle Monnin, *Ils sont devenus français*, J. C. Lattès, 2010.

one of the group's founding members, was prosecuted by the state for defamation of the police in a case that dragged on for eight years.

Leaving aside the legal dimension, it is worth revisiting the substance of this case, which revolved around the peculiar legal status of the police. An astonishing number of people do die in police vans or cells. These deaths are never ascribed a cause and so there is no agency at work, and consequently no one is held responsible. Which, in short, means that hardly anyone is ever found guilty. Deaths in custody are rather akin to the Immaculate Conception, except, of course, that something rather different is going on.

When cases against people like Hamé are thrown out of court, the state gets angry. From beginning to end, these legal actions are motivated by an obvious obsession: to make an example of the accused and thereby intimidate into silence those who would contest the government's power. Following Weber, this is a point of honour for the state: it will accept no challenge to its right to use 'legitimate force', viewing any contestation of its monopoly on violence as a challenge to its legitimacy, which is to say a threat to its very existence. One might be forgiven for thinking that the state would only go so far as to prosecute somebody for mere verbal dissent if it is being run by somewhat unhinged individuals – which as it happens was the case with Sarkozy, the minister of the interior who pursued Hamé through the courts and then became president of the Republic. But, leaving aside Sarkozy's state of mind and the specifics of that case, these utterly senseless instances of legal persecution reveal a certain disposition of the state.

A disposition which amounts to paranoia. In his reading of Deleuze and Guattari, Guillaume Sibertin-Blanc emphasises the 'extreme hysterical violence' which state paranoia can lead to.[2] It is recognisable by its complete lack of rational or practical justification, and the sheer disproportionality of the punishment sought. It is less a standard tactic of intimidation than an unbridled compulsion to crush. Could it be that it actively seeks out opportunities to express itself?

Certainly, any form of political violence is excuse enough, since such violence has a special status in the eyes of the state precisely because it is

---

2 Guillaume Sibertin-Blanc, *State and Politics: Deleuze and Guattari on Marx*, trans. Ames Hodges, Semiotext(e), 2016.

political in nature and therefore construed as an attack on the state's very essence. The contemporary state lumps its opportunities for hysterical violence into the category 'terrorism', and the compulsive nature of its response is at its most evident when it chooses not to punish but to crush and, if possible, annihilate 'political criminals' whom it has elevated to the status of *enemies of the state*. The special form of solitary confinement inflicted on Ulrike Meinhof,[3] which included sensory deprivation, was a clear instance of this process of annihilation. The same applies to the special treatment reserved for members of *Action directe*, which involved ruling out any remission of sentence. You are better off being a child murderer than an enemy of the state.

Needless to say, the deeply paranoid recognise each other and naturally enter into a sort of compulsive communion. The refusal to release Georges Ibrahim Abdallah, who has been in detention since 1984, reeks of state vengeance. Might this not be because, in assassinating a CIA agent in Paris, he became an enemy of the state? Or rather of two states, which merely goes to illustrate the solidarity of all states against the enemies of the state . . .

In a different register, one could cite Kronstadt, Makhno, Spain and so many other examples, but the list would be endless. However, if we wish to analyse the necessity of the state and its refusal to wither away, it is useful to keep such things in mind.

---

3 Ulrike Meinhof's solitary confinement was extreme: not only was she deprived of all human contact (she even had to take exercise alone) but she was kept in a featureless, soundproof room designed to induce total sensory disorientation.

Introduction

'This right, which is defined by the power of the multitude, is generally called *imperium*.'[1] The core of Spinoza's political philosophy resides in this one statement from the *Political Treatise*. *Imperium* is not to be despised, nor is it deserving of idolatry; it merely describes a necessity. We therefore need to learn, or relearn, how to understand the word *imperium* correctly, which is to say without any unnecessary baggage – we must rein in our imaginations and put away our fantasies. We must learn not to hear in it undertones of the imperiousness of a conquering power or the imperialism of a large-scale drive to subjugate, but rather to understand it only for what it is and to hear only what it says in the strictest sense: this right which is defined by the power of the multitude. But, straight away, the problems begin. What do we mean by 'multitude'? And, above all, what 'right' are we talking about? What are its ramifications, for which *imperium* serves as the umbrella word? In other words, what is this necessity which we must conceptualise before we consider despising or idolising it?

---

1 Baruch Spinoza, *Political Treatise*, trans. Samuel Shirley, Hackett Publishing Company, 2000, Part II, 17, p. 44. Translator's Note [TN]: I have emended Samuel Shirley's translation to reflect the author's decision to retain Spinoza's choice of Latin word – *imperium* – rather than to translate it (see below, p. 65). In this instance, Shirley translates *imperium* as 'sovereignty' and elsewhere sometimes as 'state', depending on the context. Recent French translations of Spinoza opt for *souveraineté* and *état*. In all subsequent quotations, I have also followed the author in translating Spinoza's *multitudo* as 'multitude' (which Shirley translates as 'a people').

The multitude is not so much a particular collection of sundry individual elements as an expression of the collective itself. It is the reservoir of social power – and even society as power. And, for Spinoza, that is precisely what a 'right' is: power. It is not at all a legal concept, contrary to the way we usually understand the word 'right' today, but rather a capacity to produce effects – to affect things. To talk of this right which is defined by the power of the multitude is therefore to envisage a capacity for affecting things on a large scale – at the scale of the multitude. What has the power to affect an entire multitude? The answer is the multitude itself. The multitude, through the very exercise of its power – and the necessary exercise of that power, for all things necessarily enact their power, this being their essence – thus affects itself. And this self-affecting is what is generally called *imperium*. So far, there is clearly no reason to protest or to prostrate ourselves. It is simply a case of being open to the invitation to see things – through the *theoria*,[2] it goes without saying.

Of Bodies (the Elementary Structures of Politics)

And this is what there is to see: that everything which happens to the multitude comes *from* the multitude through self-affecting, which is to say through the self-reflexive exercise of this 'right', which is nothing other than its own power. And the principal thing which happens to the multitude through the effect of the *imperium* is that it assumes coherence. 'The multitude will unite . . . not at reason's prompting but through some common affect',[3] as the *Political Treatise* goes on to say in a statement which goes hand in hand with the previous citation and is just as fundamental. The common affect – the affect which affects everyone identically – is an affect on a scale which necessarily implicates the multitude itself. And that is the very point: it is through self-affecting, which produces a common affect, that the multitude constitutes itself into a coherent unity, which is to say into a political formation, rather than a disparate collection of individuals. The *imperium* is a morpho-genetic principle. It serves to mutate collections from the amorphous

2 Given that *theorein* means 'to see'.
3 *PT*, VI, 1, p. 64.

state into a political form. It is the agent of grouping and hence also of supplementing, since a coherently assembled multitude contains more than a similarly sized collection of scattered individuals. This supplement is the common affect that brings people together into a body.

Why do we need to elaborate a theory of political bodies? The simple reason, of course, is because such bodies exist! Mankind has not spontaneously formed into a unity, and humanity exists in a fragmented state – neither unified nor pulverised, but fragmented. The fragments are not the dust of individual atoms, but distinct and finite ensembles. These ensembles, as ensembles, have forms, which means that they are bodies.

We are familiar with the intellectual misgivings which the idea of a political body immediately arouses: the organicist peril of communities viewed through the prism of essentialism. This, it must be granted, is a genuine danger, since groupings themselves can get carried away, usually towards essentialist notions of identity and eternity. If theoretical discourse simply endorses such notions in academic language, it immediately disqualifies itself. And yet it would seem that the source of the danger also provides a way out. The paradox, if it is one, is that the concept of a political body is both the most vulnerable to being misappropriated for essentialist ends and the most capable of radically emancipating itself from such a fate, providing of course that we have the appropriate concept of it. And such a concept is to be found in Spinoza, because Spinoza conceptualises bodies, albeit in a very general way. In other words, he does not give precedence to the human body or relate his thinking about other bodies to it through surreptitious (and typically dubious) analogies. The political body is not 'like some large human body' and it is essential not to anthropomorphise the conception of bodies if we are seeking to conceptualise political bodies. Very generally speaking, a body – human or otherwise – is a union of parts which are arranged in a certain relation to one another (a *certa ratio*, says Spinoza in his discussion of the physical world in the *Ethics*).[4] Apprehending the body not through the essential nature of its parts but through the *relations* which structure them into a union is a way of providing us with a *structural* definition, as well as affording us a

---

4 Baruch Spinoza, *Ethics: with The Treatise on the Emendation of the Intellect and Selected Letters*, trans. Samuel Shirley, ed. Seymour Feldman, Hackett Publishing Company, 1992, Part II.

principle of singularity: *this* body (constituted object), which is a union of bodies (constituent parts) arranged according to *these* relations, is not this other body. We must disregard the parts, for they are not what fundamentally distinguish different bodies; rather, they are distinguished by how the parts are arranged in relation to each other and to the whole. We have now learned two things: firstly, that bodies assume coherence through the workings of the *imperium*, which is to say the common affect; and secondly, that they assume a distinct character, which is to say they differentiate themselves, through the relations which characterise them. The structuring relations (or *certa ratio*) which confer on them their distinct form, and the common affect (or *imperium*) which gives rise to them in the first place, are *the elementary structures of politics*.

They are elementary in that the category (which we have now established as structural) of 'political body' obtains prior to any form of morphological differentiation. Above and beyond their obvious morphological differences, the tribe, the *polis*, the empire, the absolutist state and the modern nation state are all bodies, which is to say specific historical realisations of the elementary structures of politics. What do they have in common? That they are unions of parts held together in a certain relation to one another through a common affect.

The Perseverance of Political Bodies Amid Affective Convergences and Divergences

The same principle underlies the coherence of groups and their finitude: the servitude to the passions. The multitude assembles itself through the influence of (common) affects, and affects also keep it divided into distinct ensembles. We can put this another way: the centrifugal forces of divergence arising from the passions can only be accommodated, or held in check, within a finite sphere (or rather by finite spheres, plural) and not at the scale of humanity as a whole. This is because all bodies are, in Laurent Bove's phrase, 'a locus of oppositions',[5] and therefore

---

5 Laurent Bove, 'De la prudence des corps. Du physique au politique', introduction to Spinoza, *Traité politique*, Le Livre de Poche, 2002. [TN] Unless stated otherwise, all translations of cited sources are my own.

always subject to antagonistic forces since individually the parts do not a priori strive towards the perseverance of the whole. They are only held to that goal by the *imperium*, always assuming that it successfully imposes itself upon them – that it deploys sufficient power to overcome, where necessary, their centrifugal tendencies.

For this is what is meant by the 'servitude to the passions': that people's lives, conducted under the influence not of reason but of affects, do not harbour any principle of spontaneous harmony. This is not to say that no collective order is possible, because clearly it is – the very existence of political bodies testifies to this. But such forms of order have to be won: they only exist and preserve themselves through a balance which allows the passions of convergence to prevail over those of divergence. This balance may or may not be precarious, but there is certainly no guarantee that it will last forever. The prospect of decomposition thus irremediably hangs over any composed whole – but the fact that political bodies fall apart, whether through orderly separatist tendencies or through civil war, is of course something we knew already. What, then, are the chances of finding a common locus of the passions whose cohesive force would be sufficient to sustain a global political community? Extremely low, given the many grounds for divergence and the likelihood, at such a large scale, of critical fluctuations, which is to say centrifugal motions which are impossible to contain. Even if it existed, a global *imperium* would in any case also be founded on the passions, and at such a scale it would not necessarily be a pretty sight to behold – indeed, in the form not of genuine universality but of a *specific* global uniformity of the passions, would it even be desirable?

However that may be, the union of bodies poses a problem and is certainly not a natural given. Spinoza tells us that it is dependent on the interplay of the antagonistic affective tendencies which both bring people together and drive them apart – the interplay of convergences and divergences. For, unless our anthropology ignores half our nature, both these possibilities enter into what we must problematically refer to as 'human nature' – providing once again, of course, that we conceptualise it appropriately (which is absolutely essential, bearing in mind some of the monstrous pronouncements which have been made on the subject). People agree under certain relational circumstances and disagree under others. For example, they come together when they are inspired by pity or when they need to pool their efforts to have a better chance of survival;

they tear each other apart over objects which can only be possessed by one person or when they hate through affinity (which is to say by emulating the hate which one of their peers feels for another). Stated more generally, this is the expression in interhuman relationships of two (quasi-)primary affects:[6] love and hatred. One would have thought that accommodating both these tendencies would be straightforward enough, but, instead, political anthropologists have tended to retreat into monistic conceptions of man as intrinsically good or bad. So, on the one hand, we have Leviathan for the bad man, and on the other the promise of social horizontality for the good man.

The Precarious Balancing Act of Social Horizontality

The formation, perseverance and decomposition of political bodies cannot be analysed without reference to the clash of these antagonistic tendencies and the contingent outcomes of this clash. We also need to look at the process of formation and the fully-fledged form. What volume of state, legal and institutional apparatus does our collective existence call for? The answer to this question will depend in a critical way on a dual balance: the balance, between us, of convergent and divergent forces; and the balance, within us, of reason and passions. Can this dual balance be modified? Yes, it can, because (and this needs to be stated unambiguously) a capacity for modification is the chief property of human nature, when appropriately conceptualised.

It nevertheless remains the case that, where servitude to the passions prevails, the divergent component acts as an impediment to social horizontality. This is because social horizontality, correctly conceptualised, is a form of existence that is free of institutions (institutions being synonymous with verticality). It therefore presupposes the possibility of spontaneous, and durable, harmony. People come together in order to achieve something and then they stick together: that is the promise of social horizontality. The real question is whether common desire, which

---

6 *Quasi*-primary, for Spinoza designates as primary the affects of pain and pleasure (*Ethics*, III, 11, scholium, p. 110). However, love and hatred are immediately derived from them, as they are respectively defined as affects of pleasure and pain accompanied by the idea of an external cause (*Ethics*, III, 13, scholium, p. 112).

is what brings people together in the first place, can act as a sufficiently strong glue. It will certainly have to contend with other affects and struggle against other desires that are more idiosyncratic, less widely shared and less compatible with the common interest, since 'in so far as men are subject to passive affects, to that extent they cannot be said to agree in nature.'[7] Even if they do concord in their shared desire, this does not *in itself* prevent individuals who have come together willingly from disagreeing in other relational circumstances. Nor, if no other cohesive principle is at work, does it shield the group thus formed from the contingent outcomes of its antagonistic passions, which can give rise to great instability – as many a collective which has shattered apart will testify.

What can be said, then, about collectivities which are *large in number*, beyond the fact that none are able to sustain themselves in the absence of some vertical principle, or rather in the absence of some variation on a single vertical principle: the *imperium*? It is only through the vertical that the group perseveres if circumstances are such that, when in servitude to the passions, an irreducible divergence deprives the horizontal principle of the means to produce, and above all reproduce, the group's cohesion, thereby depriving it of any chance it has of *enduring*. Or, alternatively, if the group does achieve that cohesion, it is because it has in its turn engendered a vertical principle and so, by metamorphosis, has moved beyond the unstable order of flat associations and entered the order of structured and coherent political bodies. The *imperium*, that right defined by the power of the multitude, is thus the only force capable of containing *over the longer term* the centrifugal tendencies which the servitude to the passions, in its divergent forms, constantly recreates. And this force is a vertical principle.

Sobering Up to Certain Realities

Let us approach this from a different angle. There is probably no simpler way of going down well with a critical left-wing audience than by

---

7 *Ethics*, IV, 32, p. 170. [TN] Shirley renders Spinoza's *affectus* as 'emotion', as do most English translations. I have, however, followed the author in translating it as 'affect' throughout. For the important distinction between *affectus* and emotion, see Frédéric Lordon, *Les affects de la politique*, Seuil, 2016.

announcing the simultaneous advent of internationalism, the withering away of the state and radical horizontality. It would be easy enough to mock 'internationalism' for advocating almost exactly the opposite to what it thinks it is advocating, since internationalism – inter-national-ism – concerns what happens between nations, thereby confirming that there *are* nations, but let us leave that to one side for the time being. The important, and painful, point is that all of these things, which are very desirable in themselves, are also highly problematic. Indeed, one must wonder if, when rigorously conceptualised, they are even attainable – and accept that the answer is, in fact, no. However, and here is the deci-sive point, acceptance of this fact does not equate to hasty surrender, as is the case with conservatism.

Internationalism is an unfortunate misnomer since, understood in terms of its true intentions, it aims for a post-national world. But what can this mean except the complete unification of humanity, given that any intermediate group would still be a nation – a merger of former nations, perhaps, but ultimately just a larger nation (which, along the lines of a hypothetical European Union, would be nothing but a nation-state bloc on a continental scale)? Speaking very generally, post-nation-alism seeks to surmount the fragmented state of mankind, and that is certainly a bold aspiration. For unless we fall into the blinkered anthro-pology of man as naturally good and thus into a wilful ignorance of affective divergence, the obstacles to achieving such a goal are obvious, and they call for convincing counterarguments, or at least something better than a few homely declarations of principle and extrapolations from local experiments. In addition, while we know what post-nation-alism rejects, it is rather less clear what it affirms. We have no clear idea, for example, of the actual political form that a unified humanity would assume. An atomistic structure on a planetary scale? But that is not even a form, and in truth is such an absurd notion that we should dismiss it out of hand. A federation of associations of associations like Bakunin had in mind (and Althusius, many years before him)? Even if we were to admit this scenario, it would still be no less a state: a global, federal state, no doubt structured very differently to our own, but a state nevertheless. Thus, at the very moment when post-nationalism is achieved, the withering away of the state goes out of the window and social horizontality along with it, which should really come as no surprise, given that all three problems are intricately linked.

The common challenge is to contain divergent tendencies and to identify the forces capable of doing so (for forces can only ever be contained by other forces). It is worth repeating that this does not mean that there are no spontaneously convergent forces in people's affective complexions, because there are. What is doubtful is whether they are sufficient to hold in check the centrifugal tendencies or capable of sustaining a *durable* collective order. What history does show us, however, is that it is possible to resolve the 'problem', and it does so by furnishing examples of groups which remain stable over the longer term, though their longevity is doubtless relative – greater than that of simple, volatile associations, but of finite duration all the same. After lasting for a certain period, groups fragment, or fade away, or are absorbed into bigger entities, and so on. In short, history does its work of ensuring that nothing lasts forever . . . Notwithstanding this, the force mobilised for 'durable' stability is always the same: the force of the collective, or the *imperium*. However, the *imperium* is simultaneously a principle of verticality and a resource which is there to be appropriated, and hence it is a building block of a state – in the broadest sense, and regardless of the varied historical forms which it may assume. The *imperium* is ultimately the agent which enables distinct and finite groupings to cohere and so it is also – much to our disappointment, no doubt – the methodical negation of a horizontal post-nationalism characterised by a diminished state.

Rejection and Analysis

Zeev Sternhell characterises the Counter-Enlightenment as 'the cult of all that differentiates and divides men'.[8] He is quite right, at least so long as the rejection of the cult does not entail the rejection of analysis, which regrettably it often does. Many, no doubt anxious to avoid accusations of either grandstanding or else gullibility, adopt the easy option of rejecting all options, including that of thinking, as if analysing something unpleasant were tantamount to endorsing it. There are many logical errors attached to the debate around state and nation, since the state in

---

8 Zeev Sternhell, *Histoire et Lumières. Changer le monde par la raison*, Albin Michel, 2014, p. 193.

the sense in which we understand it today (and which, as we will show, by no means exhausts the concept) and the nation are the specific historical form which political bodies assume *today*. Foremost among these errors, and one may call it a methodological error, is to fail to appreciate that the refusal of 'the cult of all that differentiates and divides men' necessarily requires us to engage in analysis, and possibly to contend with unpalatable conclusions. For the fact of the matter is that, though divisions between people continue to arise, they are clearly not divided over everything for otherwise we would never observe any kind of collective formation. They do therefore know how to unite, even if it is generally around confused points of convergence or else under the influence of forces that they do not fully grasp. In any case, at best they only unite at a regional level in restricted ensembles, and, even then, these groupings are constantly beset by internal divergences.

We would do well to scrutinise these many types of division and to understand what underpins them if our political agenda is, if not to transcend them *completely*, then, at least, to reduce them. To analyse the coherence and specificity of political bodies – to analyse the fragmentation of humanity into finite groupings – is not to 'rehabilitate the nation', contrary to the hasty conclusions we can expect from certain commentators whose perspective on the world is incorrigibly axiological and allergic to all empirical analysis. There is certainly no shortage of addlebrained commentators on the left who believe that analysing the state amounts to 'loving' the state.

We may not be able to thread a camel through the eye of a needle, but we can create a rather larger opening in the form of a question which is ultimately Kantian: with the gift of salvation repatriated from heaven to earth, what are we entitled to hope for? For if neither internationalism, nor social horizontality, nor the withering away of the state are within our reach, is there then nothing to hope for at all? Through a sort of logical car crash, this is the kind of 'deduction' which paradoxically unites the most divergent camps, though each of course has their own interpretation: for some, it is a cause for celebration (that such horrors might actually happen is their worst nightmare); for others, it is a chance to gauge the forces of reaction while continuing to believe that their dream is about to become reality, or already has.

Thinking according to a Certain Desire

There are things to discard but also things to retain in these maulings of logic. What we should retain, or shall we say appreciate, is that one only ever thinks under the impetus of a certain desire and that, when all is said and done, thoughts diverge according to the particular desire underpinning them. Thinking is not an exercise in intellectual representation, detached from everything else – it is the effect of the *activity* of a mind, the affirmative projection of an individual complexion which apprehends the world in the realm of thought, and moreover informs the world, according to its own particular nature. This is what Spinoza is essentially saying when he states that 'the mind, as far as it can, endeavours to think of those things that increase or assist the body's power of activity.'[9] As Deleuze astutely observes, thinking is not a form of passive reception of the world but rather an *effort* – the effort of an active mind. And this effort, which is nothing other than the *conatus* itself, is necessarily accompanied by affects and desire. Proposition 12 of Part III of the *Ethics*, which ought to be read as the proposition par excellence concerning ideology, indicates that we need to relate thought to a desire to think: the desire to think *in a certain direction*. Thought is the inclination of a desire to think of something determinate, towards which the mind turns its power and *endeavours*: towards immanence or transcendence, order or emancipation, determinism or the event, etc. Where desires themselves might take shape is anybody's guess – the only sure thing is that we will observe them being tenaciously pursued, in an attempt to order the world according to their code.

Thus, affects are always the departure point for thinking, though it is to be hoped that we can move beyond that point and avoid thought becoming the simple re-expression of those affects. One must therefore declare one's desire and hold on to it, but without omitting to develop it through thought. In this context, desire is emancipation. The word 'emancipation' has become something of a catch-all, but it remains solidly anchored in the project of ending the varied forms of social domination – though whether we can actually put an *end* to them remains to be seen, and that is precisely the problem. Take for example state domination – is it possible to put an end to it? That we will put an

---

9 *Ethics*, III, 12, p. 111.

end to it in its present form – the modern bourgeois state – is certain, but only trivially so, insofar as it is certain that, ultimately, we will always put an end to intrinsically transient products of history. The nation state is a recent creation and its disappearance is preordained, so to speak. But if the modern bourgeois state is only the particular product of a much more fundamental principle, where does this leave us? It leaves us with the fact that it exists, and that it exists because large multitudes assemble into coherent bodies through the effect, and the formal expression, of their collective power – indeed, to such an extent that this power becomes available for appropriation and institutionalisation, which is to say domination.

We can observe the phenomenon and feel unhappy about it, but this is preferable to not liking the phenomenon and therefore deciding not to observe it. Needless to say, there are also those who observe the phenomenon and who delight in it, but such people are of less interest to us, or rather it is a question of different initial affects, as ever. The delighted have theirs, and theirs are not ours. Ours primarily take the form of an aide-mémoire which is designed, should it be necessary, to remind people of exactly what the state is *also* capable of. Our desire is to put an end to all of that, or at least to go as far as possible *in that direction*. But, in order to do so, we must look squarely at what it is that we want to put an end to and we must prepare for disappointment, for we will find ourselves having to rein in our project of emancipation (in any case, from state domination) and to redefine it as a regulating principle. What is a regulating principle? It is a principle wherein an effort to think in a particular direction takes account of the inevitable tensions and seeks a form of unification. As it happens, we know this ideal to be unattainable, but remain committed to it all the same. It is not because emancipation, in the full political sense, cannot entirely coincide with our concept of it that we must celebrate the nation, idolise the state or deprive people of any possibility of governing themselves. Indeed, we must pursue the opposite path, knowing full well that the path is neverending but also that anything which *can* be achieved along the way is well worth having: the dismantling of hierarchies, subsidiarity, self-governing local entities, the flattening of structures, and so on. For as long as we are under the regime of the servitude to the passions, we can never extricate ourselves entirely from verticality. However, verticality is a general principle whose specific forms are not predetermined, and some of those forms are assuredly better than others: namely, all those which advance us in the direction of our regulating principle.

One should not be vexed by the idea of political bodies – firstly, because the simple fact is that they exist; and secondly, because reflecting on a body immediately raises the question of what that body can do and therefore the question of what conditions are necessary for it to be able to do more. In due course, we will see that, just like human bodies, the primary property of political bodies is that they are *modifiable* – for better or for worse, needless to say. Certainly, when Spinoza analyses bodies, it is with a view to their empowerment. He asks what is required to encourage bodies to operate to a greater degree under the guidance of reason, for conduct of this kind affords us the greatest empowerment. It so happens that such conduct, lessening our servitude to the passions, has the potential besides to progressively emancipate collective life from the framework of states, institutions and laws. And it also enhances our ability to gain knowledge of the second kind, namely of common notions – in other words, knowledge of those things through which we can truly reach common agreement.

PART I

Groupings

1

The Paralogisms of Exemption (Affiliated to Nothing?)

Analysing political bodies, and hence the notion of affiliation, firstly requires us to disperse the polluting fog which invariably surrounds discussions of affiliation, that locus of very intense and conflicting political affects best circumvented if we are to stand a chance of revisiting these subjects in a more serene frame of mind. It must be said that affiliation does not enjoy a good reputation. This is hardly surprising when one considers how many horrors have been perpetrated in its name. 'Affiliates' have often evinced a murderous nature, and indeed critics of affiliation would argue that 'they are necessarily like that'. This, however, is to commit two errors in a single phrase. The first is a lack of awareness, or an act of denial, since critics of affiliation have their own affiliations, even if they don't own up to them. However unwillingly, they themselves are implicitly conceding that there exist modes of affiliation which are unthreatening, or at least distinct from the modes which they are criticising, and which they endorse de facto as their own. The second error follows directly from the first: the fact that critics of affiliation have their own affiliations suggests a certain necessity and points to the contradictions inherent in the notion of *exemption*, that implicit or explicit contention that 'one is affiliated to nothing'. For this reason, the first task when addressing the question of affiliation should be to suspend certain axiological reflexes in order to examine this element of necessity – not to heap opprobrium on it or to glorify it, but to conceptualise it. Needless to say, we should exercise extreme intellectual vigilance when addressing the topic of affiliations, for it is well known where they can lead. However, such vigilance should not reduce the matter to an axiological debate – an approach rarely conducive to the examination of empirical evidence. It should not be necessary to add, though we will do so nevertheless, that an analysis of the empirical evidence is in no way tantamount to its endorsement, nor its acceptance as a deterministic reality to which we must succumb. On the contrary, appreciating the internal mechanisms of affiliation affords the only means of transforming them or of altering the way they function.

The Paradoxes of 'Good' Affiliation

Intuitively sensing the necessity of affiliation and its captive power merely requires us to be sensitive to the ordinary realities of our social lives, even at the smallest scales. Take, for example, the school playground, where somebody says 'Let's split into teams' and teams are chosen to play a game of some kind. The children, although they find themselves in a particular team based on tenuous or indeed arbitrary affinities, nevertheless embrace their group and engage in the contest to the full, displaying a commitment to the cause of the group which is characteristic of affiliation, despite the fact that their affiliation is thoroughly contingent – they would have shown the same commitment had they found themselves on the opposing side. Similarly, one gets the distinct impression that a supporter of such-and-such a football club, who spends his time heaping abuse on another club and even getting into fights with its supporters, could so easily have been one of those rival supporters himself, had circumstances been different. If the fans in the stands at a match between Paris Saint-Germain and Marseille can be seen as kindred souls, it is because what they deep down have in common is the intransitive joy of formal affiliation, which has nothing to do with the contingent nature of its object – it is the sense of belonging itself that brings people alive, and often it matters little to what one actually belongs. If individuals are capable of throwing themselves headlong into chance affiliations, though they might very easily have thrown themselves into contrary ones, this has to be the result of an emotional mechanism whose power we need to understand, making sure we take into account all the different ways in which the social context determines both their tendency to be absorbed into affiliations and how they declare that affiliation (avowed or denied, peacefully or aggressively).

Observable on a very wide range of social scales, affiliation only assumes its full polemical value when it becomes a national affiliation, which is the situation where collective identities have demonstrated most appallingly their capacities for discrimination and, indeed, for slaughter. Once again, there is much to recommend the position which defines itself as 'post-national', both in its desire to avoid rigid categories and pigeonholing individuals and in its historical consciousness of the contingency of collective geographies, in particular the idea that current nations, which are after all only a recent development, are unlikely to be history's final word. But granting all these points does not mean that we also have to accept all the paralogisms and non sequiturs, generally laden with value judgements, which are usually brought to bear on a subject which instead requires an empirical approach (the subject is often, in fact, dismissed before it has even been addressed).

Alain Badiou is typical of this tendency when he writes that ' "people + national adjective" is not of much value',[1] which is a curious affirmation in itself, given that the 'value' invoked is of uncertain status and in fact manifestly polemical, and also given that one could at the very least grant the phenomenon an empirical status, which is to say something to be elucidated, potentially with a view to altering the forms it takes. Badiou, moreover, admits that the phenomenon *can* have value, but only under quite specific conditions: 'people + national adjective' once again becomes 'interesting' when it is a case of throwing off colonial oppression in order to achieve self-determination, which of course is national in character. Another example would be overthrowing a dictatorship through an act of revolution, though always on the proviso that this value evaporates as soon as self-determination or the overthrow of the regime is achieved and that 'people + national adjective' is instantly demoted again to insignificance through an abrupt rupture (the mechanism of which remains obscure).

In truth, it is evident enough that this affirmation of non-value is closer to a performative contradiction than it is to an empirical analysis, for, after repeating in traditional vein that 'the proletariat has no

---

1 Alain Badiou, 'Vingt-quatre notes sur les usages du mot "peuple"', in *Qu'est-ce qu'un peuple?*, La Fabrique, 2013, p. 11.

homeland' and observing that the proletariat of today are immigrants from the world over, Badiou then proceeds to ask: 'To which people + national adjective do they therefore belong?'[2] This is a rhetorical question to which the answer is supposed to be obvious, but the evidence for it nevertheless needs to be tested, and this can be done straightforwardly enough by, say, posing the question directly to those concerned and seeing how they respond. Alternatively, one could challenge the assumption through a thought experiment whereby a match is held in France between, let us say, the national teams of Mali and Senegal and we imagine how the Malian and Senegalese proletarians in the stadium would behave. Such an experiment would permit us to observe whether today's proletarians do indeed have no homeland, or as tenuous a homeland as the proletarians of the early twentieth century did in the eyes of the Marxists of the time, who were then staggered to see these same people waging savage 'patriotic' war on each other.

Leaving aside thought experiments and turning to real situations, the 'proletarians who have no homeland' cooped up in the ignominious conditions of the Calais Jungle fought each other along the lines of national groupings: Sudanese against Eritreans, Eritreans against Syrians, etc. It would appear, therefore, that they had retained some sense of homeland, in this case for the worse. Where intellectuals seem eager to discern a new international proletariat, there is, in fact, a collection of uprooted national proletarians, which is not quite the same thing. One might be tempted to object that Marx defines the proletariat as having no specific attribute and as a class without specific interests, automatically meaning that they are destined for universal status in a classless society which does not have specific attributes. If one defines them like that, however, one is forced to conclude that the proletariat does not exist.

We find a contradiction which is formally rather similar (though taken to a more explicit level) in the otherwise fascinating book by Guillaume le Blanc devoted to 'the foreign condition'.[3] While the intent of this work is to call into question national forms of affiliation in the light of the (wretched) fate which they reserve for the foreigner (the 'outside' necessarily being constituted by the withdrawal into itself of the

---

2 Ibid.
3 Guillaume le Blanc, *Dedans, dehors. La condition d'étranger*, Seuil, 2010.

national 'inside'), the dynamic of his own argument leads him to encounter affiliation once again, but this time from the 'other point of view', namely that of the migrant, and affiliation is now perceived as the nostalgia of exile – it is no longer discriminatory arrogance but something which has been painfully lost. Exile, as Edward Said confirms, is a loss: 'the unhealable rift forced between a human being and a *native place*, between the self and its *true home*' (my emphasis).[4] Le Blanc himself makes the same observation: 'There is an experience of exile which equates to a loss (of national qualities).'[5] We thus find a remarkable interplay of opposing currents of affiliation: in the country of destination ('The Homeland' inhabited by 'The Native', with totalitarian capital letters),[6] affiliation is infinitely problematic and repulsive; but when the point of reference is the country left behind, it becomes a legitimate sentiment of having roots followed by the painful experience of being uprooted, to which one readily applies words which would sound shocking if uttered by 'The Native', such as 'native country' and 'true home'.

In other words, national affiliation is only a good thing when it has been lost and may only be exalted in nostalgic mode. Just as with Badiou, for whom 'people + national adjective' becomes something detestable once the act of revolution has occurred, so this approbation of national affiliation paradoxically rests on notions of abandonment and departure. Affiliation is only a good thing when one is torn away from it. The incontestable sense which migrants have of being uprooted clearly flies in the face of a domestic discourse which rejects the notion of national affiliation, for does not talk of being uprooted imply that there is indeed such a thing as roots? Migrants do indeed suffer, and, more precisely, they suffer from a lost affiliation. Logically speaking, then, this value should be transmitted across all the links of the chain of argument: if the painful experience of migrants is deemed legitimate (and how could it not be?), this legitimacy must extend to the causal object of their suffering, which is affiliation; lost affiliation it may be, but 'lost' here is a secondary predicate and one cannot assign to a secondary predicate – loss or possession (of affiliation) – the job of making an axiological

---

4 Edward Said, *Reflections on Exile and Other Literary and Cultural Essays*, Granta, 2001.

5 Le Blanc, *Dedans, dehors*, p. 30.

6 Ibid., p. 29.

distinction in relation to affiliation itself. The discourse that seeks both to reject domestic affiliation and, quite rightly, to recognise the tragic condition in which immigrants find themselves (not merely as a minority when they arrive but also when they are forced to depart), is doomed to veer arbitrarily between emphasising (lost) affiliation and rejecting (possessed) affiliation.

This type of vacillation prompts one not so much to embrace one or other of these poles, but rather to distance oneself altogether from the perspective which gives rise to such hesitations, namely an axiological perspective which seeks to distinguish good from bad but which, in this instance, finds itself in the embarrassing situation of deeming something to be simultaneously good and bad. If affiliation turns out to be problematic when it is possessed but also when it is lost, then perhaps it is necessary, at least for the time being, to sidestep the automatic and premature tendency to frame the problem axiologically and instead to begin empirically conceptualising its workings and its connective power.

Post-Nation or Extended Nation?

Firstly, however, we need to complete our tour of the paralogisms associated with disaffiliation and post-nationalism. The crudest of these is surely the failure to appreciate that the post-national scenario so vehemently being advocated merely serves, in most cases, to pave the way for the super-national, which ultimately will possess the same characteristics – only in a worse form – as the despised nation. This is especially true of the 'Europeanist' variant of the post-national argument, which claims that current nations will be superseded and demoted in the process of constructing 'Europe'. But what could 'Europe' be, other than the redeployment of the nation-state principle itself, but on an amplified scale: a political community that declares itself sovereign and endows itself with parliamentary institutions to express that sovereignty, within borders that are admittedly extended and yet just as finite? In other words, it would remain a specific entity which is simply larger, and very far from fulfilling the conditions of cosmopolitan universality.

The particular form adopted by the institutions makes no difference in either of the two possible scenarios: either the European edifice remains incapable of crossing the critical threshold of political integration, or it does indeed cross it. In the first case, the 'Union' does not live up to the concept underlying it, because it remains at the stage of a simple grouping of nation states. The political irony here is that this downgrading of the European aspiration is presently championed by a whole neo-Kantian tendency,[7] previously known for its propensity for universalism and the sheer scope of its cosmopolitan ambitions. Now reduced to a pragmatic level of basic prudence, it abandoned the idea of a 'European state' after realising that it would lack the resources historically available to nation states for their own construction. Under these circumstances, the Union would not be a union and would hardly amount to more than what it currently is: an assemblage of nation states linked by treaties, whose constituent parts enjoy primacy because the whole has not crossed the threshold of cohesion, making it impossible to proclaim the advent of a post-national era.

In the second scenario, this threshold is indeed crossed. It is not extravagant to suppose that the resulting integrated political entity would be more likely to assume a federal rather than a unitary form, and one would have to have lost all sense of categories not to realise that a state, even a federal one, remains a state. There is little doubt that the French mind is particularly prone to this kind of distortion, having only ever associated the concept of state with its unitary and centralised form – the federal form being such an alien notion that it is taken to supersede the very principle of state. Resisting the charms of exoticism – though in truth, there is nothing specifically French about this kind of error; do not we find the same thing, indeed in more egregious form, in the writings of Ulrich Beck and Jürgen Habermas?[8] – we need to signal certain elementary truths, such as the fact that in order to be a federal republic, Germany has to be a nation state, as does the United States of America and the Russian Federation. We can therein appreciate more clearly the nature of this category error which, locked into the perspective of the constituent parts, entails imagining that the new whole of the future will be something 'quite different' and will represent a radical break in continuity. Once nation states integrate with one another to

---

7 See, for example, Jean-Marc Ferry, *La Question de l'État européen*, 'Essais', Gallimard, 2005.

8 Ulrich Beck, 'Redefining Power in the Global Age: Eight Theses', *Le Débat*, no. 125 (2003); Jürgen Habermas, *The Postnational Constellation, Political Essays*, Polity Press, 2001.

form 'something' unprecedented, the assumption is that this will necessarily be something radically different and 'therefore' not a nation state
at all: here, in all its splendour, is the paralogism of the Europeanist
post-national vision. It is incapable of conceiving the fact that a European
federal state would invent nothing new and supersede nothing, but,
instead, merely reproduce itself on a bigger scale – rather as if the
Prussians, Bavarians and Rhinelanders at the end of the nineteenth
century had proudly announced that they were superseding nations by
forming Germany.

It is, moreover, in this increase in size, or, rather, in the misunderstanding of its effects, that the deepest illusion of the proponents of
Europeanist post-nationalism lies – their belief that, in advancing the
cause of federalism (even though it does not in fact represent an
advance), they are ridding themselves of all the defects imputed to the
principle of the nation state that they wish to disown, namely the aggressive manoeuvrings of sovereignty and the 'nationalist' pathologies of
identity. The examples just cited – the United States, Russia and Germany
– should suffice to banish this futile hope and encourage a more reasoned
assessment of the logic of power. For the reality is that a taste for power
irresistibly assails large political ensembles, their very size conferring on
them a new-found degree of geopolitical influence which is proportional to their degree of integration and the extent to which this can be
converted into a unit of action. This is why we should not doubt for a
second that, were its project to succeed,[9] friendly old Europe – which
is only judged to be so now because its cohesion remains, for the time
being, a pipe dream – would rapidly embrace completely different ambitions, more in keeping with its new-found potential. This follows from
the simple fact that power tends spontaneously to exercise itself once it
becomes aware of itself. As a result, once its original constituent parts
had been 'metabolised' and its integration consolidated, it is more than
likely that the new European whole would develop all the attributes of a
sovereign entity: an essentialist notion of its identity in keeping with its
finite borders, plus assertive behaviour and the projection of its power
onto the international stage. In other words, it would develop all the

---

9 Which for other reasons I do not believe to be possible. See Frédéric Lordon, *La
Malfaçon. Monnaie européenne et souveraineté démocratique*, Les Liens qui Libèrent,
2014, and in particular Chapter 6.

characteristics of the nation state, doubtless much to the disappointment of those who believed that a change of scale would equate to a
'superseding' of what had gone before. Since the same causes lead to the
same effects, the result would be reminiscent of the United States, of
which the United States of Europe would provide a troubling echo. And
one thing that can safely be said about America is that no matter how
federal it may be, it represents in some ways the epitome of concern for
national sovereignty, in an especially aggressive variant to boot, which
suggests that a 'federalist' superseding of nationalist defects is a somewhat far-fetched notion, at least in this form.

Though they may grow in size and absorb entities of inferior status
(known as 'nations'), expanding political ensembles perpetuate the
national paradigm and, while appearing to supersede specific existing
entities, remain specific entities which have simply been enlarged. This
is why the Europeanist agenda to 'abolish the nation', in failing to realise
that the end point of this would be a new national identity (a European
identity), would have the grotesque and contradictory effect of precipitating a new form of affiliation, even as it seeks to reject affiliation.

It should be pointed out straight away that this tangle of inconsistencies is difficult to iron out by appealing to the concept of 'citizen of the
world', at least in its commonly understood meaning. This is a false way
out of the problem, which generally takes the form of a claim that is
both meaningless and boastful in that it primarily serves to parade the
panoramic outlook of the speaker, who is capable (unlike everyone else)
of instantly deploying his rational mind and his sensibility on the global
scale. Such a claim piles superficiality onto self-glorification since, on
the one hand, 'citizen' denotes membership of a city (an authentic political community, expressed through institutions) and, on the other, the
citizen of the world has literally nothing on which to draw (a global
politeia being manifestly lacking) beyond a desire to lose themselves in
dreams of non-affiliation.

The Critique of National Affiliation as a Paradoxical Mode of National Affiliation

The second paralogism of post-nationalism takes the form not of an
illusory claim to have superseded nationalism but the more subtle form

of a radical critique of the misdeeds of nationalism, or rather the misdeeds of 'their' nationalism by the nationals of a particular country. It is worth saying at this point (we will return to the subject in more detail later[10]) that collective self-analysis and a critical reassessment of one's national history is one of the best safeguards (perhaps the only one) against the dark passions of nationalism, to which the wilfully blind inevitably succumb in pouring scorn on the 'pathological contrition' of 'repentance'. But leaving this imperative to one side for the time being, it is not clear whether putting national history in the dock is incontrovertible evidence of a post-national disposition, nor whether nationals of the criminal nation itself, in rehearsing the lengthy catalogue of crimes, colonisation, massacres, aggressions abroad and repression at home (crimes all committed in the name of the nation and supposedly authorised by the notion of a superior identity or civilisation), really are signalling, as they sometimes seem to think, an irreversible rupture with 'their' nation. Paradoxically, it may be that the very violence of their criticisms belies their intended message, since true rupture would involve neutrality and an even-handed, more general criticism of the misdeeds of *all* nations, without paying special attention to any one in particular – that extra degree of vehemence which their *own* nation manifestly arouses is in itself significant. And what else could it signify but an enduring attachment which intensifies their affective reactions and betrays a continuing affiliation, despite their discourse being couched in the language of disaffiliation? This country whose legitimacy I challenge in denouncing its crimes, is, whatever I may say about it, still *my* country, because its crimes are clearly more despicable to me than those of any other country.

The paradox, then, of self-criticism (which through faulty reasoning is presented as an exercise in pure rupture) is that the violent rejection of identity in fact denotes the persistence of identity, and the avowed desire to leave reveals itself to be an inverted desire to remain. It may therefore be that people refuse (quite rightly) to tolerate the shortcomings of their own country not because they reject it but because they have a very high opinion of it – a high opinion based not on the idea of some particular quality which supposedly makes it more eminent than other nations, but, rather, on the notion of a distinctive nature which is

---

10 See Conclusion.

nevertheless destined for universality, even though the nation's actual conduct may be a source of great disappointment. Its crime-strewn history only appals them to such a degree because they feel themselves to be irresistibly implicated in it. And the degree of concern which they express in relation to this history is in itself a reflection of their close participation – the inclusion of themselves in a collective history which, whatever they might say about it, they cannot help but be a part of, and cannot help but be affiliated to.

Doubtless, there is a formally similar mechanism at work which helps us to understand the angry bewilderment of certain Jews at the spectacle of other, non-Zionist Jews voicing criticism of Israeli (government) policy; deprived of the knee-jerk accusation of antisemitism, which would be absurd in the circumstances, the only way to counter such people is to advance the psychopathological theory of the 'self-hating Jew'. But the 'self-hatred', meaning hatred of their Jewish identity, which is imputed to these Jews critical of the Jewish state might be less a rejection of identity on their part (which in any case is not what they are voicing – rather, it is being secretly voiced on their behalf) than the expression of a more elevated awareness of what it is to be Jewish – a conception which has absolutely no place for the acts of a government which occupies territory beyond its borders and applies a policy of apartheid domestically. 'Not in my name' is the cry of the critical Jew, who is in fact in excellent mental health and not at all self-hating – except perhaps in the eyes of his self-projecting opponents. Rather, he wants the epithet 'Jew' to live up to a number of universal commandments so that he can continue to assume the mantle, this time without reserve.

Impossible Disaffiliations

What, then, are the most ostentatious declarations of *exemption*, which is to say the most explicit proclamations of disaffiliation, actually worth? A declaration of the type 'I cease to consider myself as X', where X = the name of a nationality, does nothing to change the fact that the person making it still very much continues to live physically within a particular material and moral community, which may not be X in its entirety but is its local manifestation. And the conditions of existence of the self-declared disaffiliate nevertheless remain determined by this continuing affiliation: he occupies a specific place within its labour market, his social relationships are centred around this community, he reads its newspapers, and he continues to take an interest in what happens there. What is more, he derives most of his social status from it. In short, he is still fully bound up with this material and moral community which he claims to have disowned. Disaffiliation is anything but a straightforward process, and it can probably only live up fully to its (sometimes ostentatious) pretensions if the person concerned actually leaves for good. And it is this physical location of the body which so often renders the discourse of disaffiliation meaningless – bodies cannot be dematerialised or rendered virtual like electronic networks. Bodies cannot be de-localised: there is a *place* where one *lives*, and this place is itself always part of the territory of a community. And one can only exist by drawing, in one way or another, on the strength and collective resources of the community which occupies this territory.

Shlomo Sand, for example, has no illusions about his own proclamation of disaffiliation.[11] He clearly states that he no longer wants to be Jewish, but he does not deny for a moment that he continues de facto to be an Israeli. The point, for him, is that 'Jewish identity' is intrinsically problematic and indeed cannot be pinned down, once one seeks to divest it of any religious component and to recast it as a secular identity. Is there anything at all outside the religious tradition which could lend coherence to the idea of a Jewish culture? Sand maintains that the answer is no. The objective here is not to debate the validity of the argument but simply to examine its form. In asserting that a 'culture', at least given the non-religious constraints imposed, does not exist, he concludes that he is allowed to declare that he no longer wishes to be Jewish, meaning that he does not intend to be affiliated through an identity defined exclusively by its religious content. But the interesting point lies elsewhere, namely that while disowning his Jewish identity, Sand nevertheless asserts that he is maintaining his identity as an Israeli. One might intuitively have expected the exact opposite from him: that, as an intransigent critic of the occupation, it would have been Israel – the Israeli nation state – that he would have conspicuously disowned, while maintaining his Jewish identity as something distinct from Israel. But no, his

---

11 Shlomo Sand, *How I Stopped Being a Jew*, Verso, 2014.

position is quite different: I will disown my Jewish identity if it transpires that it is necessarily religious in nature, because I myself am not religious; as for my Israeli identity, how would I divest myself of it? For better and for worse, Israel is the soil which is the concrete material reality of my existence, and I would be unable to divorce myself from that. I find Israeli government policy hateful and I oppose it with the utmost vigour. But none of that means that I cease to inhabit this place or to be a member of this material and political community – I am a citizen who is distraught at the policies of this state, but a citizen of it all the same, 'in spite of myself' – though in reality because of myself, and the simple physical fact of my being *here*.

One might object that the location of bodies does not determine anything in itself, and within large territories there are smaller areas where people try to live differently. But small communities must be clearer about what they continue to owe, willingly or otherwise, to the larger territories of which they are a part – in particular the benefits of security, which is to say the legal protections afforded by the structures of the nation state. It is not hard to imagine the immediate indignation such a statement is likely to provoke, because everyone knows that the main source of the insecurity which generally afflicts these alternative community experiments is of course the state itself – the police state which, under the auspices of 'counter-terrorism', proceeds to methodically terrorise any attempt to experiment outside the social constraints of state capitalism. But the fact remains that, while its forces of law and order are a pernicious source of insecurity, the state nevertheless affords security of another order which tends to be overlooked because it is taken so much for granted: the protection afforded by one's civil status. It is therefore true to say that, contingently or perhaps even necessarily, these experiments have everything to fear from the insecurity provoked by state terrorism, but it is just as true to say that they necessarily live in constant fear of aggression at the hands of other communities: imagine an alternative community, like the one in Tarnac in central France, transposed to Iraq . . .

Whatever their nature, these little communities within larger ones cannot take the process of disaffiliation to its logical conclusion, because they are still subject to the nation-state structures within which they are de facto included, both territorially and materially. It is moreover in the very nature of those assets which economists call a 'public good' (typically, public safety and national defence) that their provision is automatically collective – it is not in principle possible to selectively exclude a few individuals from the common mass of beneficiaries, for it is not a collection of individuals which benefits but rather indivisible wholes, such as the 'territory' or the 'population'. And the disaffiliated do indeed continue to benefit from them, for all their protestations of disaffiliation.

The rejection of national identity is thus at best incomplete and in fact contradictory when one continues to derive the benefits of civil status, since for the time being that status is conferred by the institutions of a nation state. What can be the point of a repudiation of nationality, and to what extent can it *tangibly* lay claim to exemption? Such a gesture cannot be cost-free, though one wonders whether those applying for exemption are always fully aware of the nature of those costs. For, while individuals who renounce any form of nationality continue, knowingly or not, to benefit systemically from the public good of security (internal and external), the surrender of identity documents nevertheless deprives them of a whole series of rights, including, of course, the right to vote (perhaps the right which will be missed the least), consular protection abroad, the full range of welfare entitlements at home and so on (if disaffiliates fall seriously ill, where do they go for treatment?). To feel justified in doubting how fully aware they are of this, we need only look at the contrast between the fantasy of statelessness (on the part of people who are perfectly well integrated) and actual statelessness – that nightmare of absolute non-inclusion, rootlessness and zero rights, and relegation to the extreme periphery, where people are condemned to subsist in the margins of the world. The extent of that nightmare is indirectly reflected in the tenacious struggle of undocumented immigrants to obtain legal status, which is a struggle to be included and to *belong*, precisely, to the state. This renders particularly grotesque the pretensions to emancipation of the comfortably affiliated, who have become incapable of appreciating the ways in which their affiliation supports them and indeed constitutes their identity, notwithstanding the loathing this provokes in them.

2

The Social as Exceedance and Elevation

The paralogisms of exemption and post-national thinking are not merely inconsistent but also symptomatic. Symptomatic of what, exactly? What is this state of mind that is so torn and troubled by affiliation, national or otherwise, that it is led into obvious contradictions? And conversely, what is restored in the imagination by these narratives of exemption and emancipation – whether expressed in 'citizen of the world' terms or through some other claim of disaffiliation – if not that individualist sentiment par excellence of personal sovereignty: that fantasy of spurning all forms of affiliation, since belonging is perceived to be an ontological offence against one's status as subject? Is not the subject the fully realised expression of the individual? Is not subjecthood the very essence of the individual? 'Belonging' is a property of objects and would therefore seem antithetical to subjecthood. How could I be the mere object of an entity larger than myself and *belong* to it? This appears to be the principle at work behind the contemporary refusal to acknowledge that we are part of collective wholes, as if this would be tantamount to relinquishing our dignity as supposedly completely free and autonomous individuals.

Society as Societas?

One might reply that many types of disaffiliation nevertheless remain possible and that individuals do voluntarily espouse collectives and later sever their ties with them. It can also be argued that their 'identities', far from being exclusively defined by national affiliation, have for a long time tended towards the multiple and the fluid. And all of this is true. But it is when it tries to give up its greatest illusion – the illusion of an affiliation that is always optional and discardable – that exemption becomes nothing more than an individualist *flatus vocis*, a hollow declaration that merely expresses a belief in the possibility of a separate, autonomous existence, detached (or at least detachable) from everything else.

It is at this point that one also becomes aware of the deep-seated persistence of a neoliberal metaphysics among those who regard themselves as the most anti-liberal.[1] This is where we get to the heart of a social philosophy of liberalism which, based on the atomistic premise of the free and autonomous individual who is self-sufficient and separate, will never be able to conceive of society (a term which is in itself highly symptomatic) as anything other than a collection of separate individuals. I say symptomatic, because the choice of the word 'society' to describe the modern form of human groups raises questions of its own. *Societas*, a category of Roman and then canon law, originally designated not an organic whole – the word for that would be *universitas* – but an *association*, which is to say a *contingent* and *reversible* coming together of individuals of their own volition, and those same individuals will disperse again should their situation and their interests so dictate. *Societas* is the model par excellence of a collective consistent with an atomistic vision of the social world. Indeed, it is the only collective that is conceivable for a world of individuals, and so it comes to pass, highly significantly and just as inappropriately, that the word given to the social whole is . . . society. As if it consisted of nothing more than a conscious and voluntary gathering of subjects, like some gigantic limited company (or *société de capitaux*, the business world being where the word '*société*' really comes into its own[2]), but with a purpose other than added value.

---

1 See Frédéric Lordon, *La Société des affects. Pour un structuralisme des passions*, Seuil, 2013, Chapter 8, 'Les imbéciles heureux'.

2 [TN] This train of thought works more naturally in French than in English. A *société de capitaux* usually translates as a 'limited company', *société* being one of the standard French words for company (as well as the word for society). In the business meaning, we would use 'shares' in English for *capitaux*. The French term obviously evokes capital (and capitalism) more directly.

The paradigm of the association haunts all of modern thought. From the appropriately named 'social contract' theories, whose very name reflects the atomistic philosophy that underpins them, to the communist and anarchist conceptions of free associations, the associative and/or contractual paradigm sets the framework for modern thinking about groupings. People only group and bind together because they *want* to, perhaps at some initial and distant moment in the past. And this is necessarily the case because subjects that are, from the outset, free could not proceed in any other manner.

The Provisional Engagement of the Liberal Individual

So this is what the paralogisms of exemption are the symptom of: a conception of 'society' as a gathering of individuals who are fundamentally unbound and will only bind themselves together voluntarily and contingently. And that bonding process is seen as a wilful act of consent – the fruit of reflection on the part of the individual alone. It is worth pointing out straight away that this modality of bonding, of entering into a bond, epitomises the most characteristic traits of liberal individualism, for which such relationships are ultimately problematic from the point of view of personal sovereignty. The cult of exemption, of belonging to nothing and refusing to become bound, renders the principle of engagement wholly aporetic, since that would necessarily involve consenting to becoming bound. Engagement in a relationship is contradictory, in that it imposes some degree of irreversibility on an individual for whom their sovereignty as a subject implies a constant capacity to change their mind and to countenance all options, including that of disengagement. And the individual only engages in the belief that they are free to disengage at any moment, and that they are consenting to becoming bound on the proviso that they can always unbind themselves. Unsurprisingly, this oxymoronic aporia of 'reversible engagement', which lays claim to the absolute sovereignty of individual desire, finds its fullest expression in the world of business, especially the domain of finance, in this globalised age – so much so, indeed, that one could define it as a general exoneration from anything that curtails capitalist desires. In the wake of Keynes, André Orléan has shown the extent to which financial liquidity – that property of a market which allows an operator to enter *or leave* it at any time – contains a paradigmatic power in the neoliberal age.[3] It is paradigmatic because it expresses in its purest form the fantasy of the sovereignty of individual desire. Unlike physical investment, which through construction *fixes* capital (significantly, accountants speak of *fixed assets*), financial investment is non-fixed, 'liquid' and entirely reversible, since the continuous flow of stock market transactions means that capital can be retrieved and reallocated at any time according to the changing whims of investors. One can 'engage' in company A by buying shares and then withdraw a minute later, selling them in order to engage in B, C and D as one's financial desires dictate. And the nature of liquidity arrangements means that those desires are free of any constraints, of any need for patience and of any notion of irreversibility. The most revealing political equivalent of financial liquidity – and of this self-contradictory form of binding – is the conception of the collective as an association. And just as an investor only enters a market with the guarantee of being able to leave it, so the member of the collective only engages when safe in the knowledge that they can withdraw again.

The Phantasmagoria of the 'Genuine Contract'

Despite itself, for all its denials, anarchist thought is often shot through with this metaphysics of liberalism – at least in the case of advocates who deduce on the basis of individual sovereignty and free will that all groupings are based on the associative-contractual model, and indeed prescribe that model. No doubt Bakunin's idea of liberty is more sophisticated than that of 'monadological' liberalism since, in his view, the very exercise of freedom implies not merely the freedom of others but also the concrete interaction of liberties: 'Liberty is therefore a feature not of isolation but of interaction, not of exclusion but rather of connection',[4] and 'it follows that [man] only realises his individual liberty . . . by integration with all the individuals around him.'[5] And the

---

3 André Orléan, *Le Pouvoir de la finance*, Odile Jacob, 1999; 'L'individu, le marché et l'opinion. Réflexions sur le capitalisme financier', *Esprit*, no. 269/11 (November 2000).

4 Mikhail Bakunin, *Michael Bakunin: Selected Writings*, ed. and intro. A. Lehning, Cape, 1973, pp. 127–8.

5 Ibid., p. 125.

depth of Bakunin's conception of freedom is evident in the affirmation that 'man must find his liberty, not at the beginning, but at the ends of history.'[6]

However, by conceiving liberty, or more precisely the way in which liberty is realised, as connective, he nevertheless falls back on an associative-contractual conception of groupings and explicitly acknowledges the reversibility of any engagement by free consent, at every scale of the social world: 'Every individual, every association, every commune, every region, every nation has the absolute right to self-determination to associate or not to associate, to ally themselves with whomever they wish and repudiate their alliances without regard to so-called historic rights or the convenience of their neighbours.'[7] And this is not merely a 'right': it is to be seen as the only admissible way of forming groupings, regardless of their scale, and so encompasses the nation too. It is to be understood – *can* only be understood – as a *genuine* contract: 'Freedom is the absolute right of every adult man and woman to seek no other sanction for their acts than their own conscience and their own reason, being responsible first to themselves and then to the society which they have *voluntarily* accepted.'[8]

In a political philosophy of exemption like this, expressed here in its purest form, the nation is nothing more than a large association of willing members who can always reconsider their engagement (though to do what and to go where instead?). And, more characteristically, the social contract is not imaginary but very real. As Proudhon remarks: 'In J.-J. Rousseau's theory . . . the social contract is a legal fiction, imagined as an alternative to divine right, paternal authority, or social necessity, in explaining the origins of the state . . . In the federal system, the social contract is more than a fiction; it is a positive and effective compact, which has actually been proposed, discussed, voted upon, and adopted, and which can properly be amended at the contracting parties' will. Between the federal contract and Rousseau's contract of 1793 there is all the difference between a reality and a hypothesis.'[9]

---

6 Ibid.

7 Bakunin, *Revolutionary Catechism*, 1866, in *Bakunin on Anarchy*, trans. and ed. Sam Dolgoff, Vintage Books, 1971.

8 Ibid., my emphasis.

9 Pierre-Joseph Proudhon, *The Principle of Federation*, trans. Richard Vernon, University of Toronto Press, 1979.

The Exceedance of the Social (and Its Elevation)

Anarchist thinking thus accommodates only two modalities of group formation: a forced coming together under the despotic coercion of the state, or else free association based on a contract. Sociology, however, takes a very different view of 'society'. On the one hand, it asserts that the cohesive principle underpinning societies is to be understood independently of the external influence of the state, but, above all, it asserts that there is much more to human collectivities than the effects of voluntary associations and that bonds arise elsewhere than from carefully thought-through 'engagements'. Sociology's more holistic view is based not only on the idea that 'society' can exert a determining power on the individual but also on the notion that there is something additional – that there is an *exceedance* of the whole in relation to the parts. There is more to the whole than the sum of its parts, and the co-existence of parts gives rise to something extra which is not contained in those various parts. Hence society (which is a misnomer) is not a simple association, for the latter by definition adds nothing by juxtaposing its constituent elements. There is only something genuinely social, an element of 'society', when an exceedance is produced. But this is the kind of idea that liberal and anarchist thought – underpinned by the self-image of its proponents, who automatically believe themselves to be autonomous and sovereign decision-makers who freely choose the bonds they enter into – categorically refuses to entertain. This is because exceedance is something beyond their reach and their control – an unbearable proposition for a liberal individual who has decided that they are sovereign in all matters: their actions, their forming of bonds and all the consequences that follow.

Such a refusal can only assume the form of denial on a grandiose scale, for exceedance is a necessary fact. And the social is necessarily transcendence, albeit of a special kind: an *immanent transcendence*. No human collectivity of significant size can form without projecting, over and above its members, symbolic productions of every type which they have all contributed to creating, even if they are dominated by those productions and unable to recognise their own hand in them. This is the ultimate meaning of the autonomy of the social revealed by Durkheim – an order of facts that are irreducible to the conscious interactions of individuals. Before him, Marx had clearly perceived this mechanism whereby people lose control of their own productions. Even though they emanate from people, and people alone, they take on a life of their own and in a 'petrified' state tower over them. To say that humans make their own history but do not recognise that history, or rather that they are dominated by the history that is of their own creation, is perhaps the most concise summary of the notion of immanent transcendence – that essential characteristic of the social which contractual-associational thinking is bound to overlook.

Conceptualising the Social as Transcendence (an Exercise in Speculation)

By their nature, the effects of immanent transcendence are not easy to reconstruct, and for good reason: the social is always already present. Warning against the chimera of any historical inquiry that seeks to identify a starting point for the social order, Durkheim furnishes us with some definitive methodological advice: 'To be sure, if by origin we are to understand the very first beginning, the question has nothing scientific about it, and should be resolutely discarded. There was no given moment when religion began to exist, and there is consequently no need of finding a means of transporting ourselves thither in thought. Like every human institution, religion did not commence anywhere.'[10]

If the transcendence of the social is beyond the reach of any attempts to historically reconstruct its genesis (indeed, the very idea of attempting such a construction is meaningless), an insight into it can nevertheless be achieved through a different kind of exercise, which Alexandre Matheron calls *conceptual genesis*.[11] *Free of any historical pretensions*, the conceptual-genesis approach is a *thought experiment* that deliberately takes as its starting point a *fictive* original state. To seek empirical confirmations of it would thus be to miss the point. This original state is conventionally given the name 'state of nature', and it is essentially fictive because it is generally used to denote a primitive collection of atomistic

---

10 Émile Durkheim, *The Elementary Forms of the Religious Life*, trans. Joseph Ward Swain, George Allen and Unwin, 1915, p. 8.

11 Alexandre Matheron, *Individu et communauté chez Spinoza*, Éditions de Minuit, 1988.

individuals prior to any social interaction – and such a situation, it is worth repeating, can hardly have arisen in actual fact, because the social is always already there. There is no such thing as an individual who has not been socialised *ab origino*. Far from being a hindrance, however, the unrealistic nature of this situation viewed through the prism of conceptual genesis is positively an advantage, since it affords the possibility of advancing an a fortiori argument: even supposing that individuals originally coexisted in atomistic mode (which cannot have been the case), this approach demonstrates that their 'interactions' will inevitably lead, through an aggregate effect, to these collective productions which will escape their control and come to hang over and dominate them. The social is thus born endogenously (even if one insists on invoking an impossible initial asocial state).

But what exactly is the nature of these 'collective productions' that emerge through aggregate effects? Drawing on Spinoza's *Political Treatise*, of which he offers a powerful reinterpretation, Alexandre Matheron replies that it is affective. What is being collectively produced is affects. The basic mechanism of this collective production is emulation, which Spinoza describes in *Ethics*, III, 27: 'From the fact that we imagine a thing like ourselves, towards which we have felt no affect, to be affected by an affect, we are thereby affected by a similar affect.' The simple spectacle of a human individual being affected immediately affects us too – and the affect that we experience is none other than the affect which the other person experiences, 'imported' so to speak into ourselves by emulation.[12] This imitation of affects, when it takes place on large scales, can have powerfully generative properties. In a two-way dispute, as a spectator we take the side of the person whom we feel is most like us, and the affect imitation mechanism works according to the principle of affinity through similarity. The injustice suffered by the one who is 'more like' us arouses within us a sadness which is nothing other than an empathetic emulation of the sadness experienced by that other person.

Imitation, in these cases, thus induces the taking of sides and creates a chain of involvements in the initial dispute, which is to say the formation of groups with affinities which other like-minded individuals

---

12 All other things being equal, of course, as there may be other affects at work which influence our judgement of the individual in question.

subsequently join. And the formation of these antagonistic structures is aided and abetted by an increase in the yield from imitation. Bolstered by the affects which underpin its attractiveness in the first place,[13] the more individuals that one party manages to attract, the greater its power to induce affective emulation becomes and thus its ability to attract further members. Large coalitions are the undoing of small coalitions, and, over successive stages, there ends up being only one: the group has then entirely converged onto a common affect, which may, for example, serve as the basis for a certain way of feeling or of judging. It is therefore in this imitative convergence that we need to seek the basic mechanism of the *conceptual* genesis of a moral community, which is to say the formation of a group as a recognisable group. It may, for example, be characterised by the adoption of a common way of defining good and evil, or the desirable and the reprehensible. And this will impose itself on each of the members, even though none of them can recognise themselves in a meaningful way in the process of getting there or in the final result.

The Affective Morphogenesis of the Social (Common Affects and Group Formation)

It is worth stressing, once again, that it would be futile to seek any empirical historical trace in this picture afforded by conceptual genesis, and so more futile still to criticise it for lacking in realism. But what then, one might ask, is the value of a speculative argument which sets out to say something about the real world – in this case, the real nature of society – while refusing to be evaluated in terms of any *direct* comparison to the real world? Once again, Durkheim has the answer: 'But the problem which we raise is quite another one. What we want to do is to find a means of discerning the *ever-present* causes upon which the most essential forms of religious thought and practice depend.'[14] Even if it has no *immediate* connection with the real world, this does not prevent the conceptual-genesis approach from being a powerful tool for thinking

---

13 Remember that, for Spinoza, our notions of good and evil are the transfigurations in the mind of the affects of pleasure and pain by which we judge all things.

14 Durkheim, *Elementary Forms*, p. 8, my emphasis.

about the real world, not least because it can reveal the elementary mechanisms through which the social is produced. One might make the comparison with the elementary particles of matter, which are never observed separately in themselves but nonetheless enable us to understand how the macroscopic world is formed. It is no coincidence that, in this respect, Durkheim echoes Rousseau, who also stressed the intellectual nature of his project in the *Second Discourse* to return to the fundamental elements of social life without engaging in a historiographical investigation. Indeed Durkheim, who saw in Rousseau a 'precursor of sociology', quotes him on this subject: 'The investigations we may enter into, in treating this subject, must not be considered as historical truths, but only as mere conditional and hypothetical reasonings, rather calculated to explain the nature of things, than to ascertain their actual origin.'[15]

Beneath all of humanity's extraordinarily complicated, entangled and much-analysed historical productions, the common affect is the essence, the primary element, of the transcendence of the social – even though it has been rendered invisible, at least in its purest form, by the endless branching of the institutional structure in which it has so to speak been crystallised. The group affects itself, and in a way that exceeds the actions of each of its members, giving rise *from* them but also *above* them to something that transcends all of them. To this production of the social, Spinoza gives a name: the power of the multitude. Durkheim, who was immensely knowledgeable about Spinoza, consistently structured his later sociology around this intuition of what he chose to call 'the moral force of society'.[16] It is incumbent on sociology to recognise this force *sui generis* of society itself as the *real* underpinning of all types of authority, whether religious, charismatic, moral or political (real in the sense of fundamental, as opposed to processes such as elections, which those invested with authority tend to make so much of). This should not be taken to mean that a whole society is living in totalitarian unanimity beneath a crushing and inexorable force (we are well aware that the multitude is also a melting pot of variations and differences), but it does mean that there is no large-scale collective that does not proceed from this force *in the final analysis*.

---

15 *Rousseau's Social Contracts and Discourses*, trans. G. D. H. Cole, J. M. Dent & Sons, 1923, pp. 175–6.

16 Durkheim, *Elementary Forms*, p. 210.

We can even go further than the simple statement 'the group affects itself'. In truth, the common affect is in itself a generator of community, making a group exist as a group with its own internal consistency, in contrast to the phase[17] of *formless* multitude that it was in when in the (fictive) state of nature. At the end of the process, as reconstructed through conceptual genesis, a phase transition has thus occurred – a change in the state of social matter, so to speak, from amorphous to coherent. And this is driven by the common affect, which, in this respect, reveals its morphogenetic power.

The Differential Geometry of the Social: The Sheet of Immanence

This change of state is also a change in geometry. The multitude of the simple collection could fit onto one plane containing all the atomistic individuals, whereas a multitude that has become a community *through the action of its own power* has acquired a new dimension: verticality. The geometrical truth of the social is that it is an elevation. This is the fundamental difference compared to interactionism, which believes it can restrict the social to the plane of interactions and thereby completely fails to appreciate its nature. That said, the elevation of the social does not come from heaven (and sociology is not a substitute for theology): it grows out of the plane of immanence. And our challenge is to answer the following question: how can an effect of transcendence come about in a philosophy of immanence which, by definition, excludes any form of transcendence? Part of the paradox is resolved by the notion of engendering not transcendence per se, but an *effect of transcendence*. An 'effect of transcendence' describes the emergence of verticality from a substrate that must be strictly two-dimensional, as we have by definition ruled out the third dimension (that of absolute transcendence). The social is therefore more than a vertical axis arising from the plane; it is a third dimension, but engendered, so to speak, by the other two. Indeed, this is why we need to invoke a special geometry to accommodate the two terms contained within 'immanent transcendence'. In differential

---

17 The word 'phase' is being used metaphorically here, in the sense of the physical states of matter (gaseous phase, liquid phase, etc.).

geometry, a 'sheet'[18] is the word given to the generalisation of the 'classic' horizontal plane, in other words, the most general two-dimensional surface. Unlike the flat plane, the property of this sheet, or surface, is that it can be folded and scrunched such that it is elevated above itself. There is a very simple and instructive way of visualising this, namely by imagining a wave. Hokusai's wave, for example. It is from the liquid mass below that the wave forms and rises above the mass, coming to dominate it from above as it reaches the point of breaking. And, likewise, this is the peculiar shape traced by the transcendence of the social, which emerges from 'below' but rises above the substrate which gave birth to it and comes to dominate it *like* something from 'above' in a dual dynamic of ascent and descent, each moment capturing one of its terms: immanence is the ascending phase, transcendence the descending phase. The top proceeds from the bottom *in the final analysis* – that is the apparent paradox of immanent transcendence. And there is an *effect of transcendence* – and not simply transcendence – because the descending phase has been preceded (engendered) by the ascending phase. Thus, what in fact comes from the bottom is perceived and imagined as having all the attributes of coming from the top: vertical authority, affective community and incommensurable power. And yet that power is in fact that of the multitude itself, but as if separated from it. Deleuze sought to contain immanence within a plane – the plane of immanence – and one can see why there was no room for transcendence on that plane. But such a schema falls short if one wants to analyse the elevation of the social: the plane is too flat. To accommodate immanence but also encompass effects of transcendence, a more capable plane is needed: a sheet of immanence.

The Homogeneous and the Heterogeneous (Non-Totalitarian Totalities)

Unfortunately, modern individualist thought is incapable of conceptualising that geometry and cannot get beyond the antinomy of the simple vertical (the false transcendence of the priests) and the pure horizontal, which is held to accommodate all the relationships that 'free subjects'

---

18 Technically, a differentiable manifold of order two.

can form. It is assumed in the modern world that the question has been definitively decided by discarding one of these incompatible hypotheses: God is dead and with Him verticality, and so all that remains is the horizontal. While the first part of this proposition may be true, it does not follow that the second is, barring a monumental refusal to accept the verticality of the social, albeit verticality of a very particular kind.

And it is precisely this particularity that the sociological perspective – the perspective of the immanent transcendence of the social – enables us to perceive, and more distinctly still if we embrace the concept of the power of the multitude. There is no doubt that this idea is almost a personal affront to the modern individual in that it forces them to admit that they are transcended and dominated, having always affirmed that transparency to oneself should form the bedrock of individual and collective action. Acknowledging exceedance sticks in their throat, even though their entire experience of social life is a constant reminder of everything that has always escaped their control and come to impose itself upon them. Inconsistency or wilful blindness are the only ways of accommodating this otherwise insoluble contradiction between, on the one hand, the reality of a godless world and, on the other, the persistence of an incommensurable force that dominates humans – but which is none other than their own force. Even supposing that post-national transcendence has an authentic sense (and is not merely a re-enactment on an extended scale), it will not escape from the primacy of the social, which is to say the necessity of exceedance. And, in this new configuration, people will have to accept that their groupings make them exist as a body, that there is something more to that body than simple juxtaposition, and that they will never be entirely in control of that 'something extra'.

The *universitas* is more than a *societas*. This emphatically does not mean that the *universitas* absorbs and encompasses all of the relationships that people form with one another. There is no totalitarianism of the common affect, and human social life is not entirely subject to the transcendent-immanent force exerted by the whole over its parts. Under the verticality of the *universitas*, relational – and affective – human activity proliferates on every scale. Interpersonal bonds form and smaller groups come together in associative or contractual arrangements. This activity is, in a sense, the driver of internal variation within society – the seat of production of differences and divergences, but of divergences that are necessarily limited by their inclusion within the totality formed by the political group, which occupies a higher rung of the ladder. This limitation is indeed quasi-tautologous, since any divergence exceeding a critical point would, by definition, have the effect of breaking apart the group – a very possible scenario as history has demonstrated, but which would lead (*does* lead) to the creation of other groups and not to the elimination of the grouping principle.

So, although there is no totalitarianism in homogeneity, it is nevertheless true that the homogeneous and the heterogeneous operate in a hierarchical relationship, the former asserting its needs on the latter, and that the limit of the heterogeneous is the common framework in which it expresses itself. Where does that limit lie? No one is able to say, certainly not conservatives with their irrepressible tendency to detect it close at hand and perhaps overstepped already . . . But, most of the time, groups tend to agree to push the limit back in order to tolerate ever greater 'quantities of difference', as is intuitively evident from the growing ethnic diversity of contemporary societies – a mixing process facilitated by advances in transport and communications.

The Law of Large Numbers and the Self-Transcendence Threshold

The hierarchical relationship between the homogeneous and the heterogeneous, or the common and the varying, reflects the fact that the group itself is a sum total which forms a whole. But it is not a totalitarian whole, since it can tolerate a high degree of internal differentiation. As a whole, the group is *in itself* a manifestation of the exceedance of the social, though not always, of course. We are all familiar with groups that do not exceed their parts at all and in which the parts have a relationship that is on an even footing with the whole that they form, characterised by transparency and control. In most cases, the effect of immanent transcendence is an effect of size, or perhaps we should say an effect connected to size, and only groups that are sufficiently large will experience the phenomenon of exceedance. In the fictive scenario of conceptual genesis, it is the long-distance propagation of mimetic interactions that generates the common affect which brings together widely separated individuals who may not know each other, or even meet each other, and which creates the power of the multitude. And, the more numerous its parts, the more intense and the more incommensurable with its constituent parts that power is. Social bodies that transcend their parts are in most cases large bodies. Bodies wherein, by virtue of their size, affective emulations extend well beyond the visual field of individuals, none of whom can arrive at an overview of all the social interactions involved and who can only become aware passively, after the fact, of the overall structures that these interactions engender.

An increase in size merely intensifies this effect by which the multitude engenders forms that transcend it (sometimes to the extent of being unrecognisable to it) and accounts for that element of heteronomy that is intrinsic to social groupings. For there are countless practices, behaviours and habits that impose themselves on us ready-made, testifying to society's capacity to grasp hold of us. The group grasps hold of us at birth. Through the family and through school, which Durkheim memorably likened to the 'seminary of society', the group transmits its behaviours to us. Once again, this is not to suggest an irremediably determined and fixed state of affairs, nor to rule out the possibility later on of reinventing our circumstances. But it does mean that those later, conscious reinventions must necessarily take place within that overarching social framework, the influence of which can in certain instances be parried but never eliminated altogether, not least because most reinventions are collective. They are the product of the changes that the multitude continues to effect upon itself in a generalised process of self-affecting that transcends conscious intentions: it is the multitude as a whole that reinvents its behaviours.

The Synoptic Condition and the Paralogism of Scale

It nevertheless remains the case that a small number of people is the necessary (though not in itself sufficient) precondition for any collective and conscious project to control one's circumstances. The parts can only effectively control the group that they form under certain size constraints. And one might define the nature of this precondition by stating that the parts of the group cannot hope to be transparent to themselves and exert conscious self-control unless a perception of the whole is available to all – unless everyone can see everything. We might call this the *synoptic condition.* And we might describe as a paralogism of scale the error of conceiving of societies as simple homothetic transformations of communities – large groups thus being no more than small groups enlarged – and failing to appreciate that the change of scale itself produces effects and that qualitative transformations accompany quantitative increases. We have already seen the principle at work in these qualitative transformations: exceedance. Immanent transcendence is precisely that something extra which grows out of the affective synergies of large numbers of people, whereas small groups that satisfy the synoptic condition are able to aspire to the complete control of their collective productions.[19] One might speak of the law of large numbers when it comes to the social.[20] Arguing that 'what is true of a small community of friends aiming at a joint purpose is also true, on another scale, of the city aiming towards the common good'[21] is an example of the paralogism of scale in its purest form – that failure (or perhaps intellectual refusal) to appreciate exceedance which is so typical of liberal thinkers and by extension of anarchist thinkers, since both are wedded exclusively to the notion of the *plane*: the horizontality of the market and of the political contract in the case of the former, and the horizontality of association in the case of the latter. But society is not just an expanded 'group of friends' and the synoptic condition, or its absence, engenders a qualitative difference. If human groups are to be analysed at the scale of very large groupings, then they must be analysed *on their own terms* as macroscopic social entities, not simply as homothetic transformations of microscopic groupings.

---

19 In theory, at least. The American anthropologist Mark Anspach draws attention to the phenomenon of a game of tennis becoming autonomous as the players are swept up in it and dominated by it – a form of self-transcendence occurring as soon as we reach the number 2 . . .

20 This is quite separate from the law of large numbers of probability theory.

21 Pierre Dardot and Christian Laval, *Commun. Essai sur la révolution au XXIe siècle* [*Common: On Revolution in the Twenty-First Century*], La Découverte, p. 24.

The Instability of the Contractual Plane (the Failure to Recognise the Verticality of Association)

This failure to acknowledge verticality – the epitome of the anti-socio-logical mind-set – is the bane of thinking in this individualistic age, since its proponents can only imagine transcendence as something descending (and mythical) rather than as something immanent, which is to say ascending and descending (and real). 'There is no obligation between people participating in the same activity or the same task', assert Pierre Dardot and Christian Laval,[22] in complete contrast to Durkheim, who always rejected the notion of obligation as a bilateral affair – which is how liberal thinkers see it, with their contractual theories and their contracting parties who exist alone in the world. Even the most local obligation only holds through the effect of an overall force that is exterior to it, namely the force intrinsic to society – what Durkheim calls the moral force of society, which is another way of saying immanent transcendence. It is true enough that the social sciences begin with the number three, as in the presence of a third party between the two contracting parties (supposedly as isolated as Robinson Crusoe). And it is, indeed, an important third party for it is society itself, a reservoir of forces incommensurately superior to those of individuals, which alone is capable of holding them to their commitments – for the mere interplay of individual intentions and goodwill, which in most cases would mean an interplay of self-interests, would render the whole system completely unstable. And this is exactly what anarchist thinkers refuse to admit, despite their emphasis on 'values' such as altruism, cooperation and solidarity. Underpinning our actions with these values is seen as the only way of countering the strategic opportunism of utilitarian individualism (though it should be remarked in passing that, as moral productions, these values originate nowhere else but in society itself and have no guarantor other than the moral force of society).

Spinoza had, before Durkheim, already grasped the fatal shortcomings of contractualism and, more precisely, its failure to perceive the fundamental instability of the contract or any 'pact' if it depends solely on the goodwill of the contracting parties. He appreciated that it can only ever hold good through the action of a force external to its own

---

22 Ibid., p. 23.

framework. 'Even if people promise and agree to keep faith by offering sure signs of sincerity, no one can be certain of another person's good faith, *unless something is added to the promise*. For everyone can act with deceit by the right of nature and is not obliged to stand by promises except where there is hope of a greater good or fear of a greater evil.'[23] This leads Spinoza to the following conclusion: 'We conclude from this that any agreement can have force only if it is in our interest, and when it is not in our interest, the agreement fails and remains void.'[24] He is certainly not claiming that promises are never kept but rather that, unless the interests of the parties are perfectly aligned, those promises will only be kept if *something is added*, that something being extrinsic to both the content of the promise and the direct dealings between the parties. This added something cannot be anything but the force that makes us act in ways that can be at odds with our immediate opportunistic desires and thereby extends the range of what we consider to be in our interests and 'useful'; the force that extends our concept of utility beyond utilitarianism to a utility based on fidelity to certain principles, which is to say compliance with the group and its values. This force is that of the common affect, alias the power of the multitude – the principle at the root of all social rules and norms. It is the force of the ascending-descending vertical which is what really holds individuals to what they believe in, though they may think their values come from their inner selves. Visions and projects based on a notion of horizontality consistently fail to see that their moral possibilities are supplied to them by the verticality which they obstinately refuse to acknowledge. However local it may be, an obligation that ties individuals to the commons is, by its moral nature, consubstantial with this verticality. The coherence of small groups therefore necessarily derives, at least in part, from the large groups within which they are embedded, even if they continue to entertain the illusion that they could emancipate themselves wholesale from that framework.

---

23 Baruch Spinoza, *Theological-Political Treatise*, ed. Jonathan Israel, Cambridge University Press, 2007, XVI, 7, p. 199, my emphasis.
24 Ibid.

3

Divergences and Verticality

Why do people group together rather than remain scattered? And why, when they group together, do they not form one very large grouping the size of the entire planet? In other words, why are there groupings plural, rather than humanity full stop?

'It is certain that the human race merely prompts a collective idea in the mind which does not imply any *actual union* between the individuals that make it up', notes Rousseau.[1] This constructive statement hints at a way into these questions: our focus should be on *actual unions*. No doubt Rousseau has in mind the scholastic position, whose particularity and capacity for distortion Bourdieu has regularly drawn attention to, namely its fetish for ideas and the tendency to endow ideas with a reality content which they do not in fact possess.[2] Characteristic of the 'free play of the intellect' and the partial suspension of necessity in order to abstract itself from the world, the scholastic error was to take ideas about reality for reality itself and to suppose that what is conceived of actually exists, by virtue of the very fact that it can be conceived of. And so it is with the idea of 'the human race' or 'humanity', an idea that is especially attractive because it has the appeal of the universal, of which intellectuals are signally fond. But Rousseau offers us a timely reminder that it does not correspond to any *actual*

---

1 Jean-Jacques Rousseau, *Écrits sur l'abbé de Saint-Pierre*, 1756.
2 Pierre Bourdieu, *Méditations pascaliennes*, 'Liber', Seuil, 1997.

union and that, consequently, the objects to which it refers do not exist other than as ideas – in other words, they do not actually exist. It is, of course, this lack of existence, as we have seen, that points up the futility of claiming (albeit revealingly) to be a 'citizen of the world', since one is only ever an actual citizen of a political community that actually exists. For those who are unwilling to completely forego the scholastic mirages of the universal, two things need to be understood: firstly, that groupings have indeed formed; and, secondly, that they have at some point stopped growing further. People have come together but not to the point of (*actually*) forming a human race. And, so, the world remains fragmented.

A Wolf and a God

People have come together but in distinct blocks. These formations reach a point where the antagonistic forces of convergence and divergence balance each other out. The fragmented (not pulverised) nature of the world is thus the symptom of an ambivalence, of an evenly matched conflict between opposing tendencies. And this ambivalence is the very essence of man's relationship to his fellow man who, as Spinoza observes, is both a god and a wolf. These are the two rival forces which determine the elementary morphology of the human multitude to be that of distinct and finite groupings.

The plurality of finite groupings reflects the balance between the centripetal and centrifugal tendencies, which in terms of the affections of which human beings are capable can be expressed through the figures of god and wolf. It is in this respect that Spinoza's anthropology differs from that of Hobbes: though he is assuredly present, the wolf does not reign supreme over the human soul. This is because 'nothing is more advantageous to man than man.'[3] And nothing is more advantageous for the very good reason that simple survival requires us not to be alone: 'it is scarcely possible for men to support life and cultivate their minds without mutual assistance.'[4] That most basic act of persevering in one's own being – sustaining one's biological existence – is thus the primary

---

3 *Ethics*, IV, 18, scholium, p. 164.
4 *PT*, II, 15, p. 43.

centripetal force. If we are to stand any chance, survival must be organised in concert, and so people will come together out of the need to survive. This is a sufficiently powerful mechanism to form the basis in the *Theological-Political Treatise* of an outline of the genesis of civil society which is in a distinctly different vein to that of the contract which it then goes on to describe more formally. It reads more like an anticipation of the *Political Treatise,* where the contractualist argument disappears altogether in favour of the genesis of a state that is genuinely immanent, which is to say entirely produced by the endogenous interplay of the passions. In the meantime, the *Theological-Political Treatise* in fact sets out two genealogies of the state: the classic contract model is preceded by a genesis story of a very different kind, free of the artificiality of the inaugural pact, based on the division of labour.[5] 'For unless human beings were willing to give each other mutual assistance, each one's own personal skill and time would be inadequate to sustain and preserve him as much as would otherwise be possible. For people are not equally able to do everything, nor would each individual on his own be able to get what he does not have.'[6] In any case, the precariousness and perhaps even the impossibility of solitary survival, unless the environment is extremely conducive, is an experience that we can safely attribute to our fictive man in his fictive state of nature. Self-preservation supposes that we can concretely satisfy our material needs only by pooling our individual efforts in such a way that our respective skills complement each other through the collective organisation of a division of labour. The commodities of material life constitute another of the centripetal forces that prompt people to seek each other out, and this is in part why 'the social organisation of man shows a balance of much more profit than loss'.[7]

---

5 Pierre-François Moreau, 'Les deux genèses de l'État dans le *Traité théologico-politique*', in *Spinoza, État et religion*, ENS Éditions, 2005.

6 *Theological-Political Treatise*, XVI, 7, p. 72.

7 *Ethics*, IV, 35, scholium, p. 172.

The God of Pity

The forces of convergence are not, however, limited to the needs of material reproduction. In other respects, too, 'nothing is more advantageous to man than man' and man seeks out his fellows under the influence of other affective forces. The most powerful of these, as we have seen, originates in the mechanism of imitation, for this is what underpins the tendency towards compassion (as indeed the etymology of the word suggests). If the sight of another person being affected suffices to make me feel a similar affect by 'emulation', then another person's sorrow arouses sorrow in me too, and the name we give to that sorrow is pity.[8] When it assumes the form of pity, the imitation of affects is therefore powerfully centripetal (all other things being equal). It does not only lessen, or indeed eliminate, the possibility of us feeling aggressive towards this unhappy individual but may also prompt us to come to their assistance. And, as Spinoza shows, this is for reasons, or rather due to causes, that owe nothing to pure altruism: by trying to console the other person, it is in fact in the first instance myself whom I am trying to console. Through affective imitation, I have been saddened by their sorrow and as a result I am trying to rid myself of my own sorrow – in ridding the other person of their sorrow, I am ridding myself of mine. Needless to say, we should avoid falling into the nonsensical trap of supposing that this affective mechanism involves conscious and calculating deliberation. The elementary laws of the affections create a chain of cause and effect *within the body itself*, without any need for consciousness or deliberate choice to come into play, and without us necessarily forming clear and distinct ideas of these causal chains within our minds (though this could happen in certain situations). Indeed, most cases of 'altruistic' behaviour bear this out – they may be interpreted as altruistic, but this is because we are completely oblivious to the efforts *in the first person* of the conatus to soothe its *own* sadness that has been induced by the sadness of another. The moralists of the seventeenth century were unrivalled masters at correcting our blindness and forcing us to see things as they are rather than as we would like them to be, and we know that the profound egocentricity of the conatus is adept at dressing in the garb of the highest moral principles

---

8 *Ethics*, III, 27, scholium.

the pursuit of its own self-interest – though obviously in a very broad sense of the word 'interest'.[9]

However, in this case, the important point lies elsewhere. It lies in the reality of the movement that people are prompted to make towards others at the sight of their affliction, and this is a profoundly social force, even though it initially operates locally through the mutual affecting of bodies. But its local range can easily be extended, since, as the conceptual genesis model has shown us, the imitation of affects can be contagious and spread from person to person, thereby creating increasingly large groupings of individuals under a common affect – they may for instance unite in the face of a wrong done to a particular person. The imitation of affects underpins a process of empathy which finds its expression in acts of mutual support as people reach out to one another.

Divergence

The division of labour to jointly stave off the prospect of perishing, and empathetic mutual support: these are the respects in which man, even when he is not under the guidance of reason, can be a god to his fellow man. Which does not make him any less capable of being a wolf. Natural right, the other name for the conatus, does not in itself determine any form of action unequivocally. It 'forbids only those things that no one desires and no one can do', and as a result 'it does not frown on strife, or hatred, or anger, or deceit, or on anything at all urged by the appetite.'[10] This, in a nutshell, is the centrifugal power of the conatus, which renders the state of nature uninhabitable: 'Every man in the state of Nature is in control of his own right just as long as he can guard himself from being subjugated by another, and it is vain for one man alone to try to guard himself against all others. Hence it follows that as long as natural human right is determined the power of each single individual and is possessed by each alone, it is of no account and is notional rather than factual, since there is no assurance that it

---

9 See Chapter 9 and also Frédéric Lordon, *L'Intérêt souverain. Essai d'anthropologie économique spinoziste*, 'Armillaire', La Découverte, 2006.

10 *PT*, II, 8, p. 41.

can be made good.'[11] The apparent licence afforded by a natural right that 'frowns on' nothing is thus entirely illusory since it constantly collides with the natural rights of others, which are similarly unconstrained. And such encounters will inevitably come down to a simple question of power relations.

Man can be a god, yes, but we have to contend with the wolf in him too. 'In so far as men are subject to passive affects, to that extent they cannot be said to agree in nature.'[12] This statement should be read quite literally, not as some kind of exercise in style, irony or affected world-weariness: the passions, which by their nature introduce variation and diversity, cannot offer any guarantee of agreement between people. It is not that they will never agree on anything, but when under the sway of passions, it will be beyond their capacity to agree on *everything* – 'in nature'. Affective convergences, the only kind within reach under the servitude to the passions, are thus essentially contingent and unstable, and always susceptible to unravelling in a more or less violent fashion, having arisen in the first place through sometimes confused coincidences. To avoid such a precarious state of affairs, individuals would need to be guided by reason. This is the meaning of Proposition 35 (IV) of the *Ethics*, which provides the counterpoint to Proposition 32 (IV): 'In so far as men live under the guidance of reason, to that extent *only* do they always necessarily agree in nature.'[13]

However, men do not live under the guidance of reason – otherwise Spinoza would not have taken the trouble to write an *Ethics* in the hope of enabling them to perceive reason through the fog of servitude to the passions. This does not mean that on occasion, at least locally, there cannot be an element of reason in their actions, let alone that we should stop trying to step up the role that reason plays: following on from the *Treatise on the Emendation of the Intellect,* the central intention of the *Ethics* is to help us overcome our affective blind spots and aspire increasingly towards a life *ex ductu rationis*. Spinoza does at least warn us that the road leading to this goal, whether we call it bliss or liberty, is a challenging one, since 'all things excellent are as difficult as they are rare.'[14]

---

11 *PT*, II, 15, p. 43.
12 *Ethics*, IV, 32, p. 170.
13 *Ethics*, IV, 35, p. 171, my emphasis.
14 *Ethics*, V, 42, scholium, p. 223.

In the meantime (which in fact means forever), we will have to contend with people as they are: guided by passive affects. Any presupposition that ignores this basic premise will inevitably lead to political disaster; such an error is characteristic of wishful thinking and of all those grandiose schemes that are too easily inclined to see people 'as they would like them to be',[15] which is to say, as they are not. However, this is in no way to downplay the immense variety of forms – from the very worst to the not so bad to the even rather good – that the collective expression of the passions can produce.

The Workings of Affective Ambivalence

We are, therefore, forced to contend with everything that the servitude to the passions, an insuperable facet of human life, entails in terms of consequences. In other words, we have to contend with ambivalence. And there is no better example of this ambivalence than in the vastly divergent possible outcomes that can be produced by the elementary mechanism of affective imitation. For, while emulation can transform sorrow into pity through empathy, it can also mimetically induce desire and lead people to fight tooth and nail over an object that can only be possessed by one person alone, or to emulate the hatred felt towards another by somebody to whom they feel (rightly or wrongly) akin. The god and the wolf are both contained within this mechanism for emulating affects, and only the concrete nature of a particular situation will determine which one springs out of the box.

In Spinoza's view, however, such ambivalence is not synonymous with symmetry, and the confrontation between centrifugal and centripetal tendencies is not automatically an equal one. The fact that people 'cannot be said to agree in nature' means almost inevitably that in time they will come to disagree, though we have no way of predicting how intensely they will disagree nor how many of them will be involved.[16] One cannot help but be struck by the way in which the *Political Treatise*, which directly grapples with the question of the forms of collective coexistence, radicalises the argument of the *Ethics* and breaks the

---

15 *PT*, I, 1, p. 33.
16 *Ethics*, IV, 32.

apparent symmetry that one might have been tempted to read into it:[17] 'In so far as men are assailed by anger, envy, or any emotions deriving from hatred, they are drawn apart and are contrary to one another and are therefore the more to be feared, as they have more power and are more cunning and astute than other animals. And since men are by nature especially subject to these emotions ... men are therefore by nature enemies.'[18] The affective complexion of people clearly contains centripetal potential for mutual support, but without any institutionalised mechanisms for regulating violence, there is a strong probability of war. This is why the fictive 'state of nature' is chaotic, dominated as it is by wolves.

But it is not merely chaotic: it is also dynamically unstable. This is because an atmosphere that is saturated with violence triggers individual and collective affections that lead this initial state (which in fact is untenable for everyone) to transcend itself spontaneously. This is the lesson to be drawn from the conceptual genesis model, whose whole purpose is to reveal the morphogenetic power of affective dynamics arising endogenously in this precarious atmosphere of violence. We also see all the ambivalence of affective imitation at work here, for it is imitation governed by the principle of affinity through similarity – in an external dispute between two people, my compassion goes out to the one whom I judge to be most similar to me – which leads to the taking of sides and the contagion of affects. In this case, I will feel affects of pity and love for the one(s) whose cause I espouse and affects of hatred for the opposing side that carry the potential for violence. And so alliances, collective animosities and rival blocs begin to form, there are confrontations and rapprochements, and ultimately a convergence takes place through a gradual snowball effect: everyone seeks to join the most powerful group that offers them the best guarantees of protection such that through successive stages of elimination, the number of blocs diminishes and their size increases until there is only one left.

According to this speculative model, the imitation of affects thus engenders love, pity and concern for others, but also hatred and violence.

---

17 Despite the fact that *Ethics*, IV, 37 and its scholia are already clear enough on this point.

18 *PT*, II, 14, p. 43.

We are all familiar with this kind of ambivalence: when, for example, we see media coverage of a dispute between striking workers and their bosses, the mechanism of empathetic affinity prompts a sense of solidarity with one side and animosity towards the other and leads to the formation of antagonistic groupings that identify with one side or the other. And now we need to imagine the same mechanism operating without the slightest constraint in an institutional void – and what we have then is the state of nature.

The Power of the Multitude and the Formation of Groups

It is thus within this same dynamic that the chaotic violence of the state of nature finds its resolution, and the elevation which is the essence of the social is produced. The process of convergence is initially the product of common affects and is a *formative* process driven endogenously and necessarily by the power of the multitude. And, since it is a process that operates independently of the will of individuals, it is at the root of the exceedance that characterises social groupings. It is the group which forms itself in giving rise to the power of the multitude. Clearly, we are a long way here from models of voluntary association, though, of course, once the group has formed, voluntary associations may then take place. But such associations will always have as their framework the group that pre-exists them (which will also determine what potential benefits are on offer, such as safety).

The characteristic shortcoming of 'horizontalist' thinking is to systematically overlook the fact that associations which are freely entered into (and touted as the seed of a new form of politics) would not quite be able to support themselves since they would be incapable of creating the conditions for their own viability. The relevant thought experiment is not one that seeks to generalise the associative principle with reference to current entities existing in a social environment that is already constituted, structured and thus stable, but rather one that imagines these 'associations' projected into an institutional void in which coexistence is random. And it should also be noted that, when stated thus, the appealing principle of free association can also accommodate highly aggressive projects and contains no element of external pressure to cooperate – this proto-social world would be a barren steppe, prey to the anarchic and sometimes violent machinations of groups held together by nothing but power relations. 'Led more by passion than by reason' (see the next section), the stateless world is not a world of associations but of gangs.

By its nature, only the vertical can restrain violence in a large group. To convince oneself of this, one need only conduct a thought experiment which involves removing the vertical element and imagining what would result – in fact, this is the thought experiment at the core of the conceptual genesis approach. Removing the vertical would be to leave individuals, or the sub-groups they have already formed, at the mercy of their unstable horizontal relationships, which is to say pure power relations governed by the chaotic dynamics of rallying to a cause, entering into alliances and switching alliances. We can certainly analyse the coexistence of associations that is so dear to anarchist thinkers, but only if we have first agreed that the associative principle does not in itself offer any guarantee of a benign outcome. It would be obtuse to dogmatically rule out the possibility that some of these associations could significantly diverge and set themselves in opposition to each other. How would one bring an end to such hostilities, were they to break out? Asking that question inevitably leads us back to the alternative, which dyed-in-the-wool horizontalists refuse to entertain. For, either there would be a struggle between direct rivals amid general indifference until one side is brought to heel; or, the conflict would draw in third parties through affinity, leading to a more widespread unrest that is likely to rise again from its ashes at some future date, for memories of animosity leave deep traces and can easily be revived. Or else there would be an authority, formal or informal but vertical, and sufficiently powerful to hold everyone to the conditions for peaceful coexistence. Chased out the door, the rejected notion of the centre, which is to say of the vertical, reappears through the window, firstly to address the problem of coordinating the activities necessary for material reproduction,[19] but above all to deal with the question of violence. So, the group has only two options. It can submit a violent dispute between its constituent parts to those constituent parts themselves and bank on the miracle of a spontaneous resolution, which would mean constantly imperilling its own existence as a group, should the centrifugal

---

19 Or at least those relating to collective goods.

tendencies exceed their critical point. Alternatively, it can establish a central authority that is more powerful than the constituent parts and capable of containing divergences below the critical threshold at which the group would break apart, thereby preserving itself and enabling the group to exist as a group.

It is worth noting, in passing, the homothetic aspect of this situation. For, if one of the constituent parts, which in general is a sub-group, is excluded or excludes itself from the whole, it finds itself faced with the problem of persevering as a whole and is forced to (re)invent for itself what was lacking in the previous whole, namely, the resources to persevere as a group. However, this process will never reach what one might think would be its logical conclusion – a final state of complete disintegration in which all that is left is autonomous individuals – because individuals cannot themselves persevere in an autonomous state; their survival depends on them (re)organising themselves jointly at some scale or another. 'Thus the quarrels and rebellions that are often stirred up in a commonwealth never lead to the dissolution of the commonwealth by its citizens (as is often the case with other associations), but a change in its form – that is, if their disputes cannot be settled while still preserving the structure of the commonwealth.'[20] And this is precisely why there are groups, which is to say persevering wholes. Such groups have, *by definition*, succeeded in containing centrifugal divergences, as their *very existence* corroborates.

The Affective Coherence of Political Groupings

The power of the multitude arises and necessarily produces effects: common affects which are the drivers of group formation. Spinoza reveals to us that the true cement of political communities is affective. 'Since men . . . are led more by passion than by reason, it naturally follows that a multitude will unite and consent to be guided as if by one mind not at reason's prompting but through some common affect.'[21] This is an unequivocal rejection of the contract model. While the term 'scholastic error' may not be in Spinoza's vocabulary, he is

20 *PT*, VI, 2, p. 64.
21 *PT*, VI, 1, p. 64.

already aware of it and even employs the word 'philosophers'[22] with less than flattering intent. Not only do philosophers 'look upon the passions by which we are assailed as vices'[23] rather than as necessary productions of the human body and mind, but the political systems that they have imagined either involve some spontaneous harmony 'that borders on fantasy or could [only] be put into effect in Utopia or in that golden age of the poets, where there would naturally be no need of such',[24] or they are based on notions of rational constructivism whose principal instrument is the contract. Thus, the 'philosophers' live within a permanent projection of the categories of their own understanding, constantly (and unconsciously) projecting onto people their own ways of posing problems and resolving them. So, when they are not postulating a harmony which magically eliminates any problematic dimensions to politics, they are conceiving of a gigantic effort to conduct a collective, rational transaction. Explaining the foundation of the state comes down to finding an analytical solution to a well-posed problem regarding the public interest (or at least what an armchair social engineer would consider to be a well-posed problem). But neither of these two options corresponds to the real world. Life in the real world, individually and collectively, consists of human bodies with desires that are affectable. Bodies only do what they do – comply with the institutional order or overturn it, maintain ties or sever them – because they have been affected to a sufficient degree. Politics is not merely an exception to the universality of the affective condition, it is the ultimate expression of that condition – the epitome of what the 'common order of nature' produces when it comes to humans.[25]

Countering that politics is not about 'passions' but about 'values' and 'ideas' is to miss the point. Of course, politics is about values and ideas

---

22 *PT*, I, 1, p. 33. This is actually the opening word of the *Political Treatise*.
23 Ibid.
24 Ibid.
25 Given the instant revulsion that any mention of 'naturalism' in the social sciences seems to induce, it is perhaps worth directing the reader to the clarifications presented in 'À propos d'une photo' in Yves Citton and Frédéric Lordon (eds), *Spinoza et les sciences sociales. De la puissance de la multitude à l'économie des affects*, Éditions Amsterdam, 2008.

too. The common error lies in making a false distinction – ideas and values in no way escape from the common order of the affects. On the contrary, they are perfectly normal manifestations of it. Our values, for example, only arise from us subscribing to their moral content, and the act of subscribing itself (leaving aside whatever the content may be) is an entirely affective mechanism. Similarly, ideas only become effective, which is to say they only acquire the power to make us do something (adopt or resist them, defend or fight them) if they are charged with affects and lend themselves to an affective investment on our part, in the same way as values do.[26] To say that affects are the stuff of politics is thus in no way to imply that reason is absent and that all politics comes down to 'gut feeling'. Rather, it is to encompass politics, ideas and values included, within the general order of the passions – that order being the very condition of human existence and all that it engenders.

Likewise, the interplay of affects is not to be reduced to 'psychology', at least not in the narrow (which is to say, egocentric) sense of the word. As this interplay is the human condition itself, it is immediately expressed at the collective as well as at the individual level: on close inspection, there is not a single one of our affects, however private it might appear to us, that does not contain some element of the social. Politics is one of the manifestations of this affective condition, though we might equally say the same about economics, as long as we discard the misleading opposition between 'self-interest and the passions' and are capable of discerning the affects and desires underlying all the schemes of calculating rationality.[27] Spinoza does not, in fact, exclude in principle the idea of people coming together under the authentic guidance of reason, but this is something quite different to calculating rationality, whose manoeuvrings remain only too visibly subordinate to purposes that have little to do with reason. In practice, however, Spinoza accepts and indeed emphasises the fact that people do not conduct themselves by the light of reason. This is why they group together under a very different influence: the force of affects. Political communities are affective communities – and this is precisely what the

---

26 *Ethics*, IV, 14.

27 See Frédéric Lordon, 'Homo Passionalis Oeconomicus', in Eva Debray, Kim Sang Ong-Van-Cung and Frédéric Lordon (eds), *Spinoza et les passions du social*, Éditions Amsterdam, 2019.

scholastic and intellectualising projections of the 'philosophers' failed to illuminate.

Antagonistic Unifications and Persistent Fragmentation

However, we still need to explain why group formation should stop at a certain point rather than ultimately encompassing humanity as a whole. Why do human groupings not extend to the entire human race, instead of remaining limited? It is precisely because they only form under the influence of passive affects, and so there is always a risk of affective secession that cannot be eliminated. 'Men . . . are necessarily subject to passive affects and are inconstant and variable.'[28] Nothing can exclude the possibility – indeed, it is entirely probable – that an 'inconstancy' or affective variation will arise one day and lead to a divergence that the group will be unable to accommodate. One of its parts will hive off and fracture the whole (or possibly lead to its entire ruin). Once again, it would be a serious misunderstanding to interpret this as a totalitarian facet of the homogeneous group by assuming that because it is (tautologically) intolerant of certain critical variations, it is intolerant of any variation whatsoever. This is clearly not the case, and, indeed, one of the defining features of collective bodies is the extent to which they are able to produce and accommodate internal variance to their advantage and counter the threat of centrifugal decomposition. Even if people are not capable of perfect reasoning, their affective lives are capable of infinitely varied productions far beyond what we have already seen in history, upon whose spectrum we cannot impose a priori limits. But humanity *as an actual union* supposes the daunting condition stated in the *Ethics* (IV, 35) – the condition of reason, that being the only means of guaranteeing convergence in nature. And this condition is inaccessible to us. Even Kant, who went further than anyone in philosophising about the universal union of the human race, ultimately conceded that a world state was not a desirable goal.[29] Too big and too disparate, it could only maintain unity by ruling with a rod of iron and would inevitably tend towards despotism.

---

28 *Ethics*, IV, 37, scholium 2, p. 175.
29 Immanuel Kant, *Perpetual Peace: A Philosophical Sketch*.

There is also the fact that the principle of increasing returns from aggregation, which underpins group formation, simultaneously tends to separate the nascent aggregates into *types*, making it difficult for victorious entities to successfully absorb others. In other words, as they take on a more distinctive character, emerging entities become more coherent, less appealing to each other and less inclined to allow themselves to be absorbed. However, the dynamics of power relations are not so easily disarmed and realising that the limits of political growth have been reached will doubtless take some time, during which we will engage in futile wars instead. Wars in Europe in the modern age could be said to offer two lessons. The first is that our history has resulted in entities whose power is fairly evenly matched and are thus in virtual equilibrium, making it difficult and costly to push predation any further. The second is that the accumulation of idiosyncrasies has made absorption through conquest (supposing it is militarily possible) extremely difficult and too vulnerable to the risk that the centrifugal forces of the absorbed party can never be completely eliminated. The process of expansion ends only once the whole cycle of vain attempts has been exhausted. Wars are waged that are as fruitless as they are devastating, land is seized and then surrendered again (think of Alsace-Lorraine) until finally the conclusion is reached that such efforts are futile. Naturally, there are still local or bilateral power imbalances between certain entities, but these are offset by alliances and, since the twentieth century, by the deterrent of nuclear weapons and the threat of asymmetrical reprisals. It is also true that one cannot exclude the resurgence of local expansionist ambitions, as is the case with Russia today, which is busy reclaiming lost parts of the old USSR. And there remain contested territories such as Taiwan, Sakhalin and the Senkaku Islands. But a few fluctuations on the map aside, the fragmentation of the world into finite entities is in itself a stabilised state, even if 'stabilised' only indicates the current state of affairs and by no means suggests that things are set in stone.

The form of this stabilisation may change and the human continuum could always become divided up along different lines. For example, though the religious commons has been superseded by the national commons, it is certainly possible to imagine that, in certain regions, it could reassert itself and that peoples who have been split by the national principle will reassemble under the religious banner. It is also entirely possible to imagine (geographical proximity permitting?) a redivision according to social class or on the basis of an anti-capitalist lifestyle.[30] And, lastly, one can imagine the principle of absorption by a conqueror being replaced by voluntary unions of peoples, which is largely how today's nations were formed – though one might well ask how the idiosyncrasies of constituent parts could be transcended in a larger entity, when the brutal approach to homogenisation as practised by the nation states of the nineteenth century is no longer an option. The difficulties of the European Union are illustrative of this. As it grapples with its monetary policy, it is becoming more aware of the extent to which national idiosyncrasies are compatible (or as it happens incompatible).[31]

Planetary Unification through Commodities?

The resistance of specific entities to their dissolution and the probability of their rebirth – either in identical form, as in the spectacular resurgence of seemingly dormant nationalisms in the wake of the break-up of the Soviet Union, or else in novel forms – suggests that, for a very long time yet, fragmentation into finite groups will be the norm, unless a supremely powerful common affect were to emerge that is capable of dominating on a global scale all its local counterparts.

The first groupings were no doubt bound to remain localised since they were produced, and reproduced themselves, through concrete interactions whose geographical reach was limited by the material constraints of the available media – though this aspect should not be unduly emphasised. The Chinese empire got along very well without the internet, and medieval European Catholicism equipped itself with its own medium whose power cannot be overstated: a network of parishes for delivering sermons every Sunday and keeping close tabs on the faithful masses . . . A fortiori, in any case, this constraint, if it did play a role, has been lifted courtesy of a host of now-familiar channels (trade, transport and telecommunications) through which local groupings are increasingly brought into contact with one another. Indeed, they have

---

30 See Chapter 6 below.

31 For further discussion on this point, see Lordon, *La Malfaçon*, particularly Chapter 6.

been overflowing and creating commons which have perhaps not yet reached a stage of full globalisation but may well do so one day.

For better or for worse, it should be said; for, once again, the formation of a commons is not *in itself* intrinsically desirable. There are hateful commons which do not become any more pleasant to contemplate just because they are a commons. There are also stultifying commons. At present, the most dynamic (aggressive, even) candidate to become a planetary commons is the market, but it is far from obvious that, as a means of unifying the human race, we should wish it to triumph. In truth, any unification of this sort could not dignify itself with the label of 'universal', even if it were to bring together all of humanity, since it would only ever be a *specific* form of unification – the victory of a common affect which though global would remain specific among the many other possible kinds of common affect. However impressive its progress so far, this particular commons is destined for quite a while yet to coexist with local and political commons, in a relationship which is not necessarily conflictual but is unlikely for the time being to supersede those existing commons. Can we go so far as to imagine a scenario wherein cultural and national idiosyncrasies dissolve and are relegated to a rank of secondary importance, dominated instead by the planetary homogeneity of the capitalist-consumerist ethos – a process that will pave the way for a political community of the same extension, anaesthetised by the 'universal' triumph of the market society? It seems pointless to lose oneself in conjectures as to the actual probability of such a scenario – will not the planet first have to cope with a series of environmental disasters and social crises before this commons is realised? It is more suitable for a thought experiment; and besides, the important point lies elsewhere. Firstly, even if this improbable market-centred dystopia were to arise, it would merely serve to confirm that all actual communities are affective communities – one need hardly point out that the human desire for commodities qualifies as a passion. Secondly, we need to remember that the commons exists on multiple scales: there are commons (plural) at different territorial levels that overlap partially or entirely, confront each other, coexist or ignore each other (for a trite example, you can find Coca-Cola in Islamabad). And yet the great convergence of civilisations dreamt of by the champions of globalisation has not materialised. Thirdly (and this by way of an objection), we must bear in mind that affective convergences are inherently unstable precisely because a commons is constantly redefining itself into different forms, and there is nothing to prevent those forms being antagonistic towards each other, sometimes violently. This continual reworking of the group from the inside is the source of the continual variations which give rise to new (partial) affective commons that are critical or downright defiant of those already established.

Servitude to the Passions and Moral Fragmentation (Ways of Living at War)

It is when this 'inconstancy' assumes a violent dimension and different ways of living engage in a battle to the death that the union of the human race can be seen for what it really is: a Utopia that 'borders on fantasy'. At least it is so while we remain in servitude to the passions – but that is irremediably the human condition. Man 'agreeing in nature' with his fellow man is an asymptotic state involving active affects and a life conducted by the light of reason. No doubt we can get closer to this state, or at least reduce the gap a little (otherwise Spinoza would not have troubled to write his *Ethics*), but that journey is hardly linear or uniform and carries no teleological guarantee. In the meantime, who would rule out the possibility of the different commons tearing each other apart? The spectacle of the world eloquently testifies to the rather weaker probability that these commons, conceived as heterogeneous ways of living, will coexist harmoniously. And, indeed, why should we be surprised that ways of living might battle it out to the death? Life is about survival, which is a matter of life and death.

Revolutionaries should expect nothing else as they wage their battles – the dispute between their commons and the commons of the capitalist markets is hardly likely to be settled on an amicable basis. The error they then make is to suppose that they must simply weather the storm of the revolution in order to reach the sunny uplands of perpetual peace. But the grand moral convergence of humanity is hardly guaranteed; it will obviously not happen under the guidance of reason, but neither will it happen under the influence of some majestic Idea that would have the privilege of presiding over the End of History. The coexistence of ways of living should therefore be conceptualised as a *problem*, precisely because they are affective formations and so constantly open to 'diversity' and susceptible to 'inconstancy' – that indefatigable driver of agonistic variations. A problem heightened by the fact that these variations can emerge from the most varied domains: economics, religion, the way to make an omelette ... Anything can be a source of variation and potentially degenerate into a terminal confrontation. As this potential is not always realised, we might conclude that not everything leads to blood and tears. But the important conclusion to arrive at is that human groups do form and that they are necessarily *finite and distinct*, striving as best they can, with highly fluctuating levels of success over time, to carve out their niche in a world that consists not of a union of the human race but of distinct entities in coexistence. And it is the servitude to the passions which inevitably leads to entities with their own distinct identity. The only true universal is that of reason, but it is a universal that is not within our reach and thus we are left with distinct entities whose distinctness cannot be ignored. Some entities pose the question of the universal more clearly than others, aspire to it more and go further down the path towards it, but this remains an aspiration – they will always remain this side of the universal in the world of distinct entities. And that world is, by definition, a plural world.

At this intermediate stage of a necessarily linear argument, the reader may have certain reservations, or, indeed, outright objections to what is being argued, especially in relation to the notion of 'servitude to the passions', which is often (mis)understood as a thoroughly fatalistic vision of mankind which despairs of the human condition and is bereft of any hope of change or progress. In response, I can do no better than to quote Spinoza: 'At this point our readers will no doubt find themselves in some difficulty and will think of many things that will give them pause. So I ask them to proceed slowly step by step with me, and to postpone judgment until they have read to the end.'[32]

∾

---

32 *Ethics*, II, 11, scholium, p. 71.

Addendum – the Multitude? What Multitude?

Of all these potential objections, there is one at least – relating to the idea of 'multitude' – that can be dealt with straight away.

Finite and distinct groupings will persist and relations between them will be problematic, and always potentially conflictual. Does this mean that they will ultimately produce homogeneous and unified groupings? We have implied that the answer is no. The inside of a grouping is differentiated (as opposed to being uniform) and is just as much a source of conflict as relations with other groupings on the outside. But this internal conflict is of a different kind, characterised by contained divergences (if they were not contained, it would not be a group but rather a scattered array of parts). And this internal conflict goes straight to the very heart of the *problem* of group composition: in a given group, how does one triumph over affective divergence? The answer, as we have seen, is that it is the emergence of a common affect which, by overcoming centrifugal individual affects, constitutes a viable grouping that can persevere, and otherwise would be destined to fall apart. But overcoming centrifugal individual affects does not mean *cancelling them out*. And, indeed, the very fact that the coherence of the whole depends on overcoming, but not eliminating, divergence elicits the question of what we really mean when we talk of a 'multitude'. On the one hand, one might be tempted to interpret it as denoting unity, or, indeed, the unifying principle, since the common affect is the product of the power of the multitude. But, on the other, we must not lose sight of the internal divisions within the multitude – this is a given at the outset and lies at the very root of the *problem* of group formation. And it is not just a given at the outset: it is a permanent condition, since the divergent individual affects persist without ever completely disappearing. So is the multitude unified and unifying, or fragmented and divergent?

To escape this apparent paradox, we need to define more precisely the conceptual status of the 'multitude', or rather its conceptual statuses, plural. For there are two of them, and confusing them leads inevitably to theoretical errors, naturally followed by political errors. Conceptualised as the generator of the common affect, the multitude is a *philosophical* concept. The multitude as a philosophical concept generically describes the reservoir of power of the social world – one might even say the reservoir of power that *is* the social world. Leaving aside all other considerations, a grouping of people entails a pooling of powers that have the potential to generate a collective power that will exercise a morphogenetic influence over the grouping that they form. This is how the multitude should be understood philosophically speaking: as the *entity that generates the social world*. Everything that happens to people collectively is the doing of people themselves, and, in the final analysis, this comes about through a power (power being by definition the production of effects) which is the power of the multitude. Thus defined as a philosophical concept, such a multitude is, to some extent, a speculative category, which is to say that it does not have an immediate *empirical counterpart*. Try as you might, you will not find any actual philosophical multitude – it is not an identifiable real object. In this respect, it is entirely consonant with the *conceptual* genesis model of the social, whose theoretical status we have been at pains to stress:[33] it is not a historical reconstruction but a speculative thought experiment, designed rather 'to explain the nature of things, than to ascertain their actual origin'.

It would be a serious error to take the philosophical multitude for an object that actually exists. Which brings us to the other possible conceptual status of the multitude: the multitude as a sociological concept, which must by definition be tested with reference to the actual social world. And, indeed, this immediately renders it problematic, not to say congenitally null and void, for, sociologically speaking, *the* multitude, singular, does not exist. It does not exist for the simple reason that the social is always already there – the multitude is always already socialised, which is to say differentiated, structured, institutionalised and, above all, divided. This, in fact, helps to underscore the specifically abstract nature of the philosophical concept of multitude, since it denotes a situation *prior* to all of these effects of differentiation, structuring and institutionalisation which are always already in play in the empirical social world.

Empirically speaking, 'the multitude' does not exist – rather, there is society in its particular historical forms with all its internal arrangements of structures and institutions which determine the divergences within it and the mechanisms through which it seeks to accommodate

---

33 See Chapter 2 above.

them. To attempt to describe the real world through reference to 'the multitude' would thus be to invoke an imaginary entity not dissimilar to what is called 'civil society' – that ideological smokescreen designed to gloss over the inherently conflictual nature of the social by employing a misleadingly unifying term. Two uses of the world 'multitude' may therefore be in circulation, but, ultimately, it has only one possible conceptual status, namely the philosophical one. And any ill-conceived attempt to project it onto the empirical domain of sociology would be a theoretical blunder of the first order. In the final analysis, the multitude is the *abstract* driver of all social morphogenesis and every historical dynamic. But it is not, in any sense, a subject for empirical historical inquiry.

PART II
The Elementary Structures of Politics

4

The General State – *Imperium*

The instability arising from the continuous swirl of affective 'inconstancy' at every scale remains the most formidable obstacle to the advent of a genuine union of the human race. But it turns out that the fragmentation of the world into distinct and limited groupings has been aided and abetted historically by a very different kind of force: state capture.

According to the law of large numbers governing the social, capture is an inevitable feature of immanent transcendence, for the *potentia multitudinis* is a formidable resource for rulers to exploit. If, for example, the common affect converges on a belief in a God who is a 'governor of Nature',[1] the commander of men's actions and their source of salvation, there is an obvious advantage in declaring oneself to be the pontiff – and there will always be somebody who does precisely that. And there will always be somebody who declares themselves king once the principle of divine right has been established. The capturing agent inserts themselves into the ascending-descending circulation of the *potentia multitudinis* and succeeds in masking its ascending phase, thereby giving the impression that they are the source of its descending phase. Failing to recognise its own immanent productions, the multitude adopts a common conception of pure transcendence by which it imagines the capturing agent to be the 'true possessor' of what is in fact the multitude's own power. Thus transformed into a superman, since they

---

1 *Ethics*, I, Appendix, p. 58.

seem to be in possession of an incommensurably greater power, the capturing agent manages to shake off a constraint to which Spinoza frequently alludes in his political treatises: 'there is nothing that people find less tolerable than to be ruled by their equals and serve them.'[2] Is not capturing the power of the whole the best means of posing as incommensurably more powerful than the whole? 'This is why in the past kings who usurped power tried to persuade their people they were descended from the immortal gods, their motive surely being to enhance their own security. They evidently believed their subjects would willingly allow themselves to be ruled by them and readily submit only if their subjects and everyone else regarded them not as equals but as gods.'[3]

Mediated Self-Affections, Captures and Institutions

The multitude, whose power necessarily comes into being, can thus live under several regimes of common affect. This may take the form of unmediated self-affection where 'all' as a group affect 'all' individually, with no intermediary. One might cite the examples of moral norms and 'public opinion' as emanating from 'below' in the multitude and imposing themselves on the multitude without there being any formal, localised or central authority to dispense those morals or opinions. However, this is rather an idealised and hypothetical scenario, since, in practice, public opinion and even a society's dominant values are produced in structured and differentiated institutional spaces,[4] not by an undifferentiated multitude acting on itself. But, even when conceived in an idealised form, the unmediated self-affections of the multitude are diffuse, acentric and 'non-localised', so to speak. They are quite different to mediated self-affections which, as the term suggests, involve an intermediary and are thus subject to a capture (or attempted capture). In mediated self-affection, the capturing agent strategically inserted into the circulation of the *potentia multitudinis* interposes themselves

---

2 *Theological-Political Treatise*, V, 8, p. 73.

3 Ibid., XVII, 6, p. 211.

4 This is precisely why these productions are (and must be) a fitting subject for *sociology*.

between the multitude and the multitude – making it more difficult still for the multitude to recognise itself in its own productions. Though they are a simple point in the circulation, by projecting themselves as the source they convert the *potentia multitudinis* into power. We are grateful to Alexandre Matheron for having pointed out this conceptual distinction, so fundamental in politics, between power and authority, *potentia* and *potestas*, which he encapsulates in the pithy phrase: 'Political authority is the confiscation by rulers of the collective power of their subjects.'[5] Needless to say, the prospect of such a conversion brings the politically ambitious of all stripes running: is there a single would-be ruler who could resist capturing a power so formidably superior to their own and using it to affect the masses as they please? But this converting of power into authority has above all the effect of bringing the multitude under a regime governed by institutions, and indeed this could serve as the very definition of an institution: any authority which channels the *potentia multitudinis*.

Once that first capture is made, the whole institutional edifice begins to branch irreversibly – institutions engender each other in a sort of self-catalysing dynamic. For example, the original theological capture that converts the common affect of superstition into ecclesiastical authority naturally leads on to a theological-political capture whereby a temporal authority piggybacks on the spiritual institution. Later on, when the institutions of state have been consolidated, one can remove the religious skyhook. In a similar fashion, monetary institutions generally establish themselves within the immediate orbit of political institutions and mobilise to their advantage the resources of the *potentia multitudinis* that have already been accumulated. It is no coincidence that their common currency bears the image of the prince – they benefit by contiguity to the already existing political commons.[6]

As with the conceptual genesis model, this is not an attempt at historical reconstruction but rather a speculative intuiting of the institutional process in its essence, namely the endlessly branching process of capture. In the almost fractal-like swirl of its circulations, the multitude's own

---

5 Matheron, *Individu et communauté chez Spinoza*.

6 On this point, see Frédéric Lordon and André Orléan, 'Genèse de l'État et genèse de la monnaie. Le modèle de la *potentia multitudinis*', in Citton and Lordon (eds), *Spinoza et les sciences sociales*.

power becomes literally unrecognisable to it – and how would it recognise itself in the local authority of some third-rate sub-institution? And yet when a student bends to the authority of a lecturer, they are bending not to an authority which is personal but rather which proceeds from the authority of the department, which proceeds from the authority of the university, which ultimately proceeds from the authority of the state. The state is the first to capture it, and (almost) every subsequent capture derives from that first capture; Bourdieu imagined the state as a sort of central bank that is the ultimate guarantor and lender of symbolic capital.[7] And the point is that, whatever metaphor one chooses, there is nothing 'above'. In truth, to get a proper handle on this 'above' we must paradoxically return right down 'below', to the bottom of the multitude from whence, *in the final analysis*, all the powers that structure the multitude originate and are then projected towards an 'above' that it has itself given rise to.

Even though the multitude may occasionally experience approximations of unmediated self-affections, such as when a princess dies in a car crash or one's country wins the World Cup, this does nothing to alter the fact that its institutional structure consigns it for the most part to mediated self-affections. The work that society is constantly doing on itself operates by diffraction through the multiple strata of its institutional structure. Take the workings of public opinion, for example, and the way in which it changes outlooks and accepted norms. That process takes place through the media, that is, through an intermediation that powerfully informs (or deforms, depending on one's point of view, but is in any case by no means neutral) the process – it is a public space in which symbolic capital is unevenly distributed and to which there is unequal access, with pundits enjoying greater or lesser authority and capturing a greater or lesser audience share. This is a forceful illustration of the fact that the multitude lives under the regime of capture – or rather captures in the plural, affecting many walks of life but all encompassed within that original capture by the state. And this state institutionalisation of groupings gives rise to ambivalent effects, both reinforcing their internal unity and limiting their expansion.

---

7 Pierre Bourdieu, *Raisons pratiques*, Seuil, 1994.

State Capture and Unification

In fact, unification is the necessary correlate of capture: the capturing agent who establishes themselves as sovereign imposes their law. To avoid any misunderstanding, it is worth repeating that the authority, the *potestas*, of this sovereign is borrowed or rather plundered from the multitude in a misappropriation of the multitude's own power. Certain caveats must therefore be heeded when talking about the sovereignty of the state: we may grant that it has become the de facto holder of authority, while constantly bearing in mind that the true reservoir of sovereignty is located nowhere but in the multitude itself.

But the capture is a fact, and, though their authority is irremediably on loan, the sovereign capturing agent can nevertheless impose their law. As if they were projecting their own unity of purpose and even of character on the entity that they come to view as their *dominium*, that dominion tends towards homogenisation under their stewardship (and their personality). They impose what they consider to be the correct way of living on their subjects and are largely intolerant of any attempts to deviate from it. The whole historiography of the nation testifies to the vast role that the state has assumed in its formation.[8] This gives the lie to the reactionary and essentialist myths of eternal nations, and also serves to remind Hayekian libertarians that there have indeed been successful constructivist undertakings. What makes the undertaking of the nation state stand out is its sheer scale, its sheer persistence and its sheer 'success'. The term 'nation-building' does after all have a meaning, at least at the historical level and under certain conditions. For it is indeed the state – through its constant drive towards linguistic, monetary and fiscal unification, with its bureaucratic demands and educational apparatus (tellingly called *national* education) – which has been the brutal instigator of the nation, the great leveller of diversity, the engineer of an enforced commons, and admittedly, as a result, the generator of cohesion as well.

Paradoxically, this very drive to produce internal consistency and conformity becomes the source of the main obstacle to its own expansion. For, elsewhere, other coherent entities that are formally similar but

---

8 On this subject, the benchmark analysis is that of Eric Hobsbawm, *Nations and Nationalism since 1780*, Cambridge University Press, 1992 (second edition).

adhere to other types, have emerged as well. The crossing of a critical threshold of idiosyncrasy forbids indefinite extension of the process of convergence that has led to the formation of groups which are ever fewer but ever larger. Though we have stressed that the conceptual genesis model of the *potentia multitudinis* is not designed to be historically tested, we cannot fail to notice its similarities to the very real historical mechanisms identified by Norbert Elias as instrumental in the *actual* formation of European states.[9] There is the same process whereby the increasing returns of rallying to a camp result in a convergence of the competing local seats of power, the baronial fiefdoms, duchies and various sub-kingdoms engaged in the struggle for supremacy. The larger entities get the better of the smaller ones and absorb them, increasing their power for the subsequent stages of the process until there is only one left . . . which will eventually come up against counterparts that are similarly resistant.

Apparent Anachronism and an Actual General Principle

Can we, however, defend this thesis of finite distinct groupings if they are stabilised under the auspices of the nation state – an authority that lays claim to its own distinctiveness but is itself a contingent and indeed recent historical creation? Perhaps the question should be turned on its head: is it not worth reconsidering the almost overly obvious notion of historical contingency, even if the whole historiography of the state constantly warns us of the dangers of anachronistic interpretations?

No doubt, these warnings initially help us to avoid an essentialist tendency to project the present back into the past, while also recalling that what the 'nation state' immediately evokes is a phenomenon that arose quite late in history and like any product of history has a limited shelf life. But, however necessary they may be, certain methodological injunctions are repeated so often that they can become clichéd and ultimately constitute an impediment to thinking. And this may be the case with all the warnings against interpreting the nation state anachronistically – by over-emphasising its historical particularity, we may be failing

9 Norbert Elias, *The Civilizing Process*, trans. Edmund Jephcott, Blackwell, 1994.

to see an underlying general principle. For in the nation state there is indeed a general principle that is masked by the particular historical form in which we have become accustomed to seeing it. By analysing the state only in its present form, as if that form were its full scope, we fail to spot that it contains something very general and much more trans-historical (all the warnings about anachronistic thinking notwithstanding). If projecting back in time the particular form that the present has assumed is the 'anachronistic' error par excellence, failing to recognise the general principle of which the present is a particular form is to commit exactly the reverse theoretical error. That general principle is not simply derived from 'observing facts' but from the concept of the *general state* – the concept of *imperium*.

'This Right Which Is Defined by the Power of the Multitude'

Only a concept can encompass the extraordinarily diverse political forms that finite human groupings can assume and capture what they fundamentally have in common beneath their extreme morphological variety. And Spinoza provides us with this concept in his *Political Treatise*, namely the *imperium*: 'This right, which is defined by the power of the multitude, is generally called *imperium*.'[10] In his French translation, Bernard Pautrat makes the bold and, as it turns out, the most judicious choice when translating the word *imperium*: he leaves it untranslated.[11] This wise decision means that it retains its deliberately elastic double sense of state (as capturing agent) and pure sovereignty (the self-affecting of the multitude). It is not that 'sovereignty' or 'state' are incorrect translations but that, in themselves, they carry spontaneous connotations that we cannot help but associate with our historical experience of the modern nation state. Employing the word *imperium* evacuates these connotations, retaining Spinoza's more flexible term to encompass all the possible forms and thereby unleash the full power of his concept. For *imperium*, conceived as 'this right which is defined by the power of the multitude', identifies an extremely general mechanism at work in all large finite groups: the mechanism of immanent

10 *PT*, II, 17, p. 44. See footnote 4.
11 Baruch Spinoza, *Traité politique*, trans. Bernard Pautrat, Allia, 2013.

transcendence, of course, but also the likely fate of the group – that of being captured in all its forms.

The mechanism of immanent transcendence is once again present because it is another term for the production of the *potentia multitudinis* – a collective force necessarily produced by groups themselves according to the law of large numbers of the social. In the first instance, the *imperium* is the power that the multitude has to affect itself. So everything that the multitude does to the multitude falls under the concept of *imperium* – and it is the importance of what happens in this first instance that should make us wary of simply equating *imperium* with 'the State'. Institutionalised politics begins properly speaking when we ask what is to become of the power produced in this first instance. And the form that the question takes is: in whose hands will the power of the multitude fall? Or, more precisely: through which institutional structures will it be led to express itself and thereby be captured? That question relates to the threshold where all the branching occurs, at the crossroads of the possible future political paths. But it must be understood that all those subsequent paths conserve – and express in their different ways – that which was present before the threshold was reached: namely, the *imperium*. The *imperium* is not the law or the established state: it is, first and foremost, the *self-affecting force of the multitude* and *subsequently* (but only subsequently) it becomes a question of the *efficacity* of the law, if laws come to be written. The *imperium*, defined as the power of the multitude, is the mechanism via which the group, through its members, generates the power to affect its members, which is to say the power to do something to them and subsequently to get them to do something, such as complying with norms. The *imperium* is, therefore, fundamentally at play in the collective imposition of behaviours – a feedback loop in which the group constitutes itself by shaping its members into members *of the group*.

This process of self-formation, by which members conform to the norms of the group under the generic common affect of the *obsequium* (a common affect of recognition and compliance), can be called the general state. Understood thus, the 'general state' is a borderline political category in that, by identifying the fundamental mechanism at work in the formation of human groupings as the self-affecting power of the multitude, it assumes a socio-anthropological character. The general state indicates that the multitude rules over the multitude, or more precisely that the multitude formed by individuals rules over the individuals who make up the multitude, and that this is indeed an instance of sovereignty, but in a very general sense. It is a sovereignty that is pre-institutional, and thus socio-anthropological in the Durkheimian sense: the sovereignty of the social, which is to say the sovereignty of exceedance and verticality. Large groups affect their members and constitute themselves through this affection: that is the sense of sovereignty expressed by the concept of the *imperium*-general state.

The Elementary Structures of Politics (I)

So why choose the perhaps rather unexpected term '(general) state' to refer to a structure that is essentially socio-anthropological and predates any form of institutional politics? Firstly, to bring out the common denominator of all specific historical forms of established and institutionalised political groupings. And, secondly, to emphasise that the *imperium* is the source of all forms of authority in the social world.

The general state is the structure from which all institutional politics is born and that is why, although it is a socio-anthropological category, it is also a borderline political category, since institutional politics cannot be defined otherwise than as the capture of the *potentia multitudinis*. 'General state' is, in a sense, the generic term for that which lends itself to institutional capture. In this respect, the general state is not merely a socio-anthropological structure but also the *elementary structure of politics* – it is the nucleus of immanence in politics. When, like La Boétie and Spinoza, we subtract all the contingent characteristics, which is to say all the secondary effects of mediation, and we penetrate to the essential, what remains is this: '[The Sovereign] has no authority over you except through you.'[12] The foundation of state authority, and of all other forms of authority within society, resides in this elementary structure of politics that is the self-affecting of the multitude. The state only rules by channelling this self-affecting of the multitude. The *imperium*, that ascending-descending power arising from the multitude

---

12 La Boétie, *Discours de la servitude volontaire*, Vrin, 2002, p. 30.

and through which the multitude affects itself, is the origin of all authority. Authority is based on a strategy of interpolation, which is to say the capture of the power of the social, which is thereby converted into a localised capacity for the capturing agent (whether an individual or an institution) to do something to the multitude and subsequently to get it to do something. The general state is the elementary structure of politics because it expresses the ultimate truth about politics: that through the capturing agent the multitude subjugates itself to its own power. Authority, as Matheron observes, is nothing but an appropriation of the self-affections of the multitude.

And this capture extends well beyond a single political authority – all forms of authority within society proceed from it. And authority (as opposed to power) is indeed the right word to use, as Durkheim does to describe the effects which the social engenders. The social, which he sometimes calls the 'moral force of society', is the origin of all authority: the political authority of the state but also the authority of moral values, the authority of monetary tokens, and the authority of those acknowledged as experts – in short, that authority to which Bourdieu gives the name 'symbolic capital'. All these types of authority have as a common foundation the power of the multitude. All are variations on the theme of the self-affecting of the multitude: they are products of the multitude self-affecting itself to believe in the legitimacy of the state, the sanctity of moral commandments, the value of monetary tokens, the word of religious devotees and ultimately the duty to comply with all the dictates of institutions. Though this only holds, of course, for as long as the capture of the *potentia multitudinis* remains effective – these objects must continue to be sustained and invested with the power of the multitude and remain the focus of its self-affecting. That is the *sine qua non* of their retention of authority. If this condition ceases to obtain, it will signal the collapse of authority, which is to say a crisis in the institution.[13]

The varied nature of these authorities – and the fact that they extend beyond the field of politics in the strictest sense – does not detract from the pertinence of the concept of the general state, not least because the general nature of this 'state' is in keeping with the generalised instances

---

13 For a more comprehensive Spinoza-inspired analysis of institutions and their crises, see Lordon, *La Société des affects,* particularly Chapter 6, 'La puissance des institutions'.

of authority of which it is the source. But we can also employ the term 'general state' more specifically to denote the origin of the 'political' variety of authority. This variety of authority is absolutely distinct from the rest, because it is in a sense the primary instance of the *potentia multitudinis* being captured, from which all subsequent captures that sustain institutional authorities derive. The latter are all to some degree grafted onto the primary Authority with a capital A: monetary tokens use the image of the regime, symbolic capital often derives from positions conferred on the individual by the state, state law underpins almost every institution, etc. One can thus argue that, insofar as it denotes the fundamental process of the multitude affecting itself, the *imperium* is the elementary structure of *authority*, since ultimately every kind of authority proceeds from it. And one can further justify qualifying the *imperium* as the 'general state' insofar as it is conceived as being the source of all *political* authority, whatever the form it takes. The general state is the elementary structure of politics.

The General State and Its Historical Forms

It should be said that, whereas the concept of general state applies to all groups that bear out the law of large numbers of the social, the risk of anachronistic thinking that historiographical methodology warns us against only applies to the phenomenon that we have become accustomed to associating exclusively with the category of 'state', namely *our* state: the modern state, or indeed the modern bourgeois state. By refusing to speak of the state in any other context, we deprive ourselves of the opportunity to perceive a much deeper structure embedded in our state which, conceptually speaking, considerably outstrips it and of which our state is only one historical manifestation – a particular form produced by a mechanism which is much more general. Admittedly, these particular forms may superficially appear to differ entirely, and this indeed is why they seem to defy any rapprochement, why they prompt warnings of 'anachronistic' interpretations, and why it is impossible for a casual observer to perceive the common anthropological mechanism that unites them. One might make a comparison with the periodic table: its elements appear disparate, but they are part of a single series. Any finite human grouping that is sufficiently large enacts the mechanism of the general state. This is why, although it would be an obvious category error (obvious to the point of triviality) to speak of a 'state' in relation to Venice, Genoa or the Roman Empire (at least if we have in mind our modern states), it is not a mistake to apply to them the category of general state, of which they are particular expressions historically located in time.

Indeed, throwing all historiographical caution to the wind, we should go further and state that all political groupings are states in the sense of the general state – in the sense of the *imperium*. Although his intention was to speak of the state of his time, since his political thought was constantly grappling with that reality, in Chapters II to VI of the *Political Treatise* Spinoza arrives at extremely general conceptual intuitions of the state which extend well beyond the specific characteristics of *his* state, the Dutch Republic. And he has no hesitation in applying them, without any contradiction, to political entities of the past such as Rome, Aragon or indeed any type of city. In this context, it is entirely legitimate to speak of the tribe, *polis*, empire and city, as well as feudal, absolutist and modern bourgeois societies, as states – and that is by no means an exhaustive list, unless we seriously underestimate the prolific creativity of history.

Some will object, even granting that no historiographical solecism has been committed, that such a generalisation merely clouds the issue by applying a superfluous common category to that which is genuinely diverse (and interesting for that reason). But it is worth repeating that the primary virtue of this approach lies precisely in revealing the mechanism that operates between the multitude and its constituent parts in absolutely every large human grouping: the *imperium* through self-transcendence. Perhaps this virtue becomes more obvious if we revisit the question of the viability of notions of political horizontality and in particular the notions advocated by proponents of voluntary association, who resolutely claim to escape from the 'state' without appreciating that they cannot escape from the general state. It may be true that when they speak of the 'state', they have in mind our modern state. And, in fact, we can unreservedly concur with them that 'our state' is not *ours*: the modern bourgeois state we live in is not a state that we possess – it is a State that leaves us in a state of dispossession. But the point being made here is of another order: it is that the *imperium*, understood as the effect of an immanent common affect, is so general a phenomenon that it is highly flexible morphologically speaking and may emerge where we least expect it – or, more precisely, where our acquired conceptual representations, closely based on the modern state and inclined to assimilate the modern state with the state in general, least expect it. If it is sufficiently large, even the most free and (would-be) horizontal community, however attached to an egalitarian network structure and however determined to resist institutional capture, will engender the exceedance that is characteristic of the general state. And, almost tautologically, it will only hold together if it possesses (or rather, continuously produces) a mechanism of cohesiveness – a common affect – which simultaneously constitutes the group and shapes individuals into members of that group, thereby conferring on the group a coherence and longevity that distinguish it from reversible associations.

Are 'Stateless Societies' Really Stateless?

Invoking the work of Pierre Clastres, one may be tempted to assert that 'stateless societies' do nevertheless exist.[14] When they are not erring, like Kropotkin, by searching the animal world for anthropomorphic confirmation of cooperation in nature,[15] anarchist thinkers believe that they have found in ethnological studies of pre-state societies one of their best arguments to defend the notion that stateless societies *are* possible, which tends to go hand in hand with the hope of recreating them in the present.

However, it is as well to discard the type of argument that first proceeds by identifying 'models' (whether social, economic or political) and then proposes to 'import' them. This approach has given rise to a veritable ragbag of applications and, like most errors of thought, has attracted economists first and foremost (one has lost count of the 'models' – 'Japanese', 'Scandinavian', 'Anglo-Saxon', 'German', etc. – under whose spell they have fallen), but it is now conquering new, more unexpected territories. We are now urged, for example, to convert to the Gaia

---

14 Pierre Clastres, *Society Against the State: Essays in Political Anthropology,* trans. Robert Hurley and Abe Stein, Princeton University Press, 1987.

15 See Chapter 8.

principle or to resurrect the *politeia* of the Guaraní tribe. The obvious fault common to all these projects of raw importation lies in an ignorance of the contextual variables – decisive in terms of the viability of the 'model' in the place where it was originally implemented, but notoriously absent in the place where the aim is to transplant it. For a 'Mother Earth' policy to work, one would have to sign up to a whole symbolic order of myths, beliefs and cosmogonies that is unlikely to be widely embraced in the 'importing' societies, unless of course one is tempted to embark on the mythogenic and somewhat hazardous undertaking of recreating it in situ.

Similarly, the tribe without a central authority analysed by Clastres derived its viability from a fabric of social relations shaped by a subsistence economy, a very limited division of labour, and a very specific symbolic environment, which (it is worth reminding would-be mythogenic engineers once again) is completely unreproducible. The unavoidable conclusion is that these 'solutions' (for the eagerness to replicate 'models' is the epitome of 'solutionism', that regressive functionalism in political thinking that often searches for 'solutions' very far afield), when deprived of the original conditions that made them possible, become unworkable ... Perhaps it is the troubled context of the early twenty-first century that is giving rise to this proliferation of regressive solutions advocating a 'return to' Mother Earth, the Guaranís, the village communities of yore and suchlike. And yet Marx and Engels comprehensively dismantled this jumble of nostalgic aspirations in *The Communist Manifesto*: the social and symbolic relations of the past belong to the past. Those relations were what sustained ways of living that are now of anachronistic interest to some. The point is that institutional and symbolic systems are holistic – you cannot wander around picking and choosing as you would in a self-service canteen. As a result, unless we were to embark on the madcap project of recreating this past in its *entirety*, these vestiges are of no contemporary political use to us. It is up to us to *invent* new relations that are not simple imitations of those of the past.

However, the central point and interest of this discussion lies elsewhere. The fact that 'stateless societies' are free of a separate state apparatus and their leadership is systematically denied the power of coercion (at least in times of peace) has been so well established by Pierre Clastres that there is no need to revisit the matter. The point is to draw attention to a different problem, namely that of the presence of a moral force in the group capable of dominating all its members and imposing itself upon them. This is the problem of the *source* of any State with a capital S: in other words, what is the state that precedes the State and indeed enables it, through capture, to exist in the first place? By stripping the State back to the fundamental mechanism on which its viability rests, namely the power of the multitude, and to its elementary structure, namely the self-affecting of the multitude, what we are left with is the general state. And it is clear that the general state is also at work in 'stateless societies'. Indeed, having got to this stage in our argument, we might even say that this is trivially true: in any large human group, the general state is the group-formation mechanism which also infuses all of the group's collective productions, including the production of authority. For, as Clastres clearly shows, although the leader has no power of command, he is by no means entirely lacking in authority: he possesses symbolic and moral authority. But what is this normative power if not a capture of the power of the multitude (by a single individual in this case)? Like the political power to command others, in its own distinct way symbolic authority is an authority that allows one to affect others and to get those affected to do certain things – or, in rigorously Spinozan terms, it is a power, and, in the final analysis, a power capable of affecting everyone can only be the power of everyone. Symbolic authority – the capacity to impose one's truth with authority – is thus, in itself, a characteristic manifestation of the *imperium*, 'this right, which is defined by the power of the multitude'. 'The general state, *c'est moi!*'[16] is something that the Guaraní chief could legitimately say. He is the individual capturing agent of the *imperium* through which the tribal multitude has entered into a mediated regime of self-affection: it is the affective force of the multitude itself that is channelled through the chief to affect the individuals in that multitude.

David Graeber himself, another leading figure of anarchist anthropology, could not avoid encountering this vertical action of the social that constitutes the *imperium*. He analysed the power exerted by fetishes in certain African ethnic groups, including the *nkisi* figures common in the Congo Basin whose powers ranged 'from the policing of marketplaces

---

16 [TN] See p. 163 below.

to the protection of property rights to the enforcement of contracts.[17] Graeber relates how the contracting parties drove nails into *nkisi* statuettes, which would suffice to keep them to their reciprocal pledges. And it should come as no surprise that this sufficed, since a fetish is nothing other than the material expression of the entire group's symbolic order and derives its efficacy from the power of the group being invested in it. More interestingly still, Graeber reports cases of fetishes that are capable of 'preventing a war of all against all'.[18] Leviathan is demonstrating here just how varied are the forms it can assume: a wooden statuette is a long way from a separate, coercive state. The true Leviathan, conceptually speaking, is not the Hobbesian modern state but, rather, the general state.

As the general state applies to human groupings in the most generalised possible way, it is a fortiori the case that so-called 'stateless societies' are general states. Though constituting a borderline category and appearing to be the radical antithesis of our own modern state in their neutralisation of the leader's power and their determination to avoid capture (and division), such a society is nevertheless a general state in the sense in which we have defined it. In fact, we ought to question the very idea that capture has been eluded since, by virtue of possessing symbolic power, the chief is clearly a capturing agent. It is the *form* of capture, which is to say the nature of what the capture produces, rather than the fact of capture itself, that distinguishes 'stateless societies'. That distinction notwithstanding, such societies by no means live up to the ideal of horizontality that eager contemporary political anthropologists would confer on them. Here, then, is the reality of 'stateless societies': they are as vertical as any other, and for a good reason: all cohesive groupings accommodate the principle of verticality in their own way. They are in no position to eradicate it since the vertical, the *imperium*, is the very mechanism to which they owe their cohesiveness and hence their existence. The group only perseveres to produce, and reproduce, its own normative commons, which is to say to reproduce itself as a general state.

---

17 David Graeber, *Possibilities: Essays on Hierarchy, Rebellion, and Desire*, AK Press, 2007, p. 129.
18 Ibid.

The General State and a Way of Living in Large Numbers

There is, no doubt, more than enough here to offend certain crusading anarchist thinkers who will be horrified to see their acentric projects assimilated with the category of state – the very category they are so keen to make a *radical* break from. But the intention here is not so much to horrify them as to gently remove their rose-tinted spectacles, not least because we can share without reserve their loathing of institutional captures, their dread of the nationalist nation and their horror of the police state. However, it is essential to show them what they do not want to see: that individuals who believe themselves to be free and sovereign are subject despite themselves to the powers of the collective. The very existence of durable groupings attests to those powers and places everyone within them into the category of the *general* state. There are two possible scenarios: either the collective, *regardless of its form*, crosses the threshold of cohesiveness, thereby enabling itself to persevere in its own being, or it does not cross it. If it fails to cross it, it is merely a contingent, unstable and temporary assembly of individuals which will break up at the first serious flare-up of affective 'inconstancy' – this is the destiny of free associations and all 'pacts', which will fall apart 'unless something is added to the promise'. If it does cross it, it is a general state stabilised by the verticality of a common affect that durably endorses a certain way of living through its institutions (for it will necessarily have institutions).

However, one does not endorse a way of living simply through a free and rational decision: such an endorsement is an affair of the passions. It is worth repeating here that the passions should not be construed as blind and obscure forces emerging out of the pre-linguistic darkness and radically alien to the logos. For a start, affects are accompanied by their ideas, since the mind 'perceives not only the affections of the body but also the ideas of these affections'.[19] Indeed, ideas only ever come to us enveloped in affects or conveyed by affects (or else they go in one ear and out the other without affecting our bodies). The driving force of an idea, by which is meant its capacity to set us in motion and make us do specific things that conform to that idea, correlates directly with its affective intensity. Even if it looks to us like the consequence of our 'free will', the endorsement of a way of living, like any motion of our body in

---

19 *Ethics*, II, 22, p. 81.

fact, is the consequence of an affective determination. And it differs from the reversibility of transient adhesion by its very intensity and durability, such that it inscribes in our bodies a *habit*, in Spinoza's words, which is to say ways of feeling, judging and desiring which taken together constitute a way of living. Unless we cleave to the notion of a mind in sovereign command of its decisions, these intense affective determinations are better described as a seizing of our being than as an 'endorsement', for it is not so much that we are subscribing to a way of living but rather that a way of living is taking possession of us. And these affective determinations necessarily have the intense force of the collective – a force capable of sustaining the group over time, even as its parts are replaced by new ones.[20]

Chiapas: From One State to Another

It is also possible to test the hypothesis of the general state in relation to recent and even ongoing historical experiments, by once again deploying the paradoxical resources of a fortiori argumentation. For it might seem obvious that the political experiment in Chiapas eludes the 'State'. It certainly eludes the Mexican bourgeois police state that is waging war on it (all bourgeois states wage war on those who explore the outer fringes of their capitalist order). But does it elude any form of state whatsoever, that is, the general state, too? No more so than any other political formation. Both internally, with its governing councils arranged into a hierarchical territorial network, its dispute resolution and policing authorities, and its educational institutions, and externally with its army (the EZLN), Chiapas displays all the constitutional and military attributes of a state structure.

The importance of the presence of a military institution cannot be overstated, for it is the concentration of a force which is perhaps the most eloquent expression of the organic unity of the collective – its conatus striving to persevere in its being, in this instance in the face of external elements which are threatening to destroy it. And then, of course, there is the obvious fact of the intimate link between an army and a state. It is worth noting in this respect what EZLN stands for:

---

20 See Chapter 5 below.

Ejército Zapatista de Liberación *Nacional*,[21] which affords additional confirmation that even if one eludes certain specific forms, one does not elude general principles – in this case the principle of the nation state (conceptualised in its most abstract form). We might conjecture that Central and Latin America, less burdened than Europe with a long history of ethnic and nationalist ravages, can envisage the idea of nation more serenely, not least because the 'Zapatista nation' was originally born out of a very different idea of the nation to ours, namely a nation of the indigenous. And we know what a powerful and politically effective idea that can be in that part of the world – the example of Bolivia springs to mind.[22] But this was only the case at the outset, one of the distinguishing features of the Zapatista nation being that, from this ethnic wellspring, it has since defined itself as an open, inclusive nation, keen to incorporate anyone who identifies with the way of living that it has established, regardless of their origins – provided they identify with that *particular way of living* and are similarly keen to belong. In other words, provided they are immediately placed under its common affect and demonstrate their espousal of that common affect, not through some solemn, grotesque declaration but by living their daily lives in accordance with the community's principles of collective existence. And this is unquestionably an instance of nation-building, albeit very different to the aggressive nation-building that seems to be a congenital disease of the modern European nation state. Nevertheless, its very coherence, even if we approve of its anti-capitalist radicalism, has a restrictive downside: the Zapatista nation's way of living will only be accommodating towards those who subscribe to its project. It is by no means certain that it would be so welcoming to a group of neo-entrepreneurs – every nation has its outsiders.

Fleeing the (bourgeois) state, the Zapatistas have rebuilt a state; a different state no doubt, but nevertheless a state which is a fresh variation on the general state. It should not ultimately be so difficult to distinguish between the underlying mechanism and the forms it gives rise to (or, to use traditional philosophical language, between essence and accidents). Accordingly, it should not be so difficult either to accommodate

---

21 My emphasis.

22 An idea that is not without its problems, however. See Franck Poupeau, *Les Mésaventures de la critique*, Raisons d'agir, 2012, Chapter 3.

both the necessary persistence of the general state beneath the Zapatista form and the specific and explicitly stated project to ceaselessly resist the ever-renewed threat of capture. In its own way, compared to other contemporary forms of the general state, it is a unique project in its attempt to form a state that eludes so far as is possible the curse of division and dispossession. But it can only do this so far as is possible, which is to say, never completely.

5

What a Political Body Is
(What a Political Body Can Do)

Limited groupings are bodies. Stated thus, this assertion does not come across as especially original. Do we not often speak of social and political bodies? But it is one thing to use familiar language to describe this or that, and quite another to associate a concept with that habit. Without the concept, a 'collective body' remains a metaphor. Admittedly it can be a striking one, like the famous frontispiece of *Leviathan*, for example, but it still remains only a metaphor. However, there is a barrier to getting beyond the metaphorical stage, which has largely been erected by the contemporary social sciences. It stems from a wariness (to some extent justified) of organicist interpretations of society and their cortege of biological analogies, often loose and sometimes outrageous. But – in a characteristic swing of the pendulum to the other extreme, driven, in part, by the individualist turn – in guarding themselves against the organicist peril, the contemporary social sciences now refuse to acknowledge the inner coherence of collective entities in keeping with the Popper–Agassi principle, which rejects the notion of groups having any goal or self-interest *as groups*. But it is precisely their functioning 'as groups' (rejected by individualist nominalism) which needs to be analysed if we are to render a social fact like the nation state conceptually intelligible. This does not, however, mean falling into the clumsy trap of hypostasis whereby the nation is endowed through simple projection with all the attributes of a human being, such that it becomes in some sense merely the individual writ large.

In this respect, the Popper–Agassi principle erects something of a straw man: unless we are seduced into taking the facile analogy of the group as an enlarged human being literally, why would we be tempted to ascribe to it attributes of consciousness such as goals or self-interest (when there is no obvious locus for such attributes)? Unfortunately, this understandable aversion to dubious analogies has had the broader effect of curtailing any attempt to analyse collective entities in their collective dimension. And, indeed, this is the challenge of a theory of collective bodies: we need to persist in conceptualising social entities in terms of their inner collective coherence and allocating a mode of existence to them detached from organicist notions of essentialist communities or of social entities as simply the human individual writ large. This of course means avoiding the most obvious error of attributing to them psychological traits through unwitting anthropocentric projection, but we must nevertheless stick with the task of analysing their capacity for perseverance (as for any mode). And this, it turns out, is a *corporeal* capacity, not a fact of consciousness.

Towards a General Theory of Bodies

The first step, then, is to overcome the natural and unconscious tendency to take the human body as the implicit reference point for any possible body, as this approach inevitably leads to aporia when we realise that non-human bodies cannot in fact be conceptualised in the same way as human bodies. But we must avoid drawing the erroneous conclusion that they cannot be conceptualised as bodies *at all*. This is why a theory of collective bodies calls for a *general* theory of bodies, stripped of all anthropomorphic elements but still able to accommodate the human body as one of its specific instances. Since he accords man no exceptional status among the things of nature, and, indeed, does not attempt to conceptualise man's essence per se (meaning, it should be said, that it is unclear if it is legitimate to speak of an *anthropology* in his philosophy),[1]

---

1 While Alexandre Matheron points out that there is 'no problem speaking in a very broad sense of a Spinozan anthropology', in answer to the more specific question of whether Spinoza attempts to characterise 'man per se', he suggests that the answer is no. Alexandre Matheron, 'Une anthropologie spinoziste?', in *Études sur Spinoza et les philosophies de l'âge classique*, ENS Éditions, 2011.

Spinoza is better equipped than anyone to resist the analogy of the human body when it comes to thinking about bodies in very general terms.

Often quoted is his statement that 'nobody as yet has learned from experience what the body can and cannot do'.[2] First, one would need a clear idea of what a body is. Spinoza provides this in a less cited but extremely important passage in Part II of the *Ethics*. After explaining that the mind is the idea of the body and that man consists of the union of mind and body, he goes on to say: 'But nobody can understand this union adequately or distinctly unless he first gains adequate knowledge of the nature of our body'.[3] Here, Spinoza is laying the first stones of the thesis known (inappropriately)[4] as 'psychophysical parallelism' by deducing that if the mind is the idea of the body, then 'in proportion as a body is more apt than other bodies to act or be acted upon simultaneously in many ways, so is its mind more apt than other minds to perceive many things simultaneously'[5] – a thesis that will culminate in Proposition 39 of Part V.[6] We can be sure that Spinoza is not referring to just any body. Admittedly, in Part I of the *Ethics*, he does not once refer explicitly to 'man' (except in the scholia). However, his intentions become clear enough in the few lines that introduce Part II: while he has thus far only addressed very generally the infinity of things that follow from the essence of God, he now declares that he will henceforward address 'only those things that can lead us as it were by the hand to the knowledge of the human mind and its utmost blessedness'.[7] And this is where man comes in.

---

2 *Ethics*, III, 2, scholium, p. 105.

3 *Ethics*, II, 13, scholium, p. 72.

4 Chantal Jaquet has most clearly highlighted the inappropriateness of this label, which I use merely as a convenient shorthand. See Chantal Jaquet, *L'Unité du corps et de l'esprit. Affects, actions et passions chez Spinoza*, 'Quadrige', PUF, 2004.

5 Ibid.

6 'He whose body is capable of the greatest amount of activity has a mind whose greatest part is eternal', *Ethics*, V, 39, p. 220.

7 *Ethics*, II, Introduction, p. 63.

The Body Not as Substance but as Relation

Nevertheless, the generalising spirit continues to predominate. The scholium of *Ethics*, II, 13, though dealing explicitly with *human* bodies, is careful to specify that 'what we have so far demonstrated is of quite general application, and applies to men no more than to other individuals, which are all animate, albeit in different degrees.'[8] Thus, when Spinoza declares the need for 'a brief preface concerning the nature of bodies',[9] we should not be surprised that three-quarters of his treatment is devoted to bodies in general. Only the last six postulates deal specifically with the human body.

So, what is a body in general? It is an ensemble of parts that will remain united with each other by preserving *a certain relation of motion and rest*: 'When a number of bodies of the same or different magnitude form close contact with one another through the pressure of other bodies upon them, or if they are moving at the same or different rates of speed so as to preserve a certain fixed relation of movement among themselves, these bodies are said to be united with one another and all together to form one body or individual thing, which is distinguished from other things through this union of bodies.'[10] The parts, which are themselves bodies, therefore make up a 'union of bodies' according to a certain relation (*certa ratio*) between themselves which is distinct 'from other things'. In Spinoza's eyes, then, individual things are divided, but he pays no attention to this (false) problem. What matters to him is to highlight the composite nature of bodies, to insert each one into a grand hierarchy of composition that culminates in the supreme individual thing that is the whole universe (*Totius Facies Universi*), and, above all, to make their divided-composite nature compatible with individual instantiations of activity and perseverance: though they are composites, there are still individuated loci of power that are distinguishable from one another.

And this individuation is defined in completely fresh terms, namely in structural terms. What is an individuated body? It is a *certain relation*

---

8 *Ethics*, II, 13, scholium, p. 72.

9 Ibid.

10 *Ethics*, II, definition, p. 74. [TN] I have slightly emended the Shirley translation and followed RHM Elwes (1951) in translating *certa ratio* as a 'certain fixed relation'. Shirley translates it as an 'unvarying relation'.

(*certa ratio*) according to which the parts are arranged. The rupture with the familiar essentialist conceptions of bodies could not be clearer, and indeed Spinoza makes this perfectly explicit: 'Bodies are distinguished from one another in respect of motion and rest, quickness and slowness, and not in respect of substance.'[11] Spinoza is no doubt thinking within the mechanistic framework of the natural philosophy of his time, and our twenty-first-century mentality automatically leads us to question the conceptualising of bodies in terms of 'motion and rest'. But dismissing Spinoza's thinking as mechanistic would be unfairly reductive of his philosophy. For the idea of preserving a certain relation between motion and rest has nothing essentially mechanistic about it, and indeed the way in which political bodies preserve this relation serves to confirm this: human bodies, which are parts of the political body, manifestly do not do so through physical contact but through mutual affections and through affects. In any case, a body is not a substance: it is a union of parts arranged according to a certain relation such that it forms a coherent ensemble of motion and rest.

The Politics of the Human Body

It is perhaps in this respect that the overlapping of the physical and political is most evident, something consistent moreover with Spinoza's uncompromising naturalism.[12] We can intuit that there is a physical dimension to politics by reconceptualising politics as a landscape of powers. Invoking 'ideas' to counter this vision of politics as driven by forces is a very feeble objection, for ideas have no efficacy unless borne by affects – it is only by virtue of being borne by affects that ideas acquire any efficacy at all. And affects themselves fit very naturally into this general grammar of power, as suggested not merely by their definition as variations in the power of the affected body but also by the way in which confrontations between them are settled, with the strongest affect winning out over the weaker one,[13] and by the view of affects as properties

---

11 *Ethics*, II, 13, lemma 1, p. 72.

12 On this question of uncompromising naturalism, see Citton and Lordon, 'À propos d'une photo'.

13 *Ethics*, IV, 7, p. 158.

pertaining to the mind rather than as unruly emotions to be derided.[14] Politics is the factory churning out the products of collective affective forces.

Likewise, there is a political dimension to the physical. We can already intuit this from the definition of the finite mode as the expression of the infinite power of God, and so a finite delegation of power which is then confronted with other modes, in relationships of power involving concord and alliance or discord and dispute – that is, in a political relationship. Is not the conatus, by definition, an *effort*? And if perseverance necessarily assumes the form of a striving, it is because the world does not consist solely of concord, and one is obliged to struggle against contrary forces – such is the politics of things.

And now we can see that there is also politics in bodies themselves by simple virtue of the fact that a body is a union of parts. Alexandre Matheron; and Laurent Bove; have taken this line of thinking to its logical conclusion by proposing that we should regard all bodies, including the human body, as federations, since the parts can only make up a body if the body is capable of retaining its parts.[15] And it retains them in a relationship on which its existence depends and whose nature should by now be clear: it is a relationship based on sovereignty. A body can only exist if it is capable of subordinating its parts to the sovereign effort of persevering (perseverance and subordination, it is worth repeating, being a matter of bodily forces and not of conscious will). If the parts are there to be subordinated by this body, then they could just as well have remained scattered or entered other competing bodies, but instead they have been subordinated into this one. And, indeed, bodies do battle for parts every day. When a human (or other animal) body eats, it dispossesses another body of its parts and assimilates them; in other words, it brings them within its own subordinating sphere and reorders them accordingly. The body only perseveres for as long as it extends its *imperium* over its own parts – 'I only accord a right to the sovereign over his subjects to the extent that through his power he is able to dominate them', writes Spinoza in his letter to Jarig Jelles, and exactly the same applies to the particular

14 *PT*, I, 4, p. 35.
15 Matheron, *Individu et communauté chez Spinoza*; Bove, 'De la prudence des corps. Du physique au politique'.

politics of the human body, where seditious organs wanting to live for their own sake may win out, or cellular rebellion may occur. The conatus is the sovereign of its parts in so far as it can subordinate them to its own effort to persevere. If its *imperium* begins to weaken and the forces of divergence regain the upper hand, its fate will be decomposition. But 'to the extent that through [its] power [it] is able to dominate them', it is the regulator of their coexistence and the dominant principle of its own composition.

The Body as Form, and Its Configurations

Exactly what this relation is that constitutes the essence of a body Spinoza does not say – except that it is a relation of motion and rest. But his analysis of the physical world in the *Ethics* affords some vital additional clues to his conception of bodies. Firstly, the fact that a body retains its nature even as its parts are replaced by new ones (lemma 4, p. 74). Secondly, that it will also retain its nature as it grows (lemma 4, p. 75). And, lastly, that its nature will remain intact in multiple configurations (lemma 7, p. 75).[16]

To take these points in order: the body is not reducible to specific parts. If a part is lost and replaced by an equivalent part, this makes no difference so long as the replacement part enjoys the same relation to the whole. This is the old problem of the ship of Theseus: wear and tear results in all the wooden parts being gradually replaced until none of the original remains: is it still the same ship? Of course, says Spinoza, because the nature of the ship does not derive from the wooden parts themselves but from the relation in which the parts stand to each other, and that has not changed.

Secondly, the body is invariant under a homothetic transformation (in mathematics, a homothety is a transformation that conserves the same ratios). A body can thus grow and remain the same, provided it is not excessively deformed as it grows.

---

16 'I don't know how they really cohere and how each part agrees with its whole; to know this I would have to know the whole of Nature and all of its parts.' Letter 32 to Henry Oldenburg in Jonathan Bennett (ed.), *Correspondence – Baruch Spinoza*, earlymoderntexts.com, 2017, p. 24.

Thirdly, and most importantly, the same relation of the parts to the whole is compatible with multiple configurations: for example, a human body sitting down, standing up or doing a handstand against the wall is still the same body but in manifestly different configurations. Here Spinoza introduces a fundamental conceptual distinction between form and configuration. 'Form' is the name given to the relation of parts to the whole that forms the essence of a body (lemma 4, proof, p. 75). But this form only ever materialises 'concretely' through a given configuration – indeed, Lorenzo Vinciguerra asserts that there is no such thing as a form that is not configured: a form is always already configured.[17] This is because configurations are the affections of form, and every mode is always already affected. Form, as a union of parts, reveals here one of its principal properties: configurative plasticity. The law of internal composition that constitutes the relation of the parts to the whole (the form) can (literally) be configured in multiple ways, on condition that the relation of its parts that defines it remains intact. Form is deformable (into its configurations), but only up to a certain point, beyond which it will disintegrate: a (human) body will endure the rack up to the point of dislocation, and then it is not the same body – that body has simply ceased to exist.

The Elementary Structures of Politics (II): The *Certa Ratio*

The body defined as a 'certain relation' (*certa ratio*) and not as a substance, and which retains its nature as its parts are replaced and in its varying configurations: these are the principal elements of a general theory of bodies that is applicable to political bodies. This entails certain important consequences when conceptualising social entities and trying to tread a middle ground between outright denial and the trap of essentialist communities. For, in refusing quite rightly to fall into identity-based essentialism but lacking any other means of conceptualising the nature per se of collective bodies, certain intellectuals find themselves cornered into denying that distinct social entities exist at all . . . It is also the case that they are incapable of understanding a collective entity as anything other than a totalitarian form of affiliation – and it is amidst this muddle

---

17 Lorenzo Vinciguerra, *Spinoza et le signe. La genèse de l'imagination*, Vrin, 2006, p. 142.

of antinomies that their analysis of political forms inevitably goes astray. The objective of a structural theory of bodies in general, and political bodies in particular, is to untangle this knot of (false) problems.

And, first, we need to complete the list of the elementary structures of politics. The first was the *imperium*, which is to say the self-affecting of the multitude, which is the wellspring of all authority in the social world and above all the mechanism through which political groupings acquire *coherence*; it is this which can be categorised as the 'general state'. The *certa ratio*, that structural relationship according to which the parts cohere into a union of bodies, is the second. The *certa ratio* is the formal structure of bodies in general and political bodies in particular. It is the principle which confers on them their *distinctiveness*. This relationship according to which the parts cohere constitutes the individuality of the whole – and that individuality is distinctive. Such-and-such an individual thing is not the same as another thing: each has its own characteristic *ratio*. It is therefore by the same mechanism – the constitutive relation of parts to each other and to the whole – that a body both distinguishes itself from a simple collection (an absence of relation) and from other bodies (that are structured according to different relations). As François Zourabichvili writes: 'The existence of a proportionate communication of the parts (in terms of motion and rest) is the reason for any structure and the criterion that distinguishes it ... from a simple aggregate.'[18] And also, we might add, from other structures whose parts likewise cohere according to a certain ratio (proportion) of movement and rest. Juxtaposing parts into a cluster amounts to nothing – what is needed is the structure that composes them into a (political) body according to a certain relation of the parts to one another and to the whole. And this union has nothing to do with substance, as is made perfectly clear in *Ethics*, II, 24, proof (p. 82). Although the subject of this proposition is the human body, the assertion is clearly of general application: 'The component parts of the human body do not pertain to the essence of the body itself save in so far as they preserve a certain relation of motion with one another.' The nature of the parts plays no role in the definition of the nature of the whole that they will form: it is the relation of the parts to one another and to the whole which defines the whole.

---

18 François Zourabichvili, *Spinoza, une physique de la pensée*, 'Philosophie d'aujourd'hui', PUF, 2002.

Are the political implications of this structural definition of a collective body sufficiently clear? If they are, we should not shy away from accepting the consequences that naturally follow from it. The first step is to accept the principle of differentiation that necessarily follows from the individuation of bodies. If we are capable of conceptualising that which constitutes, in its structural essence, an individual, we must admit the existence of individuals, plural, and in this instance political collectives of individuals. This gives an interesting new complexion to Rousseau's assertion that 'the human race merely prompts a collective idea in the mind which does not imply any actual union between the individuals that make it up', his 'actual union' acquiring here a curiously Spinozan resonance.

Non-Totalitarian Totalities and Porous Enclosures

It will be easier still to accept this principle of the individuation and differentiation of political bodies once we appreciate that the principle is one of only partial enclosure. Leaving aside fantasies of the human race, political bodies, which only consist of certain parts and not all parts, are admittedly totalities and hence enclosures, but they are only partial enclosures – there is no totalitarianism in a totality. As Alexandre Matheron notes: 'In a finite individual, each constituent body can effect motions other than those that it communicates to other bodies within its whole according to a *certa ratio* – it can communicate those motions to exterior bodies or to other constituent bodies according to other *rationes* or even according to no invariable ratio.'[19] The citizen of a nation-state totality can experience with their fellow citizens motions and communications of motion that have nothing to do with the certain relation (*certa ratio*) through which they constitute that totality. In other words, not all the deeds of the citizen are subordinated to the coherence of the *politeia* to which they belong. I can entertain with my fellow citizens relations that have nothing do with our shared citizenship, such as relations based on friendship, a shared neighbourhood or religion, or membership of the same club. Moreover, the deeds of a citizen can

---

19 Alexandre Matheron, 'L'État, selon Spinoza, est-il un individu au sens de Spinoza?', in *Études sur Spinoza*, p. 419.

perfectly well contribute to the (structural) coherence of another collective body that is distinct from the one of which they are initially a part.
Through the communicating of motion and rest, one may contribute to
the composition of the political body that is a nation state, but also and
simultaneously to the composition of another collective body, such as a
religious congregation, whose contours do not overlap with those of
nation states. One can even communicate one's motions within two
bodies of the same kind – and have two passports. It may be that some
of these simultaneous affiliations require certain conditions to avoid
being self-contradictory, but that is not to suggest that they are impossible in principle. The structural definition of a body does not require
that 'all the activities of the constituent parts can be deduced from the
laws of the whole'.[20] And, 'as their integration into the whole is never
complete, they can also accomplish other motions and communicate
them to other parts or to external bodies according to other laws that do
not relate to the whole'.[21]

This communicating of motions outside the body of reference reveals
the nature of the enclosure that the body constitutes: it is a necessarily
porous enclosure. If the general theory of bodies initially enabled us to
conceptualise the political body without reference to the human body,
conversely it also enables us to revisit certain properties of the human
body in order to throw light on the properties of the political body, for
the porosity of the enclosure is nowhere more visible than in the case of
the human body. The human mode, which is famously finite, can only
live in symbiotic interaction with other finite modes. There are the
elementary nutrients without which simple biological perseverance
would be inconceivable but also, and above all, the other finite human
modes with which it jointly organises an expanded form of perseverance that extends the exercise of its powers and will potentially lead it to
the 'true virtue and life of the mind'.[22] The human mode, as a part of
nature, is connected to other parts of nature and engaged with them in
an existence which is necessarily relational. One can immediately see
how deluded notions of 'individualism' are when conceived as autarchic
sovereignty. By contrast, Étienne Balibar, borrowing from Simondon,

---

20 Ibid., p. 419, Matheron's emphasis.
21 Ibid., p. 435.
22 *PT*, V, 5, p. 62.

draws the logical conclusions of the theory of the finite mode by stressing that there is only the transindividual.[23] So, although there is something like a structural enclosure of the human individual, it is a necessarily porous enclosure. One might even risk the oxymoron of affirming that it is an open enclosure: under the law of the transindividual as it applies to the finite mode, the closed enclosure is simply doomed to perish.

At the same time, above and beyond what they have in common (the structural definition of their essence in relational terms), we should not forget what the human body and the political body respectively conserve, and we should not treat them as exact equivalents. Pierre-François Moreau reminds us of the difference between unions that are biological/human and those that are political:[24] the former proceed from the integration of functional differentiation (of the organs), and the latter by the convergence of similar parts (citizens). Nevertheless, while acknowledging these pertinent differences, the principle of the porosity of the enclosure applies in equal measure to both the human and the political body. Although the porosity of the political body arises primarily from its incapacity to subordinate its parts *completely*, it also proves positively beneficial to it. That said, extremely closed political totalities can also be viable, and it is perhaps in this respect that the difference between the human and the political body is clearest; the Hebrew state analysed by Spinoza in the *Theological-Political Treatise* is one of the most notorious examples, its internal cohesiveness being partially based on a rigorous collective enclosure and a religious hatred of the foreigner. While porosity is not the imperative for the political body that it is for the human body, and although this type of extreme enclosure is conceivable in principle (and indeed attested to in history), it nevertheless remains the case that, in line with the argument that Spinoza develops regarding the human mode, the complexity of the body (that is, the broad spectrum of its affectabilities) determines the amplitude of what it can do – in other words, the extent of its powers. The complexity of the political body derives above all from the diversity of its parts, provided of course that

---

23 Étienne Balibar, 'Individualité et transindividualité chez Spinoza', in Pierre-François Moreau (ed.), *Architectures de la raison. Mélanges offerts à Alexandre Matheron*, ENS Éditions, 1996.

24 Pierre-François Moreau, *Spinoza. L'expérience et l'éternité*, 'Épiméthée', PUF, 1994.

they remain subject to its organising principle. But that organising principle – the structural relationship that it imposes upon them – is elastic. And that very plasticity can be exploited to allow it to assume new configurations – for example, through the arrival of new parts that give fresh impetus to the group's constant reshaping of its own collective complexion.

The Eternal Nation Does Not Exist (France as the Spanish Poet)

The structural theory of political bodies allows us, then, to avoid the slippery slope towards essentialist communities in two respects: by the nature of the theory itself, of course, but also through the insight which it affords into the demise of bodies – an insight that explodes the fantasies of the eternal to be found in the national narrative. Some might argue that if there is one respect in which a difference must be acknowledged between the human and the political body, then it is in respect of death. How could a single concept of death be accommodated within a general theory of bodies that would apply to all types of body? But do we really know what the death of the human body consists of? In a quite remarkable scholium, Spinoza explodes the conceptions that we hold to be incontestably obvious on this subject: 'I have no reason to hold that a body does not die unless it turns into a corpse'.[25] It is the kind of sentence that makes one sit up with a start, and Spinoza seems aware of this. He abruptly terminates the scholium with a teasing admonition: 'But I prefer to leave these matters unresolved, so as not to afford material for the superstitious to raise new problems.'[26]

And yet he has suggested the outline of a solution to this problem, so we should not dismiss it as a mere aside. Indeed, it is entirely consistent with the remarks preceding it that pertain to his general theory of bodies: 'But here it should be noted that I understand a body to die when its parts are so disposed as to maintain a different proportion of motion and rest to one another. For I do not venture to deny that the human body, while retaining blood circulation and whatever else is regarded as essential to life, can nevertheless assume another

---

25 *Ethics*, IV, 39, scholium, p. 177.
26 Ibid.

nature quite different from its own.'[27] Here, we need to be sensitive to the word 'disposed' – 'when its parts are so disposed' – in order to appreciate the scope of its possibilities. The constitutive relation of a body is the certain way in which the parts are *disposed* in relation to each other. And death as we know it (or think we know it) does indeed consist of a new way of them being disposed in relation to one another, namely in scattered form. Ashes to ashes, dust to dust – this is a different disposition of the parts. But why should this scattering be the only such transformation that a body can experience? If we read the scholium of *Ethics*, IV, 39 with the attention it deserves, this is the very logical question that arises. There is, indeed, no reason to hold that, even if the external appearance of a body remains the same, its parts cannot be disposed in a very different way, for their disposition is not merely a question of spatial location but of mutual relations and the communicating of motion and rest to one another – to the extent that the same ensemble of parts or their fungible equivalents, rearranged in a new relationship among themselves, can constitute a new body. This means that the body that they formerly constituted no longer exists – it is dead.

Spinoza gives a striking example of this process of decomposition and recomposition through which (without passing through the 'corpse' stage) the same collection of parts are rearranged through a radical transformation of their organising principle (the relation of the parts to the whole) from one body into another which involves the death of the first and the birth of the second: 'I have heard tell of a certain Spanish poet who was seized with sickness, and although he recovered, he remained so unconscious of his past life that he did not believe that the stories and tragedies he had written were his own. Indeed, he might have been taken for a child in adult form if he had also forgotten his native tongue.'[28] How are we to recognise this radical structural change, which is to say, death? The answer is through the erasure of a substantial fraction of the body's memory. The Spanish poet has not completely lost his memory because he has retained his native tongue, in contrast to the Croatian teenager who came out of a twenty-hour coma having completely forgotten her mother tongue and

---

27 Ibid.
28 Ibid.

speaking German fluently – a language she had only just begun to learn. (Was she dead too?)[29]

In Spinoza, memory has to be understood in a wider sense than that of the familiar 'reservoir of memories'. Memory is a bodily inscription. Our individual experiences leave traces that confer on a body its particular disposition or configuration, which Spinoza calls our *ingenium*. The *ingenium*, the product of vestigial traces inscribed in the body, is the memory of the practices of a body, the durable stabilisation of its habits and the re-expression of its affective susceptibilities in their contemporary complexion. If it is sufficiently profound, a change in memory is thus a reconfiguration that exceeds the elasticity threshold of the form. Form is deformable through its configurations, but only within certain limits. Beyond those limits, form is no longer reconfigured but simply destroyed and the body dies. The excessive scale of the reconfiguration that results from the radical modification (in this case the erasure) of the Spanish poet's memory is not compatible with the maintaining of its form. We are now dealing not with the previous form configured differently but with another form, which is to say another essence and literally another body. In the transition between the two, a death has occurred. Though the parts appear to be the same, we are no longer dealing with the same individual.

This new conception of death, though implacably logical, may well leave us utterly disconcerted when it comes to the human body, but it puts us on the right track when it comes to conceptualising the death of collective bodies. We can now conceive of a scenario whereby they can die other than through the death of all their parts. Spinoza's thinking is close to that of Aristotle on this point. 'For inasmuch as a city is a kind of community, . . . when the *form* of the government has been altered and is different it would appear to follow that the city is no longer the same city, just as we say that a chorus which on one occasion acts a comedy and on another a tragedy is a different chorus although it is often composed of the same persons, and similarly with any other common whole or composite structure we say it is different if the form

---

29 'Une adolescente croate sort d'un coma en parlant allemand' (Croatian teenager comes out of coma speaking German), Nouvelobs.com, 15 April 2010.

of its structure is different.'[30] So, for Aristotle, the state is a 'kind of community'. He does not go so far as to suggest, at least not as explicitly as Spinoza does, that it is an individual thing per se, but a 'kind' of community nevertheless means 'not any' community. In other words, not any human aggregate constitutes a city, and even a common location does not suffice, 'for it is said that when Babylon was captured a considerable part of the city was not aware of it three days later.'[31] Contrary to appearances, Babylon was not therefore properly speaking a *city* – to translate this into Spinozan terms, we could say that certain motions failed to be communicated from one part of the city to another. In a similar vein, 'if one were actually to bring the sites of two cities together into one, so that the city-walls of Megara and those of Corinth were contiguous, even so they would not be one city.'[32] For a group of people, even if they are located in the same place, to constitute a city, something else is needed: they need to be composed within a form. Provided we understand it in a sufficiently broad sense, 'constitution' is the word for this form when it comes to politics: 'It is clear that we must speak of a city as being the same city chiefly with regard to its constitution; and it is possible for it to be called by the same or by a different designation both when its inhabitants are the same and when they are entirely different persons.'[33] A city is defined by its constitutional form, and we can say that it remains the same even if its parts are entirely replaced. Conversely, if the parts are retained but composed within a different form, it is a different city.

For both the political body and the human body, there comes a point when changing into something that is not just different but *completely* different signifies death. We can therefore now conclude, with the Spanish poet in mind, that 'countries' do indeed die – even if a misleading sense of continuity over time gives us a mistaken impression of enduring identity. Though it would probably be futile to attempt to situate this death precisely in time, we can be sure that our current habits

---

30 Aristotle (*Politics*, Book III), *Aristotle in 23 Volumes, Vol. 21*, trans. H. Rackham, William Heinemann Ltd., 1944. [TN] I have emended Rackham's original translation ('inasmuch as a state is a kind of partnership') so that it concords with the *cité* and *communauté* of the French translation which the author cites. My emphasis.

31 Ibid.

32 Ibid.

33 Ibid.

and mutual communicating of our motions have very little in common with those of what we (inappropriately) call the France of ten or twelve centuries ago. Such a shift in the memory of our behaviours and practices – such a reconfiguration of the collective *ingenium* – prevents us from maintaining the fiction of an unvarying social totality even if we are speaking figuratively. The same applies to these totalities as to Spanish poets: they die without us noticing, and it is merely the retrospective power of the imagination that invents a permanent state that in reality has fallen apart (several times, perhaps). There is no such thing as an eternal France, and the national narrative that has invented it is for the birds. Needless to say, it is the essentialist conception of communities that gives rise to such fantasies: indefinite duration is supposed to be one of the predicates of 'substance' or 'essence', ergo if the community has a characteristic essence, then it must be eternal. But the flaw is inherent in the premise: political bodies are only a substance in the imagination. As with any body, there are, instead, *forms* – and mortal forms at that. And, when it comes to the 'countries' of today, they will probably already have experienced death, perhaps several times.

Reality – and Falsity – of the Imagination

We now, therefore, have two ways of arguing against the mythologies of an eternal national substance, but they are not equally persuasive: one is to simply deny that such a thing exists, and the other is the structural theory of political bodies. Incapable of conceptualising the specific nature of political bodies, and understandably haunted by essentialist nationalism, thinkers on the left find that they have no option but to downplay the issue: that which they are unable to conceptualise to their satisfaction they decree to exist only in the inferior mode of a mistaken fiction. There is of course plenty to say about the relationship between fiction and the real world. But, as we know, Spinoza refuses to set the two in opposition; on the contrary, he grants an empirical status to the products of the imagination: for him, those products are real. What individuals imagine is the product of their bodies and minds in a real sense. Indeed, these products are so real that one can in principle reconstruct the generative process, and Spinoza has no hesitation in doing so, showing us for example how we spontaneously produce the fiction of free will.[34] But we have arrived at a state of extreme confusion if we are no longer capable of distinguishing between the degree of (non-)truth of products of the imagination and their degree of reality. If people in a group imagine a mythical past that serves to hold them together, that product of the imagination *in itself* exists in reality, and it *really* holds them together. Benedict Anderson does not downplay nationalism when he seeks the key to it in the imagination.[35] We might debate whether this perspective exhaustively captures the phenomenon in question, but we can unhesitatingly dismiss the notion that it is somehow downplaying it.

Determined not to think in terms of bodies, which, in their eyes, smacks of organicist essentialism, intellectuals on the left have limited empirical resources for conceptualising a grouping of the national type and tend instead to settle for normative statements such as '"people + national adjective" is of no interest'. And yet surely there is scope for conceptualising political groupings, and national groupings in particular, without being beholden to categories of good and evil. The aversion to consecrating in intellectual form the imaginary discourse that people invent about their nations is understandable. But this should not, for want of an alternative discourse, entail giving up on trying to conceptualise the phenomenon other than through a normative lens that a priori downplays it – not least because we have far from exhausted the resources for an empirical treatment of the subject. The structural theory of bodies can hardly be accused of pandering to the esoteric discourse of the national imagination, since it methodically challenges essentialist tropes. Yet, at the same time, it fully acknowledges the existence of such political groupings by advancing a concept of their form which in turn allows us to conceptualise their individuation and thus their differentiation from their equivalents.

---

34 *Ethics*, I, Appendix.
35 Benedict Anderson, *Imagined Communities: Reflections on the Origin and Spread of Nationalism*, Verso, 1983.

What a Political Body Can Do

A further point needs to be made on this subject in order to prepare us for a transition towards more normative questions (which we are by no means discarding – we will come to them in due course): namely, that the Spinozan theory of bodies leads us naturally on to an analysis of their power. As we have seen, when Spinoza speaks of bodies, he is always asking what they can do. That question, which relates to the ontology of power, applies to all bodies, political bodies included. The answer to what a political body can do lies in the contemporary configuration of its from. What a body can do depends on the configuration of its *ingenium*. Look at its folds and the behaviours that have become stabilised as habits, and you will know what it is capable of. La Boétie asks how we are to explain voluntary servitude, and the answer is that we have acquired the habit. All submit to one because, having submitted many times before, they have completely lost the *habit* of freedom. Pride in sedition is no longer in people's habits and so that fold has been erased from the collective *ingenium*. In its place a habit of submission has formed: 'The primary reason for servitude is custom.'[36] The fold of custom forms quickly, and when it is one of submission, it radically erases the previously existing folds: 'It is unbelievable, once they are subjugated, how the people forget freedom so suddenly and so profoundly that it is impossible to awaken them to reclaim it.'[37] And one is tempted to wonder whether this deep sleep that renders an old habit inaccessible, having erased the memory of a whole range of practices (in this case, the practices of freedom), is not tantamount to the death of a political body in the fashion of our Spanish poet.

For Spinoza, habit forms from the permanent traces left in the body by certain experiences which, precisely for this reason, can be described as 'marking' us. La Boétie makes the same point in different words: habit is a question of *nourishment*. The habit or habitus of freedom or servitude is a dietary matter. Tell me what you have been fed on and I will tell you what your 'custom' makes you capable of. 'Nourishment moulds us in its own fashion' – there is an extraordinary

---

36 La Boétie, *Discours de la servitude volontaire*, p. 35.
37 Ibid.

simplicity to this phrase, and also an extraordinary depth.[38] When two Lacedemonians are asked to pledge allegiance to the Persian king Xerxes by one of his lieutenants, they explain that they have tasted freedom and will never subjugate themselves. La Boétie comments on their mutual inability to understand each other: 'It was not possible for the Persian to regret freedom for he had never had it, nor for the Lacedemonian to endure subjugation, having tasted freedom.'[39] He goes on to add: 'Both parties spoke as if they had been fed.'[40]

What a body can do is dictated by its *ingenium*. If it is badly folded, it is sometimes capable of so little that its impotence is experienced as the mirror image of a particular power. It is subjugated but content to be so, and thus a happy subject – that epitome of impotence which in Spinoza's words leads men to 'fight for their servitude as if they were fighting for their own deliverance.'[41] La Boétie makes the same point about a subjected people: 'Seeing them serve so earnestly and willingly, one has the impression not that they have lost their freedom but that they have won their servitude.'[42] This is the tautology of power: the (political) body can only do what it is capable of, and no more. But it is in fact a false tautology, or at least, if it is one, it is a tautology in the same profound sense that we encountered in our discussions of immanence: a being knows no reserve, which is to say that every action of every mode expresses at every instant *the full extent* of their power. They always do what they can do to the full, and there is no left-over reserve that regrettably remains unexploited. Sometimes they can do very little, but what they do do (however limited it may be) is the exact and perfect measure of their power at that particular moment.

As with any mode, this applies to the collective individual that a political grouping constitutes. A structural conceptualisation of bodies, insofar as it naturally raises the question of their power, thus allows us to analyse in a more rigorous fashion the conceptually erroneous but heuristically fertile intuition that political bodies 'only ever get what they deserve'. Getting Sarkozy for president in 2007 is exactly what

---

38 Ibid.
39 Ibid., p. 37.
40 Ibid.
41 *Theological-Political Treatise*, Preface, p. 6.
42 La Boétie, *Discours de la servitude volontaire*, p. 35.

France 'deserved' at that particular time. Italy, when it gave itself up to Berlusconi, 'deserved no better'. We should hold on to this intuition but rid ourselves of its inapt formulations. There is no court of just deserts and no fault to be attributed to the people – there is merely the quantitative reckoning of their powers. Sarkozy and Berlusconi (and Hollande and Renzi, for that matter) are not the sanctioning of some fault: they are the exact measure of what those political bodies could do at that moment in time, which as it happens was not a lot. If one wishes, one can, of course, seek get-out clauses or mitigating circumstances: Sarkozy was a foreseeable result within the institutional frameworks of the Fifth Republic, etc. But those are only secondary variations on the general theme of 'power'. Is not living within such an institutional framework already in itself a measure of the power, or rather the impotence, of the political body in question? Only a feeble body can give itself such a form of parliamentary government as a framework for its political life – perhaps not as feeble as a body that has given itself up to a king ruling by divine right, but, nevertheless, a body that is still very wedded to servitude. For, apart from its customs, the laws and institutions that a political body gives itself are indisputably involved in the constitution of its *ingenium* and endow that body with its particular configuration as expressed through its degree of power – a degree of power that is susceptible to variation as the collective *ingenium* is reshaped and new folds are formed, for better or for worse, needless to say.

For example, one tends to attribute to the British people a keen attachment to civil liberties, and yet they have acquiesced to the invasion of their streets by CCTV more readily than any other nation, and are apparently rather relaxed about it. What experiences and self-affections did they have to pass through to lose their power to such a degree? How does one get to a stage where power has been so thoroughly lost that one abandons oneself to the servitude of omnipresent surveillance? Other countries apply the death penalty, allow their citizens to arm themselves and then watch them kill each other, seemingly helpless to do anything about it. Even the high school carnages make no difference – do they not have the morbid impotence of a death cult? In a reflection of just how much power they have lost, the citizens of neoliberal societies accept without flinching the proliferation of advertising lies that would have scandalised them a few decades ago. They have made concessions that would have outraged more powerful political bodies, ending up with a servile media, two-a-penny 'intellectuals', the flagrant corruption of cultural life and the bankrupt discourse of politicians. Neoliberal poisoning has made political bodies capable of less and less, which is no doubt the point of the exercise. More precisely, they are being led to redeploy their powers according to a new 'portfolio', for there are certain things they have nevertheless become more capable of, such as dulling their senses with commodities and devastating the planet. By contrast, they are becoming ever less capable of things like cultivating the 'true virtue and life of the mind'. But being able to do a greater number of aberrant things and fewer things that are 'useful to us'[43] means quite simply being able to do less. Whatever particular individuals may think of this, they nevertheless have to acknowledge that the whole of which they are a part has lost some of its vitality. That is not the *fault* of anyone but rather the *measure* of their power or impotence as a body. Since power must exercise itself in the present moment, if a particular political body could have done more, it would have done more. It would have done something else. The fact that it did not is a reflection of its impotence.

The *Hilaritas* of the Political Body

With important consequences, Laurent Bove has transposed into the order of political bodies Spinozan concepts which had automatically been assumed to be reserved for human bodies, and whose general application had not previously been appreciated.[44] For example, titillation (*titillatio*) and happiness (*hilaritas*) are affects of pleasure that are related to the body, but the former only affects some parts of it whereas the latter affects all parts 'equally'.[45] The drunkard knows only *titillatio*: he is a simple mouth and throat and knows pleasure only through those parts – the rest of his body lies fallow. Spinoza constantly insists on the fact that only the balanced pleasure of the body in all its parts is unequivocally good under the regime of passive affects.[46] Although it is

---

43 *Ethics*, IV, definition 1, p. 154.
44 Laurent Bove, 'De la confiance politique: construire l'*Hilaritas* démocratique', EuroNomade, no. 23 (January 2014).
45 *Ethics*, III, 11, scholium, p. 110.
46 *Ethics*, IV, 42.

a pleasure, *titillatio* only affects certain parts of the body and can lead to imbalance.[47] One can imagine the modern reader's reaction on hearing Spinoza talk about *titillatio* in all seriousness like this, and the idea that this could be applied as a political concept might strike them as more implausible still. And yet the point being made is an entirely serious one. Like any body, the political body can fall prey to unbalanced developments wherein the affects of pleasure only relate to some of its parts – and once expressed in those terms, the concept immediately becomes a fertile (and serious) notion again. The confiscating of authority by the few, who are the only ones to experience the pleasurable prerogative of taking decisions, and the economic inequalities which reserve monetary pleasures for a tiny minority, are entirely serious examples of the political *titillatio*. By deviating from the principle of *hilaritas* in order to deny most of its parts access to sources of pleasure, the political body unbalances itself and harms the development of its collective power. In the final, unfinished chapter of the *Political Treatise*, Spinoza describes democracy as *omnio absolutum imperium*, or the completely absolute state.[48] Had he had time to finish the work, might he have stated explicitly that this is because it is the political realisation of the principle of happiness (*hilaritas*)?

There is surely no more fundamental political question than that of how far the powers of a political body can extend and what it is capable of achieving in terms of freedom. But, first, we need to have recognised that politics is individuated into distinct bodies that are nevertheless transformable and extendable – in short, modifiable in all the senses that this word conveys in Spinoza's conceptual lexicon. To know what a body can do, we need to know what it is in its form and its configuration, which is to say that, at the very least, we need to have recognised that it is a body.

---

47 *Ethics*, IV, 43.
48 *PT*, XI, 1, p. 135.

6

The Affects of Politics

There are two elementary structures of politics: the self-affecting of the multitude (*imperium*) is the mechanism by which political groupings cohere, while the certain relation (*certa ratio*) that structures their form is what differentiates them as distinct bodies. These two structures are in fact two sides of the same coin. What determines the form that the group coheres into? The *certa ratio*. Conversely, what makes the parts maintain that certain relation to each other which constitutes the political body? The affects of the *imperium*. In a sense, one can adopt one of two perspectives on the political body: the perspective of the whole or the perspective of the parts. The point of view of the whole is that it determines how its parts are disposed in relation to each other. The point of view of the parts is that they are affected according to the relation in which they stand to the whole. The relational form which defines the political body concretely derives from the common affect which brings the parts together – in a certain way. Envisaged from the viewpoint of the parts, the political body is thus a question of affects. Human individuals do not form political groupings through some rational, contractualist process of deliberation: it is affects which hold them together, and it is worth repeating that these affects are the vehicle for ideas, values and a common symbolic realm.

And now, we come to a delicate juncture: according to our own rules, we ought not in principle to apply our thought experiment to the contingent realities of our age. But the age is notably obsessed with the question of the national, which is almost instantly reduced to a question of 'national identity' and swamped in normative statements. The only reaction to traditional national celebrations, for example, is to organise alternative events that dispute their legitimacy – there is no common ground between the two. So, talking of affects in relation to the nation doubtless runs the risk of being immediately interpreted as an apology for intrinsic national identities. Discouraging knee-jerk reactions and posturing is an uphill struggle, but the first step is to point out that, if affects are the very stuff of social life,[1] then it would be unwise to treat them with excessive intellectual contempt, not least because empathetic engagement is not what is required. Affects lend themselves to an entirely quantitative treatment. Consistent with his uncompromising naturalism, Spinoza states the case, still pertinent today, for discarding the familiar stance of moral sentimentalism in favour of a physical analysis of the passions: 'So I have regarded human affects such as love, hatred, anger, envy, pride, pity, and other agitations of the mind not as vices of human nature but as properties pertaining to it in the same way as heat, cold, storm, thunder, and such pertain to the nature of the atmosphere. These things, though troublesome, are inevitable, and have definite causes through which we try to understand their nature.'[2] This alone ought to give the pious 'internationalists' pause and start bringing them round to the idea that judging is an activity best preceded by understanding, and that describing the interplay of affects does not amount to an endorsement. Such things should ordinarily go without saying, but intellectuals with a tendency to cultivate an extreme sense of their own singularity are particularly in need of the reminder. They are inevitably offended by the idea of being themselves included in the 'masses', or the mass of common affect – in other words, by the very idea of belonging to a totality. Such a temperament is aptly sublimated in their refusal to conceptualise groupings as anything other than gatherings of singularities (of any kind), or to acknowledge that anything could transcend their desire to associate of their own volition (as this would somehow amount to a surrendering of their identity).

---

1 For further discussion on this point, see Lordon, *La Société des affects*.
2 *PT*, I, 4, p. 35.

Conceptualising the (National) Wellspring of Our Thinking

Repugnance for affiliation does not always entail this level of blindness. Alain Badiou, whose universalist beliefs are hardly in doubt, acknowledges with refreshing candour that he feels 'French to the core'.[3] This statement could be interpreted in several ways, probably not all of them consonant with his intentions, but one interpretation has the virtue of reminding us that, however emancipated we may feel from any national affiliation, we are never emancipated from it entirely. The very simple reason for this is that we are wrapped in the nation from the day we are born and such formative, deep and archaic folds can never be smoothed out entirely, however much we might wish it. There will always remain something of our socialisation from childhood on (whether or not we wish it or acknowledge it), including, of course, our language and the habits of thought that are inevitably attached to it – we can say without fear of contradiction that Alain Badiou is a French mind. But then there are all the other folds we have acquired in this 'seminary of society', which is a national society. The individual *ingenium* is formed in the group and most of the biographical affections that comprise its dynamic constitution derive, to some extent, from within the group. Family and school transmit common behaviours, and this transmission is for the most part unconscious since parents and teachers speak and act spontaneously out of the habits which they have themselves acquired through the exact same mechanisms as those they are now reproducing. Though capturing its youth is the first and surest means for a nation to ensure that people's *ingenia* conform to its type, countless later affections then serve to deepen the folds: administrative procedures, documents attesting to civil status, election campaigns, the nation-centric character of public debate, etc. It is through an affective enterprise that is as intense as it is underestimated that the nation-state body continuously produces 'nationals' – are those who contemptuously dismiss affiliation aware of just how much they too 'belong'?

Bourdieu observes that the state is probably the most difficult object to apprehend because those likely to be conceptualising it are products of that state: they have been educated within it, and, at the

---

3 Alain Badiou and Marcel Gauchet, *What Is to Be Done? A Dialogue on Communism, Capitalism and the Future of Democracy*, trans. Susan Spitzer, Polity, 2016, p. 6.

outset, the intellectual tools at their disposal are the schematic representations and categories that have been forged by the state itself.[4] As a result, our thinking is always to some degree a state-like way of thinking, though for the most part unconsciously and unintentionally so. All else being equal, it is the form of thinking least capable of achieving the kind of critical distance needed to avoid becoming subservient to its subject matter, namely, the state. Socialisation is an education – another name for the 'folding' process – and even our intellectual habits bear traces of the way of living (first and foremost, that of the nation state) that is their wellspring, and whose form they duly express. So how do we conceptualise an object when our concepts derive from that object? The answer is that it is not easy, and there is a persistent risk of inadvertently ratifying those concepts if we do not reflect on our own habits of reflection. Marcel Detienne has been startled to observe how often French historians of the nation have allowed themselves to be enlisted – enthusiastically, and without the slightest critical reserve – into celebrating the nation.[5] They have allowed themselves to be led astray and influenced by the very object from which they should have established a critical distance at the outset – rather like a science of myths that merely inserts itself into those myths and lends credence to them.

However, the obstacle is not insurmountable: Bourdieu does manage to conceptualise the state. But, aware that he, like everyone else, is caught up in the gnoseological net of the state, he starts by unlearning to think within the framework of the implicit assumptions of a national thinking about his nation. The first stage in this methodological exercise is to become conscious of the influence under which we are labouring. Perhaps one needs to be a sociologist – aware of the factors that determine behaviour, including the behaviour of sociologists – to avoid falling into this grandiose philosophical idea that we are free and emancipated from everything. We may then perceive more clearly those commonplace and run-of-the-mill processes at work within all of us and in which we are more 'caught up' than we would willingly admit. To perceive in oneself that national or state fold, having perhaps vehemently

---

4 Pierre Bourdieu, *On the State: Lectures at the Collège de France 1989–1992*, ed. Patrick Champagne et al., trans. David Fernbach, Polity, 2014.

5 Marcel Detienne, *L'Identité nationale, une énigme*, Folio Histoire, 2010.

criticised it in (other) people's thinking, is the first step towards a more rational analysis founded on an awareness of the power of the affective mechanisms underpinning national affiliation. For it is indeed through affects that the nation holds us in its sway: even those who are least sympathetic to the nation are much more 'national' than they would care to admit.

The Affects of Collective Perseverance

Above and beyond salient sporting and military events and suchlike, which on the whole tend to nurture a chauvinistic form of the national common affect, what is the affective basis of national affiliation? On the basis of which regular affects does affiliation sustain itself?

As we have already seen, and contrary to the impression that too cursory a reading of it might create, the *Theological-Political Treatise* does not entirely subscribe to the social contract model to account for the genesis of the City. If, as Pierre-François Moreau argues, Spinoza moves entirely beyond contractualism in the *Political Treatise*, we can already detect this shift in Chapter V of the *Theological-Political Treatise*, which suggests a sort of mechanism by which the endogenous interplay of the passions (rather than the artifices of the contract) give rise to the grouping of people into political communities.[6] These primitive associative passions relate to material survival, which ultimately is only possible in concert with others. It is in order to persevere in their being in the most basic form – that of biological reproduction – that people are prompted to come together and stabilise their groupings. This argument is present in the very earliest attempts at political philosophy: it is impossible for man to satisfy all his needs on his own, and so the division of labour imposes itself as the most practical solution and as a principle of self-interested solidarity. In the first instance, then, it is people's sense of the precariousness of their own situation and their mutual material dependence which holds them together.

One might object that there is no reason why this very general mechanism should only be at work in the national space (the definition of which, moreover, is very recent). Has it not been established that the

---

6 Moreau, 'Les deux genèses de l'État dans le *Traité théologico-politique*'.

division of labour now extends into the international space and that the 'global market' has completely overspilled the borders of the modern nation state, making it a dispensable grouping *in terms of this mechanism*? But the whole point is that this international space is international, meaning that even though the circulation of commodities does extend beyond borders, the conditions under which those commodities circulate remain regulated by nations – witness the political and legal dispositions (accords, treaties) that have to be negotiated in order to extend circulation, dismantle barriers, revise norms and so on. Though their borders may have been overspilled, nation-state groupings nevertheless remain the entities of reference in this more generalised circulation – international trade is only ever an extended version of national trade.

Can one thus argue that subnational and even very local spaces are also amenable to hosting forms of the collective organisation of material reproduction (communes or communities, for example)? Up to a point, yes, but only up to a point. This is because material reproduction at the local or community level can never pretend to complete autonomy and will continue to depend on the larger national state space to which it de facto belongs. This is not merely a question of the extended collective infrastructure (roads, energy, water) whose production is beyond its capacity – the key point is that communes, by definition, are not themselves in a position to create the conditions for their own external security. This remains the prerogative of the entity which encompasses them and stabilises their coexistence – an entity we shall call the state, regardless of its form.

But the gains achieved by the institutionalisation of material reproduction at the national level are so deeply integrated that it would probably require their destruction in a major crisis before we were once more able to experience the affects that gave rise to them. And, in any case, as one would imagine, it is affective mechanisms, which are anything but material, that underpin national affiliation. But what are these mechanisms? Spinoza has a gift for bringing us back to what is most elementary – to stripping things down to the bone. And, in this case, that means the love of ourselves and the hatred of others.

Symptomatic Pride

Although he does not formulate the problem explicitly in the idiom of affects, Vincent Descombes takes us back to the heart of what he appropriately calls 'the moral psychology of the citizen'.[7] This is, naturally, a collective psychology whereby the individuals of the nation find solidarity in their grand sense of collective stature and react fiercely to any attempts to impugn it. He quotes Rousseau on the subject: 'As soon as this multitude is so united in one body, it is impossible to offend against one of the members without attacking the body, and still more to offend against the body without the members resenting it.'[8] That individuals might feel pride in the grandeur of the whole that they jointly form, or take personal offence at the indignities this whole may suffer in the course of its existence, is a point that the logicians of Port-Royal were unable to grasp: 'And it is this that reveals the nature of the vanity that individuals derive from the fine actions of their nation in which they have played no part, which is as silly as that of a deaf ear basking in the reflected glory of the sharpness of the eye or the skill of the hand.'[9] But it is the nominalist, truncated logic of an atomistic social perspective, by definition little inclined to apprehend collective entities in their own right, that leads to this kind of blunder, rejecting an affective reality as having no place in its analysis since it is so obviously a 'rational' aberration.

And yet Rousseau directly experienced this rational 'impossibility'. When he was critical of French music, the whole nation came down on him (despite, one may suppose, it not being composed exclusively of virtuoso musicians): 'The letter on music was taken seriously, and incensed against me the whole nation, which thought itself offended by this attack on its music.'[10] Admittedly, as Descombes points out in citing this passage, Rousseau's 'whole nation' should be understood as a metonymy for the cultivated public. Nevertheless, these 'cultivated

---

7 Vincent Descombes, *Les Embarras de l'identité*, 'Essais', Gallimard, 2013, p. 228. My argument here is based on Chapter IV, 'Les identités collectives'.

8 Jean-Jacques Rousseau, *The Social Contract & Discourses*, trans. George Douglas Howard Cole, J.M. Dent & Sons, 1920, p. 28.

9 Antoine Arnauld and Pierre Nicole, *Logique de Port-Royal*, Librairie de L. Hachette et Cie, 1846, p. 157.

10 Jean-Jacques Rousseau, *Confessions*, Book VIII, Outlook, 2018, p. 32.

minds felt offended as French people, not as musicians or connoisseurs of literature.[11] Just as the Port-Royal ear was indignant that the people had put their finger in 'its' eye.

What the truncated rationality of the atomistic outlook cannot understand is the extended rationality of the *intelligere* of the passions, which can give access to those passions. For affects are properties of human nature which are objective in the same way that heat and storminess are objective properties of the atmosphere. Spinoza makes the following observation: 'If we think that someone loves, desires, or hates something that we love, desire, or hate, that very fact will cause us to love, desire or hate the thing more steadfastly. But if we think he dislikes what we love, or vice versa, then our feelings will fluctuate.'[12] We thus meet again the genetic power of the imitation of the affects[13] that was at the core of our speculative model of the formation of the power of the multitude,[14] but this time in relation to the national common affect: we love and we hate together. 'As lovers, let our hopes and fears be alike. Insensitive is he who loves what another leaves', comments Spinoza by way of Ovid.[15]

The Amalgams of the Affectio Nationalis (the Loves and Hates of Fellow Citizens)

Loving and hating together is part of the national affect – loving each other and hating outsiders: 'If anyone imagines that someone similar to himself is affected with hatred towards a thing similar to himself, which he loves, he will hate him.'[16] Perhaps there is a need here, more than anywhere else, to put Spinoza's lexicon into perspective since, on a prima facie reading, it may leave the reader perplexed or even shocked. 'Love' and 'hate' need to be appreciated in their broad sense and with clinical detachment: they are, respectively, the affects of pleasure and pain

---

11 Descombes, *Embarras de l'identité*, p. 124.
12 *Ethics*, III, 31, p. 122.
13 *Ethics*, III, 27.
14 See Chapter II above.
15 *Ethics*, III, 31, corollary, p. 122.
16 *Ethics*, III, 45, p. 130.

accompanied by the idea of an external cause.[17] One can thus speak of love for one's partner but also for chocolate; hatred for the rival whom one would like to kill, and also for the stone in one's shoe. The difference lies only in the intensity – and, needless to say, the various actions that these varying intensities determine. Somewhere along this spectrum of intensity, at points that can vary depending on place and time, are national affects.

Secondly, when Spinoza speaks of 'someone similar to himself', he does indeed have in mind another human being. On the one hand, the finite human mode is only one thing among all the other things of nature – admittedly it has superior capacities to a pebble, say, but they share the same ontological status: *pars naturae*. On the other, as he shows, the mind-body reacts when it identifies morphological similarities. The imitation of affects is predicated on relations of resemblance: it is thus at its strongest in the case of another human being, quite strong for the great apes (in whom 'we recognise ourselves'), less so for a quadruped (though there remains a similarity in the body plan), and negligible in the case of an earthworm. But 'similarity to oneself' is not merely a question of physical morphology: there are also, of course, imagined 'similarities' which lead us to see a fellow citizen as 'similar' and a foreigner as 'different', despite the fact that they are physically equivalent.

If therefore something like an *affectio nationalis* prevails among citizens (which of course by no means excludes the possibility of hatred and conflict existing between them), another individual who is ostensibly similar to us but hates someone similar to us whom we love (all other things being equal, we love our fellow citizen through *affectio nationalis*) will incur our hatred. Those sceptical of such love between fellow citizens might consider the different reactions in a country when an executed hostage is a fellow national as opposed to a foreigner, and the different levels of hatred that this provokes. We need to appreciate the clinical literalness of the Spinozan lexicon as it applies to the world.

In the following proposition, Spinoza identifies the guiding principle of national, and above all inter-national, passions: 'If anyone is affected with pleasure or pain by someone of a class or nation different from his

---

17 *Ethics*, III, 13, scholium.

own and the pleasure or pain is accompanied by the idea of that person as its cause, under the general category of that class or nation, he will love or hate not only him but all of that same class or nation.'[18] International affects (and affects between nations) thus arise out of this fundamental mechanism of amalgamation whereby the imagination spontaneously links distinct things on the basis of simple resemblances and in the absence of any actual causal connection. And this linking process obtains equally for love and hatred. Indeed, there is no reason in principle why hatred should characterise relations between nations – relations between the nationals of two different countries can in principle be characterised by love instead. As we know from experience, nothing prevents different nations from lovingly cosying up to each other, but this affective love is completely unstable and at the mercy of external events which can rapidly terminate it, or indeed transform it into hatred, since imitations of affects between nations tend to intensify those affects. For a banal illustration of the changing currents of international affects (would that it never got any more serious than this), the Americans started out loving *French fries*, but when they felt themselves betrayed, they renamed them *freedom fries* before eventually reverting to the original name.

Clearly there are ample opportunities for hatred . . . One thinks of Pierre Clastres and his *Archeology of Violence*, whose subtitle 'War in Primitive Societies' is incidentally very poorly chosen, for Clastres does not address war *in* primitive societies but rather *between* them – as with all anarchist anthropology, of which he is a kind of figurehead, the existence of war *within*, of internal war, is consistently denied, all the better to argue that the state is dispensable. Leaving that aside, *between* primitive societies there is indeed war and Clastres aptly correlates this with the very constitution of the groups, which is to say the insertion of people into a collective identity which can only be defined through difference – 'we are *not* those others' – and a relationship of opposition that will inevitably spill over into war.[19] Though he does not attach the same inevitability to it, as indicated by *Ethics*, III, 46, Spinoza is well aware of this affective mechanism. The strongest cement holding

---

18 *Ethics*, III, 46, p. 130.
19 Pierre Clastres, *Archeology of Violence: War in Primitive Societies*, trans. Jeanine Herman, Semiotext(e), 2010.

together the Hebrew state, whose formation he analyses in the *Theological-Political Treatise*, is the religious hatred felt towards non-Jews. And the contemporary world is certainly not short on examples of a state of war being of functional benefit to certain societies, providing a powerful – and affective – boost to their internal cohesion. As with the primitive societies that Clastres describes, nationalist hatred continues to do much for the affective life of nations.

Collective *Acquiescentia* in *Se Ipso* (or the Pooling of Self-Love)

There is, however, a flip side to this hatred, and that is the affect of pleasure through which individuals develop their attachment to the nation and consequently their sense of 'personal' offence when the whole group has been insulted (or so they imagine). This affect originates at the individual level and Spinoza calls it 'self-contentment' (*acquiescentia in se ipso*), which is synonymous with 'self-love'.[20] The mind feels pleasure when it regards its own self and its power of activity.[21] And this pleasure increases through the imitation of affects[22] when the individual 'imagines he is praised by others'.[23] If he is praised, it is because he has been the cause of pleasure in others; this pleasure becomes his own through imitation,[24] and as a consequence of the idea of himself as cause 'he will regard himself with pleasure'.[25]

A national group thus serves to increase *acquiescentia in se ipso* by giving us the opportunity to love ourselves more, collectively as well as individually, through the imaginative participation in the achievements of the group. From this affective perspective, the sense of national attachment derives much of its force from offering, so to speak, a form of pooled *acquiescentia in se ipso*: a process wherein the desire to love oneself becomes a shared experience, offering more opportunities to 'regard [one]self with pleasure' even if only in the imagination. If one is able to suppress for a moment the (very

---

20 *Ethics*, III, 55, scholium, p. 136.
21 *Ethics*, III, 53.
22 *Ethics*, III, 27–30.
23 *Ethics*, III, 53, corollary.
24 *Ethics*, III, 27.
25 *Ethics*, III.

sociocentric) impulse to mock or execrate the national affective complex and to consider it empirically, one will acknowledge that pride is one of its principal elements. Indeed, it is perhaps the national affect par excellence. Loving ourselves collectively and taking pride by association, even if we are perfectly aware that we have played no concrete role in the achievements we are taking pride in, is the affect above all others that binds individuals to the group, as Rousseau discovered to his cost by unwisely casting aspersions on 'French music' – an unforgivable offence that scandalised even French people who did not know the first thing about music. Needless to say, this affect binds individuals to differing degrees, and from the mass of national achievements each individual selects those with which they identify and in which they will take pride, according to the folds of their *ingenium*. Those things can vary greatly from one social group to another, but they are all formally the same: it is as a result of the same affective mechanism that some are proud to be French on account of the Commune and others on account of the 'nation of Clovis'. And, of course, the intensity of the affect of pride in the affective life of each individual is a function of the dearth or abundance of the pleasure of *acquiescentia in se ipso* that they have previously experienced in their lives.

Collectively Dispelling Axiological Anxiety (Reassuring Ourselves about Our Customs)

We do not love ourselves collectively through our nation's achievements alone, but also through our common customs. It as if, through collective self-reassurance, we are trying to dispel a crippling axiological anxiety over the value of our objects of desire and our customs. If, as Spinoza asserts in *Ethics*,[26] we do not desire a thing because we judge it to be good but, rather, we judge a thing to be good because we desire it, then there is no objective, intrinsic property of things that indicates that they are worthy of being desired. It is always from the outside that they are designated as being such, by the judgement of others,[27] and this orientates

---

26 *Ethics*, III, 9, scholium, p. 109.
27 *Ethics*, III, 27, pp. 118–9.

our own judgement and serves to confirm that the thing does indeed have the value that we ascribe to it. 'If we think that someone loves, desires, or hates something that we love, desire, or hate, that very fact will cause us to love, desire or hate the thing more steadfastly', Spinoza observes.[28] This is why people engage in aberrant exercises in proselytism, seeking to incite in others a desire for the things they themselves desire as if to confirm those desires, even if it means unleashing envious rivalries: 'It is in everyone's nature to strive to bring it about that others should adopt his attitude to life; and while all strive equally to this end they equally hinder one another.'[29]

Customs, however, are things of a particular kind which have the property of not being 'rivals', as the economists say: the fact that one individual adopts such and such a custom in no way prevents others from adopting it too. Indeed, the individual will actively work towards this end, since 'it is in everyone's nature to strive to bring it about that others should adopt his attitude to life'. How better to confirm ourselves in our own customs than to eagerly encourage their adoption by those around us? This mechanism may not be unequivocally 'virtuous', since others will make similar but opposing efforts centred on different customs, and Swift's Little-Endians will inevitably enter into conflict with the Big-Endians. The wars of religion are a textbook example of the war of customs (how should we conceive of God, how should we worship Him, etc.), and much international hatred derives from the same source. The European Union, for example, is at loggerheads over monetary customs. One country – Germany – has come out the winner in the struggle to 'bring it about that others should adopt [its] (monetary) attitude to life'. There are other nations, such as Greece, which no longer want to live according to this custom that has been imposed upon them.

However, when it does triumph in its proselytising struggles, the convergence of customs (on account of the mechanism of confirmation by imitation) has an unrivalled power of collective cohesiveness insofar as it is a power that soothes the axiological anxiety through the force of the collective: as a part of the whole community that has adopted them, each individual can judge with certainty that those customs, which are

---

28 *Ethics*, III, 31, p. 122.
29 *Ethics*, III, 31, scholium, p. 122.

also their own customs, are indeed the right ones. Thus, the nation not only offers a medium through which our self-love can be inflated by our imaginary participation in national achievements; it is also a community with axiological confidence in its own customs.

The Way We Live by Our Customs

The fact that they can both weld a community together and trigger fierce proselytising battles reflects the ambivalence of customs when it comes to war or peace. This tension between opposites is a direct consequence of the axiological effort that is necessitated by the fact that objects of desire (broadly understood) lack intrinsic properties of value.[30] This is why the way in which customs actually coexist can assume highly varied forms, in each case determined by particular historical circumstances. In the *Theological-Political Treatise*, Spinoza uses the example of the Hebrew state to illustrate the extremes of the spectrum that these historically determined forms can come to occupy. Leaving aside certain secondary social stratifications, the citizens of that state were united in a community of completely homogeneous customs, whose necessary correlate was the hatred of the outsider. What came next in the history of nations has hardly avoided this 'coherent' configuration of internal homogeneity and outward-directed animosity, but in principle there is no reason why this should be so.

Indeed, it is possible to cite counterexamples. Spinoza's Amsterdam was a city open to outside influences where different types of people coexisted on good terms. Matheron sees it as an environment that was conducive to doing philosophy:[31] seventeenth-century Amsterdam increased the probability of a Spinoza emerging . . . In other words, it is not just a question of customs but of meta-customs: the *way* that one lives by one's customs. Stated in normative terms, this can mean aggressively or amiably, with a closed or an open attitude; stated in more neutral terms (which is doubtless preferable), in a fixed or a fluid way. Fixity when it comes to customs is the correlate of an imagined essentialist identity and an eternal nation. And in many cases even that fixity

---

30 *Ethics*, III, 9, scholium.
31 Alexandre Matheron, *Le Christ et le salut des ignorants*, Aubier, 1971.

is imagined, since social bodies will spontaneously ingest and assimilate external elements, often without realising that they are doing so (one might say that they are heterotrophs). Take the example of Japan, which has cultivated an extreme sense of its own insularity and idiosyncrasy, seemingly oblivious to the many borrowed elements of its culture (its language from Korea, and kanji, Zen and the martial arts from China, all imported before the Meiji era was even reached).

It is trivially true to note that the movement of populations is what gives rise to these borrowings, but perhaps a less obvious point to make is that they reveal a crucial property of bodies: their potential for modification. Like all finite modes, including the finite human mode, the political mode is modifiable. Like all bodies, the political body is a configurable form that is always already configured and always open to reconfiguration, according to its affections and within the limits of its plasticity (the elasticity in the relation of its parts to the whole). This modifiability is the property which adherents to notions of essentialist communities and identities will always systematically ignore.

The Modification of Customs

Prosaic examples can be useful in this context. While culinary customs, for example, may not come with quite the same stakes attached as the customs for worshipping God, they illustrate rather neatly the principle of modifiability. They may even give us grounds for hoping that more modifications are possible further into the future, not least because they are one of the most accessible and ultimately successful examples of 'internationalism'. They are also a good example of the traces that are continuously left on the body by our experiences (and we should not think that culinary experiences are a peculiar case by being so obviously bodily in nature – as we have seen, the principle applies very generally). It is in any case true that, if it is a happy experience, the chance exposure to another cuisine will arouse a joy that sparks a desire to repeat that experience.[32] As foreign restaurants gradually began to spring up, nationals discovered new ways of eating – and they saw that it was good! New experiences, new delights, new folds. New customs

---

32 *Ethics*, III, 37, proof.

are thus integrated into the pre-existing set of old customs and this reworking of the *ingenium* is an extension that opens it up to new affectabilities. This may be a trivial example, but it is nevertheless a clear illustration of the dialectic of form and configuration: it is still the same body and the same relation of the parts to the whole, but the configuration has been modified. There is nothing dramatic or radical about this, since the plasticity of the form can accommodate the reconfiguration in question. By extension, we may also note that the French have not ceased to be French by dint of eating Italian, Chinese, Japanese, Turkish and Algerian food. They have simply broadened their customs. And that is a key property of modifiable modes: their customs are not fixed but extendable.

Admittedly, what individual and collective conditions are required for these extensions to arise remains an open question, and it is these conditions which regulate the direction, speed and limits of possible extensions. Some new customs may well be less accessible than others to the contemporary *ingenium* – it is fairly unlikely at present, for example, that the idea of eating cats and dogs would go down very well with the French, but there is nothing in principle to say that one day they will not change their minds. The possibilities afforded by modifiability are always likely to outstrip our imaginations, though no doubt our affectabilities would have to be considerably extended before we start eating cats and dogs. Adopting the reverse perspective (and even if it may seem unthinkable today), can we exclude the possibility of a reactionary, nationalist rearguard action in the culinary sphere decreeing a return to some eternal French gastronomy (forgetting that the French did not even invent wine) and driving out foreign restaurateurs? Modifiability, particularly at the collective level, can always undo what it has done and can as easily give rise to the worst-case scenarios as to the best.

Customs or Partisan Stances?

The passions, which are the stuff of politics, obviously focus on other matters besides the contents of our plates. But we must always bear in mind that, since things are not intrinsically desirable in themselves, even the most bizarre can be elevated into a collective matter of life and death. Swift's portrayal of the dispute between the Big-Endians and the

Little-Endians over the correct way to crack open an egg is an imaginative literary illustration of the possibilities of modification.[33] And to cite a recent and very real case, were not the stakes in relation to the '*apéros saucisson-pinard*' perfectly obvious to everyone?[34] But, while culinary communities for the most part coexist peacefully (when there are no other issues at stake), the same cannot always be said of all communities united by shared customs. And this is why the internal divisions within national ensembles, and their mutual relations in the international space, constantly raise the question of meta-customs – the way we live by our customs. Forgetting that those customs have always necessarily been nourished by external influences, and denying the fundamentally heterotrophic nature of social bodies, results in the embrace of imaginary notions of the immutable and eternal nation and the conversion of customs into *partisan stances*. It is one thing to have customs but quite another to elevate them to a superior status as the only admissible customs, so that we not only live by them but adopt them as partisan stances in opposition to the customs of the rest of the world. Spinoza makes no secret of the fact that he finds this degeneration of customs into partisan stances to be a probable outcome – 'it is in everyone's nature to strive to bring it about that others should adopt his attitude to life'[35] – and he outlines the consequences: 'He who from emotion alone endeavours that others love what he himself loves and live according to his way of thinking acts only by impulse, and therefore incurs dislike, especially from those who have different preferences and who therefore strive and endeavour by that same impulse that others should live according to their way of thinking.'[36] It is a war of customs that have become partisan stances – customs that have been press-ganged into the service of proselytising meta-customs.

Contrary to what one might think, the idea that *by nature* people wish for others to live according to their own way of thinking does not lead to an inevitable outcome. Spinoza merely says that it is a natural

---

33 *Ethics*, III, 9, scholium.

34 [TN] This is a reference to groups gathering for an apéritif in public (and consuming cured pork sausage and red wine). Some of these gatherings were organised by far-right and Islamophobic groups in predominantly Muslim neighbourhoods in France.

35 *Ethics*, III, 31, scholium, p. 122.

36 *Ethics*, IV, 37, scholium 1, p. 174.

affective inclination. And what one affective mechanism can produce, a contrary affective mechanism can contain or indeed undo. Historically speaking, the hybridisation of customs suggests that efforts to enforce partisan stances do not always win the day. Those efforts may be ongoing, spurred on by the desire to fend off axiological anxiety, but sometimes they will not succeed in preventing customs from coexisting in a different relation to one another. To what extent is this the case? As ever, the answer to such a question depends on extrinsic historical circumstances: the general nature of relations between nations and the collective conditions within nations, whose ability to develop the affective forces of friendly meta-customs and to mitigate partisan stances – that is, to achieve a peaceful coexistence with other customs – varies. These conditions are themselves subject to sociological influences: the diversity of customs is experienced differently by the inhabitant of a large city who is comfortably established in life in the broadest sense of the term (possessing economic, cultural and other sorts of capital) and the person who is relegated to (and cooped up in) the most run-down environments and leading a precarious and highly vulnerable existence. Besides, even the conditions necessary for an acceptance of diversity are always subject to an 'all else being equal' clause; we are all aware of thoroughly bourgeois instances of racism and the counterexamples of different communities coexisting peacefully in disadvantaged neighbourhoods. Though we need to avoid too mechanical and simplistic a sociological perspective, it is nevertheless essential to identify what extrinsic factors socially and affectively determine meta-customs – that is, the way in which we live by our customs. This question lies beyond the reach of moral exhortations based on an abstract universalism; conscious and virtuous transformations in this domain are only achievable by taking into account the social and historical, concrete but contingent, conditions that determine whether the peaceful coexistence of customs, characterised by their distinctness, is possible. And that peaceful coexistence is the precondition for transcending those customs and reaching towards the universal.

The Constant Reworking of Political Bodies

It would, however, be a mistake to imagine that this conflict of customs is limited to relations between groups (nations) – it is present just as much internally. Indeed, this was the original premise of our analysis: that there is affective divergence. A political grouping is never anything other than regulated divergences. A body maintains its parts in a *certa ratio* to the whole only through the workings of a common affect that contains divergence. And this means that its ability to persevere is constantly at risk of being compromised, as experience confirms: bodies can indeed decompose. But, in established groups, decomposition rarely assumes the configuration of violent chaos, of all against all. It is more a case of secession by blocs.

Reminding ourselves that divergence is constantly present, or at least constantly possible, serves also to emphasise once again that political bodies are non-totalitarian totalities. This potential divergence, which the body must contain in order to persevere, and the irreducible self-detachment of its individual parts, who if not in mutual conflict are always ready to rebel against the sovereign, mean that political bodies are totalities that are constantly being *reworked*. The apparent stability of political formations, including of nations, is misleading: their perseverance is hard-won amid the constant struggle between centripetal common affects and local centrifugal affects. Counterintuitively, it is the state of crisis that reveals the truth of the institution: the nature of a body's composition, which is masked when the institution is operating effectively and its existence is taken for granted, is never so clear as when it starts to decompose. The truth of the nation is separatism. It is the truth of a body composed in an unpredictable manner of antagonistic affects whose balance is always vulnerable to being critically disrupted. And observers only become aware of the contingent nature of this affective balance when it falls apart. Europeans looked on with stupefaction as Czechoslovakia was partitioned and now contemplate with dread the secession of Scotland, Catalonia and Flanders.

Splits within the *Potentia Multitudinis*

And yet Spinoza is quite clear as to the contingent nature of the power relation that enables the sovereign to maintain himself in place and ensure the coherence of the whole. He spells out the precondition for this in his letter to Jelles, namely that the sovereign's power must be sufficient to win out over that of his subjects. The *Political Treatise* is more forthcoming on the details: 'The King's will has the force of law just as long as he holds the sword of the commonwealth . . . he cannot hand over his sovereignty to another without the acquiescence of the multitude *or its stronger part*.'[37] We have already seen that the natural right of the sovereign ensues from the successful capture of the power of the multitude. Logically developing his algebra of power, Spinoza specifies here that in fact it suffices to capture the 'stronger part'.[38] This is an important qualification with several consequences. Firstly, this evocation of a 'stronger part' of the *potentia multitudinis* indicates a more general truth about a totality: the common affect that binds it to its sovereign is by no means experienced unanimously. Secondly, what other name could we give to the 'weaker part' – the part that has not been captured – but 'dissidence'? Thirdly, who would be so reckless as to rule out the possibility that the weaker part might one day grow in strength and become the stronger part? This might well happen, according to Spinoza, should the sovereign abuse his power and provoke an affect of 'indignation': 'matters which arouse general indignation are not likely to fall within the right of the commonwealth [which we could alternatively call the 'power of the sovereign']. It is without doubt a natural thing for men to conspire together either by reason of a common fear or through desire to avenge a common injury. And since the right of the commonwealth is defined by the power of the multitude, undoubtedly the power of the commonwealth and its right is to that extent diminished, as it affords reasons for many citizens to join in a conspiracy.'[39] A conspiracy driven by a common affect of indignation at the sovereign is what sedition is. And it will be a case of common

---

37 *PT*, VII, 25, pp. 88–9, my emphasis.

38 It is worth repeating once again that natural right in Spinoza is *not* a legal concept: it is power. *Ethics*, IV, 7.

39 *PT*, III, 9, p. 52.

affect against common affect: the dissident common affect versus the *obsequium* (the common affect of compliance), the rebels versus the adherents, the perpendicular versus the aligned – in short, the affective forces of divergence ranged against those of convergence. If ever the power of the multitude was one, it has ceased to be so and has split into two antagonistic movements. And the outcome, as ever, will be decided by the existing power balance. The sovereign could weather one part of the *potentia multitudinis* not supporting him so long as he continues to have enough power to prevail over the dissident bloc. It is tautologically the case that his capturing capacities are threatened as soon as he finds himself less and less able to capture power and ultimately becomes a minority holder of power. Too large a part of the power of the multitude has been diverted away from him, or indeed has directed itself against him: having lost the affective affiliations that previously shored him up, his downfall is imminent. He has been undone by contrary affiliations. What one common affect has produced (an established political order), another can undo.

In established political ensembles, then, affective divergence does not take the form of a return to the state of nature or of the atomistic chaos of a war of all against all – it plays out as confrontations between blocs. And these are blocs of customs, whether political, religious, cultural, or otherwise. In long-standing, well-established, structured, institutionalised and 'customised' societies, divergence adopts the form of civil war. All revolutions and all the great uprisings begin as a configuration of Spinozan sedition: the coming together of a large number of people in a common affect of indignation. And this is backed up by a 'common hope'. The Communards were indignant at the betrayal of the Republicans on 4 September, and then came the common desire for self-government and a social and universal republic. It is a memorable example of a split in the power of the multitude. The Communards were defeated because they remained the 'weaker part' of the multitude.

Viability as the Ultimate Criterion (or the Tautologies of Existence)

Other convulsions that we are likely to find less admirable proceed from this same splitting of the *potentia multitudinis*: splits along ethnic lines (Rwanda), religious lines (Iraq, and to a lesser extent Yugoslavia) and 'identity' lines (Ukraine, Crimea), though 'identity' is a notoriously catch-all category whose meaning is anything but precise. Indeed, going against the grain of how the word is generally used, we would have to say that secessions which are properly speaking political also fall within that category. This is because secessions are formations based on common affects and *eo ipso* are generators of affiliation, which is to say identity. The Commune was an identity – it may have radically reorientated and complexified the national split, but it was nevertheless a distinct identity, whose distinctiveness was, as so often, defined in opposition to something else: the way of living of the Versaillais. The Commune invited everyone to join it, without distinction of any sort – providing that people sincerely subscribed to its *own* way of living, which is to say its own identity. The invitation was even extended to the Versaillais, again on condition that they became Communards and thus assumed the identity of the Commune. One can, of course, insist on the universality of the Commune's principles and its generic appeal to all humanity, but there were concrete processes at work: the affective affiliations on which it *actually* drew, and the common affects that made it a collectivity based on affiliation. The Commune was an affective community.

'Impure' cases confirm this a fortiori. Scottish separatism, which came close to winning the day in the 2014 referendum, combines affective determinations of many kinds. Naturally, there is everything that is generally bracketed under 'identity' in the cultural and nationalist sense of the term. But in addition to the kilt there is the politics: Scotland consistently votes for left-of-centre representatives and policies (in the traditional sense of left, as in more public services, more generous social security, etc.), whereas this is not the case of the bulk of the United Kingdom as a whole. The fact that it forms a relatively coherent but minority sub-grouping within a vaster ensemble of which it is a part has probably been the major driver in Scottish separatism: if we form a relatively homogeneous collectivity whose scope for political expression is systematically curtailed due to our situation as a minority, then we aspire to living separately, since separation holds out the possibility of finally living in accordance with our principles.

Counterintuitively, once again, it is the threat of separation that reveals the reality of the union, which is to say the frequently overlooked prerequisites for the perseverance of parliamentary 'democracies'. The principle underpinning the existence of these 'democracies' is the law of the majority, that is the presupposition that the minority component will nevertheless continue to adhere to the community. But, for this attachment to hold fast, specific conditions are required which are, in a sense, the affective transcendence of the law of the majority: namely that there exists a sufficiently powerful common affect at the scale of the whole to contain potentially divergent common affects at the scale of a region, and specifically the minority region (from which it is clear that this region is not defined primarily in geographical terms). The coherence of the whole is therefore dependent on containing the potential of the *potentia multitudinis* to split – in the form of secession in the best of scenarios, and of civil war in the worst. This containment operates according to a certain hierarchy of scale in terms of common affects. The whole is perfectly capable of accommodating internal differentiation. The common affect that makes it cohere does not need to operate in a totalitarian and unanimous mode, for it is able to tolerate affective formations at smaller scales – provided those formations do not cross a threshold and upset the balance of power that enables the whole to impose itself on its parts, to maintain them in a *certa ratio*, and thus to preserve itself as a whole.

This situation needs to be viewed, not from the affective viewpoint of the parts which we are (parts of parts, even), but from the more detached perspective of a physical analysis of bodies which focuses on the conditions governing their composition and decomposition: a 'physics' of unions and disunions.[40] And, in so doing, we need always to bear in mind that this physical analysis of politics is dealing with the affective forces which are the very vehicle of ideas and values – it is a perspective that takes ideas and values fully into account. This 'physics' is entirely governed by the tautologies of perseverance: a whole only holds together if it satisfies the affective conditions for its perseverance. It only holds together if the force exerted by the *certa ratio* wins out over the centrifugal tendencies of the parts – in other words, if, and only if, the common affect at the

---

40 Union and disunion form the prism through which Pascal Sévérac reinterprets Spinoza's oeuvre as a whole: *Spinoza. Union et désunion*, 'Bibliothèque des philosophies', Vrin, 2011.

higher level wins out over the common sub-affects at the lower levels. The whole only perseveres if its internal hierarchy of power is preserved: that is the tautology of power. Logically following on from the conatus, the first criterion by which Spinoza judges bodies is their *viability*. Viability is the ultimate criterion of judgement for all things. Do things hold together and last, or do they decompose and fade away? Do they cohere or do they scatter once again? The eternal question is: when they move, do they hold up? Judging them by this constantly reiterated test, we will come to know how well political communities manage to deal with the centrifugal forces of human nature – those forces that can result in people being 'contrary to one another'.

Tracing Boundaries (Religion, Nation, Class . . .)

Fragmentation is a prospect with which every totality has to contend. But where are the fault lines? A priori, they could fall anywhere. A posteriori, it is another matter. A secessionist 'region' is not necessarily geographically defined, as we have seen. It might, for example, be the 'region' of those dominated by capitalism or of adherents to a particular faith, and these 'regions' can be dispersed and non-contiguous. That said, contiguity can be conducive to seditious divergence. In the case of Scotland, the divergent 'region' does correspond to a geographical region. The Commune was Parisian. These are not coincidences but rather a reminder of the force of territorial inscriptions – places of *physical* co-presence. This is one condition for interaction and above all for concerted action: being together, assembling, talking to each other and plotting coups are all characteristic of political sedition whatever concrete form it might take, from a peaceful referendum to civil war. All these things satisfy a topological condition – not a *necessary* condition but a conducive condition. The Commune sought to extend beyond Paris and spark equivalent movements in Lyon, Saint-Étienne, Narbonne and elsewhere. But these equivalents were, in each case, spatially separate: it was a *side-by-side* struggle. Scotland can only envisage itself as a separate political community because it clearly satisfies the condition of contiguity. The completely dispersed political community does not exist. It is a fantasy of social media obsessives who confuse online games with a way of living, for, at a certain point, people have to *come together*, and, if possible, not as an isolate in the middle of a hostile whole.

Are the dominated of capitalism thus doomed on account of dispersal? Not at all, for they occupy territories above and beyond national borders so densely that if the opposing side did not have the full weight of the modern bourgeois state apparatus behind them, they would be the dispersed ones. We can go further still: the dominated of capitalism *do* form a community, but it is prevented from existing as such by the coercive power of the modern nation state (and all the folds of the collective imagination directed towards the reproduction of capital). There are the folds of national affects, too, which are obviously encouraged by the modern state but also operate independently of it.

A priori, there are a thousand ways to divide up the human continuum and history has selected a number of them in turn, bequeathing to the modern era the nation state. But history teaches us that tribal, religious and imperial divisions are possible too. Communism advanced a new way of drawing the boundaries and even what it claimed to be the definitive way, prior to the erasure of all boundaries: the human race would be divided up, not along the lines of existing nations but of antagonistic classes, before giving rise to a classless society with no boundaries.

An initial objection might be to point to the blind spot of economism, which believes that eradicating economic cleavages and violence (we will grant the possibility of this scenario for the purposes of a fortiori argumentation) is synonymous with eradicating all cleavages and violence. As if violence were not deep or inventive enough to redeploy itself in new directions . . . To take just one example, are not struggles for recognition likely to arise around all kinds of interests and to propagate (non-economic) inequalities and their own forms of violence? Might not new fault lines emerge between the new 'elites' and the new 'segregated ones' according to those criteria of recognition? The notion of a unified, (economically) classless human race misunderstands the underlying mechanism that leads to fragmentation into distinct political bodies: the servitude to the passions and the constant potential for divergence. For it is the insidious power of divergence, which can resurface at any time and in relation to the most arbitrary of stakes, that fractures bodies into blocs according to inventive and unpredictable boundaries.

The Unthinkable Boundaries of What Comes Next

That said, the unpredictable often gives way to the simple retracing of the most familiar fault lines: the religious, the ethnic and the national. Their tenacity implicitly reflects the sheer difficulty of politically engineering a redrawing of boundaries – an aspiration that is often little more than wishful thinking. Their tragic failure to appreciate this left early-twentieth-century Marxists stupefied to see the proletarian internationalism of which they had dreamt swept away in an instant by the very real passions of chauvinist nationalism. In their defence, however, like all attempts at drawing boundaries, theirs was a reflection of what was thinkable in that age – a constraint that erects a powerful obstacle to conceiving anything which is heterogeneous to an age. And there is little doubt that, when it comes to political groupings, what is thinkable in our age is the nation state. What is thinkable comes to dominate to such an extent that any attempt to explore the unthinkable is seen as outrageous.

The irony, of course, is that what is thinkable today was unthinkable yesterday. The nascent nation state was initially viewed as an abomination by those who considered the Holy Roman Empire to be the only conceivable political form. The nation state deliberately ignored the primacy of religion and its characteristic boundaries and proposed, then imposed, a very different drawing of the boundaries. The solidarity of Christians against the infidels underpinned the Holy Roman Empire and served to defuse tensions between the kingdoms that formed that totality. The nation state, where religious matters increasingly took a back seat, infuriated the Catholics: the comparative impartiality of the state towards competing religions was seen as a betrayal, as was the fact that inter-state relations governed by the logic of sovereignty gave rise to rivalries where previously there had been Catholic solidarity. One sixteenth-century pamphlet lambasted 'those who endlessly cry "the State, the State" instead of concerning themselves first and foremost with our hallowed religion'.[41] Clearly, every age has its own scandals. Just as in the sixteenth century, when the modern state emerged from the realm of the unthinkable to outrage the upholders of the Christian

---

41 Sixteenth-century political pamphlet cited by Marcel Gauchet, 'L'État au miroir de la raison d'État: la France et la chrétienté', in Charles Zarka (ed.), *Raison et déraison d'État*, PUF, 1994, p. 207.

empire, so a political form other than the nation state cannot be conceived of in the present age. There is currently no equivalent threat, since the exit of the modern state from the stage of history is much less advanced than was its entrance in the sixteenth century.

No alternative tracing of the boundaries has yet acquired real coherence. Admittedly, a notion of it was floated with proletarian internationalism, but without even going into the difficulties of updating the category of 'proletarian', it remains an impotent idea if, at the level of immanence, we judge power by its effects. To retrace boundaries is to reconfigure the regime of common affects. In this case, it would require a new common affect of class to arise that was sufficiently powerful to supersede the national common affect, which is currently dominant and draws the actual boundaries. This would mean altering the hierarchy of common affects such that the common affects of class and nation stand in the same relation to each other as the common affects of nation and religion do in the modern state – possibly coexisting, but with the major subordinating the minor. The proletarian political body would thus integrate the former nations that have been 'won over', coexisting temporarily with nations still resistant to abandoning their own identity but with the expectation of absorbing them in due course. It is worth pointing out that from the point of view of these other nations, the proletarian political body would have all the characteristics of a nation.

There is nothing to rule out such a scenario in principle – as ever, it is a question of the prevalent balance of power. And when that question was first posed in 1914, it was answered in dramatic fashion. But only conservatism, ever eager to declare the end of history and having by its nature a vested interest in not seeing beyond its own age, would take this to be a definitive answer. The question will be asked once again if formations of the power of the multitude organise themselves around a post-national theme and effectively contest national common affects. The form that such a contestation will take remains an open question and it will not necessarily have the good taste to conform to our expectations: the effort to (re)constitute a caliphate beyond the national borders of the Middle East is a case in point. It is an illustration of just how intense the ongoing battle between common affects remains, with each party striving to impose its own boundaries but only succeeding temporarily – the mechanism behind a world fragmenting is clear for all to see. There is the religious affect against the national affect against the class affect, and, alas, we cannot claim that the latter is the strongest competitor in the struggle. And this is without taking into account other kinds of common affect which the inventiveness of the servitude to the passions could at any moment propel onto the stage of history – a stage which divergence ensures is perpetually revolving.

PART III
The Horizon of Horizontality

7

Capture, or, The Phoenix Rising

The elementary structure of politics, namely the *imperium* (the self-affecting of the multitude), leads to the political body experiencing capture – one of its parts internally capturing and subordinating the mass of other parts. Expressed thus, one realises that the idea of capture initially makes sense not in terms of the body itself but only from the perspective of its parts (in fact, the idea *can* be applied to the body itself, in that its power – what the body can do – is indexed on the existence and form of this internal capture, but the idea is more immediately intelligible from the viewpoint of the parts): some of them seize the *potentia multitudinis* and reign at the expense of the power of the other parts. Capture is another word for political dispossession. The question is: to what extent is it possible to resist this scourge?

Our Rulers Tire Us

'We are not tired!' This is the slogan chanted by the governed in defiance of the authorities when they want to throw off the yoke of routine and reject the role of obedient herd – it is a warning that they will have to be reckoned with all over again. Generally chanted by the younger demonstrators (with their greater reserves of energy), it is a way of reminding the powers that be that they exist. The authorities will hope to ride the situation out by ignoring them, a strategy that has its merits.

For the truth is that we *are* tired, at least in this particular configuration. Governments have a talent (or rather the means) for tiring us out and are well aware that this is their principal resource. In the division of political labour that places the rulers above the ruled, the former are paid to dedicate themselves full-time to governing the lives of the latter. They then go home, watch their exploits replayed on TV and retire to sleep the sleep of the righteous. For everybody else, breaking out of their passivity requires an injection of energy. And this reappropriation can only properly begin after eight working hours – this is the prosaic, but concrete and extremely tiring, practical effect of the division of political labour. Campaigners know from first-hand experience the consequences of having a political life at the end of the working day: there's the weariness, yes, but also all the evenings given up, the reduced hours of sleep, the other projects abandoned and the compromised family life. 'We are not tired!' is not just a defiance of one's rulers but also a minor miracle of performative self-denial.

And, unfortunately, more often than not it is a flash in the pan – mass mobilisations that come to grief as (union)[1] mediators are led astray, struggles that fizzle out on account of exhaustion, and the gradual dissipation of the initial outburst of energy as the powers that be play the long game and bank on people's passivity. We have to admit that most of the time, an institution attains its goals simply by doing nothing and waiting for the storm to pass – in other words, by waiting for weariness to kick in. Fortunately, there are some cases where people persist, do not cave in and sometimes even win (in France, examples include the government's withdrawal of new labour laws in 2004 and 2006, the successful campaign against the extension of the Larzac military base in the late 1970s, and perhaps, in future, the successful blocking of development projects through land occupation by environmental activists).

It nevertheless remains the case that a government elevated above the people is wearying, precisely because it is elevated and thus separate. Is it possible to make it less so? For Alexandre Matheron, a peerless reinterpreter of Spinoza, the question does not even make sense or at least admits only of a trivial answer: separation is *part of the concept* of government. It is *potestas* and not *potentia* – the confiscation of the

---

1 I have in mind the leadership of the union confederations.

power of the multitude. And yet Spinoza starts writing a Chapter XI of the *Political Treatise* which begins: 'I pass on at length to the third kind of state, the completely absolute state which we call democracy.'[2] *Omnio absolutum imperium*: the completely absolute state. The formulation is a shocking one to us – such an opening salvo hardly reads like a prelude to a ringing endorsement of parliamentary democracy. But then Spinoza died, virtually in mid-sentence, leaving us in the lurch. We can therefore do no better than follow Matheron's lead and pose the question differently: if non-separate government is an oxymoron, is it possible for the multitude to communicate more directly with its own power?[3] This question continues to haunt the modern political age, and with good reason: ditching the hallucinations of the Pope immediately became synonymous with autonomy and reappropriation, despite the fact that a different form of confiscation merely superseded the previous one, in the belief that it would be more readily acceptable for being secular. Nevertheless, the notion of reappropriation became lodged in people's minds and has stayed there ever since, accompanied now by an anguished impatience as that reappropriation has yet to materialise.

Could it be that this has not happened for a good reason? In other words, even though the obvious obstacles have been removed, is it possible that it *cannot* happen? It is not especially agreeable to run the risk of deflating such a grand idea, but is it really deflating it to identify precisely what the idea is capable of? Perhaps the deflation and disappointment ultimately stem from asking too much of the idea.

A first clue is provided by the fact that the phrase *omnio absolutum imperium* contains the word *imperium*, which is to say the general state. It seems clear that Spinoza is about to talk about something other than the oxymoron to which we have given the name 'parliamentary democracy'. But that something will nevertheless continue to fall under the category of *imperium*, 'this right, which is defined by the power of the multitude', which is to say a politics that is still inscribed within the horizon of verticality and the general state.

What, exactly, does this constant fact of the vertical mean? Some have hastily concluded that it is nothing but the totalitarian shroud of a

2 *PT*, XI, 1, p. 135.

3 This is in itself a problematic formulation to which we will return (see Conclusion below).

Leviathan. It is not that at all, but their minds, shaped by the modern state, can only conceive of the *modern* state when they hear the word 'state'. And their state-influenced thinking has been clouded by the circumstances in which, and above all according to which, they have learned to conceptualise the state. And, as they are also *logical* thinkers, they have deduced that, since they do not care (understandably enough) for the modern state, they ought to prefer its *opposite*, namely the horizontal. So long as this remains a preference, we can grant them that unreservedly. The question is the extent to which its realisation is possible – what actual status should be accorded to the idea?

If we take seriously the exceedance that arises from the law of large numbers of the social, the answer is immediately apparent. People are mistaken if they believe themselves to be united solely by the horizontal bonds of an association freely entered into, for they are underestimating the extent to which they are being influenced from above (even if they have themselves created that 'above' from down below). Their customs, and especially their customs for establishing relations and forming groups, are in part opaque to deliberative reflection and are inescapably shaped by the self-affecting of the multitude, which affects every one of its members. The extreme polarisation of thinking on this question of the horizontal and the vertical is such that we should not be fearful of repeating that the common affect (which is composite) does not encompass the affective lives of individuals in their entirety. In truth, it is the *particular form* that the general state assumes which determines the scope of horizontal productions, and needless to say the spectrum of possibilities is very broad. Indeed, it is impossible to say a priori how broad it is, which is a good reason in itself to strive to make it broader still. It is certainly the case that well-established nation states, which are particular forms of the general state, are not all equally well disposed to the productions of the social body that escape their control. Indeed, if truth be told, most of the time they display antipathy towards them. But this antipathy is not an inevitable state of affairs, or, rather, we should say that the political project to fight against it still makes absolute sense, even if that struggle will always be played out – and this is the point – on the stage of exceedance and in the shadow of verticality.

From Above or Below? Bodin or Althusius?

The polarisation of thinking on this issue could be summarised in two names and a confrontation: Bodin and Althusius.[4] To minds shaped by the modern bourgeois state, particularly if they are French, it is Bodin who sums up how one should look at the state, and not just because they are not familiar with Althusius. It is the reality of the modern state that Bodin captures in his analysis of sovereignty, for his sovereignty is transcendence without immanence: the complete authority of the sovereign as the agent or proxy of the divine, that authority being vertical, descending and exclusive. Hobbes completed the picture by adding the anthropological argument of violence, but the fundamental scheme is already there – a scheme in which there is a disjunction between the ruler (above) and the governed subject (below). And, above all, the diversity below contains too many centrifugal tendencies for unity to be produced except under the iron rule of the sovereign – in other words, from above. Postulating that the parts do not spontaneously cohere, the conclusion reached is that coherence has to be *imposed*. Sovereignty is presented as an indispensable act of imposition by the sovereign at the summit of the whole. There is no need to dwell overmuch on this conception of the sovereign, which is the purest form of the capture of the *imperium*: an all-pervasive authority which captures the mass of the governed and holds it under its heteronomous sway. And Bodin's achievement is to make this picture hold together without any divine intervention or assistance from the heavens. It is an intellectual construct that is as subtle as it is bold, for it retains the *formal* structure of heaven and earth but secularises heaven, chasing God out and installing the sovereign in his place.

Bodin is writing within the context of his age, which is that of an absolutist French state in the process of being formed. He bears witness to the process, giving doctrinal form to a reality that is already coming to pass. His sovereignty is thus both the theory and the reflection of a political form that is coming into being. By contrast, Althusius, who is more or less Bodin's contemporary, approaches the question of sovereignty from an

---

4 What follows owes a debt of gratitude to Gaëlle Demelemestre, thanks to whom the incomprehensibly overlooked work of the sixteenth-century German philosopher Johannes Althusius is now better known in France; see *Les deux souverainetés et leur destin. Le tournant Bodin-Althusius*, Éditions du Cerf, 2011 and *Introduction à la* Politica methodice digesta *de Johannes Althusius*, Éditions du Cerf, 2012.

appreciably different context: that of the Holy Roman Empire. This alternative political form leads him to propose a different image of authority, though in truth their two perspectives differ in every respect, including their point of departure: diversity to be ordered (from above) for Bodin, and the vitality of relations to be nurtured (from below) for Althusius. Though Bodin is seen as a philosopher of the modern political age, the more modern thinker is, in fact, Althusius, since he conceptualises the forms of authority on the basis of an original anthropology of social life. He conceives social life not as necessarily passive and heteronomous – as centrifugal agitation to be reduced or as a teeming mass to be shaped – but as a communicational activity in a very broad sense of *communicatio* and then as a source of production in its own right, which politics should seek not to subjugate but to constantly develop: 'Politics is the art of establishing, cultivating and conserving between men the social life that ought to unite them. We call this symbiosis.'[5] Before they are the subjects of a sovereign, individuals are 'symbionts'. It is the immanence of their communal life which should be the starting point of any political philosophy. People remain united not through the external action of a sovereign but through their own interactions, which continuously weave and reweave the fabric of 'social life'.

We have to step back for a moment and realise that we are by now so used to the term 'social life' that we no longer give any thought to what it means – otherwise, it will be hard to appreciate just what an intellectual rupture the term represents in a text dating from the very start of the seventeenth century. Althusius is two steps ahead, whereas Bodin is only one step ahead: the former not only identifies the secularisation of a supreme authority that acts to shape a shapeless mass but also analyses this secularisation from the perspective of the 'mass' itself. He picks apart the mass and considers it in terms of the productivity of its intrinsic power. This was not the first time that immanence had entered into political philosophy – even French absolutism was unable to curb the dissidence of La Boétie. But it was perhaps one of the first occasions on which a political philosophy was formulated so explicitly in terms of an anthropology of the immanent powers of social and institutional life, and asserted that the role of institutions was to nurture those powers.

---

5 Althusius, *Politica methodice digesta*, I, § 1, quoted by Demelemestre, *Introduction à la* Politica methodice digesta.

Althusius's conception of social life is thoroughly communicational and relational. The isolated individual does not stand a chance – entering into relation with others is both destiny and salvation. It is the sole basis of collective material and moral reproduction. It is not through the power invested in the state but through the immanent exercising of its own powers that the social body succeeds in persevering – and this has to be our starting point if we are to understand anything at all about what is going on. Althusius is consistently two steps ahead: he is already modern in exploring an individualist perspective, but he is doubly so for having recognised the impasses to which monadological individualism leads and for having posited from the outset that, though there are indeed individuals, their existence is necessarily relational. Out of this arises a doctrine of human rights (quite incredibly, considering this is 1614) that is highly original since, while positing the inalienable right of everyone to 'the preservation of their own body and their freedom in the face of fear, murder, harm, injury, compulsion by force, servitude, captivity and coercion', it is not based on the idea of subjective rights. Rather, it is founded on the concrete preconditions of cooperation for the purposes of collective preservation: to be fully symbiotic supposes freedom and integrity of the person and also, as Demelemestre notes, that 'other people are not simply a means for helping the individual to make up for what they lack but a precondition for the emergence of individual capacities and the social space'.[6] From his anthropology of the *consociatio symbiotica universalis*, Althusius concludes that politics, as a symbiosis, is necessarily a politics of free *communicatio*.

Sovereignties

The formation of institutions must therefore be conceived of as an ascending movement from the immanent base of the *consociatio symbiotica*. Materially and morally speaking, associations, or to use the term of the American institutional economist John Commons, 'going concerns',[7] are nothing other than the expression of the self-organising power of social life itself. Like individuals, and in a sort of homothetic

---

6 Althusius, quoted in Demelemestre, *Les deux souverainetés*, pp. 201, 186.

7 John R. Commons, *Institutional Economics*, New Brunswick, 1934; *The Economics of Collective Action*, University of Wisconsin Press, 1950.

replication, each of these local groupings senses its incompleteness, the impossibility of autarky, and the need to enter into relationships with other groupings. In a remarkable anticipation of anarchist thinking some three centuries later (it is surprising that anarchist movements have not recognised him as their great precursor[8]), Althusius saw symbiosis as an associative dynamic deployed on every scale in a proliferation of associations of associations. Local groups, corporations of every kind, towns, provinces and nations form a hierarchy of nested groupings governed by the twin principles of maximum autonomy and affiliation by consent to the grouping on the next rung up the ladder – one would think this was Proudhon or Bakunin speaking.

Encompassing the whole of this institutional and associative architecture is the supreme level of the community, which is merely given the generic name *universitas*. It is clear, however, that Althusius has in mind the Holy Roman Empire, in which 'supremacy' has none of the absolute authority of Bodin's sovereign. Rather, it merely designates the confederation of a political whole governed by a principle of subsidiarity, the sharing of sovereignty, and the strict delegation of powers from the lower to the higher levels. The *jus regni*, that right to govern that is the attribute of the supreme level of the *consociatio universalis*, is precisely the ascending effect of a system of mandates. In other words, coming after La Boétie but before Spinoza, Althusius perceives that authority is immanent in power – that *jus regni* is immanent in the *potentia multitudinis* – even if he does not express it in quite those terms. And, like them, he identifies the correct relationship, the right way up, between the ruler and the governed: not, as Bodin would have it, with the former above the latter, but the reverse. From where does authority emanate? From the people. And it is therefore the people who are pre-eminent. Those in power are proxies and logically inferior to those who invest them with that power: 'Whatever authority may be conceded to someone, it is always less than that of he who concedes it, and it is therefore understood that the pre-eminence and superiority of the conceding

---

8 In *Histoire de l'anarchisme* by Jean Préposiet (Pluriel, 2012), Althusius's name appears just once (p. 25), and then only as a representative of the very generic 'political philosophy of the century of Reformation' along with Machiavelli, Erasmus, Thomas More, Suarez and . . . Jean Bodin. There is no mention of his contribution to what would later become the anarchist movement.

party remains intact.'[9] The multitude is sovereign and the prince is a mere concession holder – their relationship cannot escape the logical hierarchy of instituting and instituted party. 'It cannot be denied that the superior party will be the one which institutes the other and is an immortal subject, and this is self-evidently the people. The second party is inferior as it consists of a person and is therefore mortal.'[10] Althusius then comes up with a formulation that could be straight out of the *Discourse on Voluntary Servitude*: 'To conclude, the authority of a plurality of men is greater than that of a sole man.'[11]

And that authority is not just an abstract word: since it establishes 'between the prince and the people a mutual obligation', one of the people's duties is to rebel if the prince contravenes this law of nature on which the right to self-government of provinces and cities is founded. As Robespierre would later say, 'when the government violates the rights of the people, insurrection is for the people and for each portion of the people the most sacred of rights and the most indispensable of duties.'[12]

From this, it is clear that the word 'sovereignty' on its own does not connote anything specific. Two radically different political worlds emerge from the philosophies of Bodin and Althusius, the (false) secular transcendence of authority being diametrically opposed to the immanence of social vitality from which everything proceeds in the final analysis. At the risk of transplanting the opposition somewhat brutally into our contemporary debate (and bearing in mind that 'sovereignty' on its own means little unless it is duly qualified), this sixteenth-century debate provides us with the two sides to the classic antinomy between 'nation-state' sovereignty and 'popular' sovereignty – or, to be still more direct, between the sovereignty of the right and the sovereignty of the left, for these two conceptions of sovereignty, of which Bodin and Althusius represent the poles, do indeed relate to distinct political worlds and discourses which are forever diverging. In opposition to 'national sovereignty', which should really be understood as *governmental* sovereignty (the latitude of governments to govern in full possession of

---

9 Althusius, *Politica methodice digesta*, IX, § 23–24, quoted in Demelemestre, *Introduction à la* Politica methodice digesta.

10 Ibid.

11 Ibid.

12 Frank Maloy Anderson, *The Constitutions and Other Select Documents Illustrative of the History of France 1789–1901*, H. W. Wilson, 1904.

the levers of state), stands 'popular sovereignty', which should be understood as the capacity of a collectivity to achieve awareness and mastery of its own destiny. The secularisation of sovereignty in the modern revolution merely substitutes one configuration of heteronomy for another if it remains a governmental sovereignty of the right. The modern project is only genuinely accomplished through popular sovereignty, which indicates where the horizon of autonomy lies.

The Undefined Contours of the State

'Indicates' is here the operative word, since that horizon can never quite be reached. Althusius anticipates anarchist thought to such a degree that he even perceives its ultimate shortcomings. To credit him with antici-pating the question of internationalism would perhaps be an anachro-nism too far, but Althusius, in his own way, nevertheless understood the limits on the process he describes. The ascending dynamic of associa-tions of associations does not persist indefinitely. At a certain point it stops, for its scope for extension is finite. There is a level of supreme government which encloses a certain human ensemble that is *distinct from others*. The *universitas* is not, and cannot be, entirely universal, despite what the term might imply. In the case of Althusius it assumed the particular form of the Holy Roman Empire, which propagated itself to a remarkable degree and whose size commands respect. But there existed, nevertheless, something outside it, organised into similar politi-cal ensembles which were also finite.

The distinctness and finitude of political ensembles is what anarchist and internationalist thinkers cannot, or will not, countenance. By making a link that is in fact contingent, they have come to identify Bodin's form of sovereignty with 'national' finitude and the finitude of political groupings, such that they believe that, by getting rid of the former, they will *ipso facto* get rid of the latter: eliminate Bodin's sover-eign state and the unity of the human race will be achieved forthwith. Yet the link between the two is far looser than they imagine, and, even if we explore the most varied forms of sovereignty, we cannot get beyond the necessary finitude of their jurisdiction. Even if it is firmly committed to the principles of autonomy and subsidiarity and determined to prioritise local going concerns, to respect their associative vitality and their self-organising dynamism, and to delegate mandates to a higher level rather than to accept dictates handed down from on high, a political ensemble (even one as remote as can be imagined from a homogenised whole beholden to a sovereign) will reach the limit of its extension. The most freely ascending dynamic of associations grouping together stops *somewhere*.

If the term had not been so abused, it would be preferable to call this stopping point by its proper name (in the sense given to it by Plato and Aristotle at the dawn of political philosophy): the republic. This is really the only way of conveying the specific nature of this supreme level of 'association' – a meta-association that is qualitatively distinct from all the other associations in terms of the scope or rather the *general applicability* of its prerogatives, as befits its status as the all-encompassing whole. One could describe all the going concerns and associations on the lower rungs of the ladder as '*récommunes*' or *res communes* – things that are common to a group of people brought together by a particular shared interest (concern).[13] Associations can be sovereign, though only within the limits of their concern – they are only sovereign in relation to their particular object and cannot pretend to a more general sovereignty. An association which exercises its sovereignty over a shared passion for boules is not a state . . . It is the scope of the concern and its *degree of general applicability* that make the difference – or, put another way, the extent to which it is determined or undetermined.

The *res communes* are characterised by their partial and clearly defined (determined) purposes, whereas the *res publica*, the thing belonging to the whole, is a priori characterised by the *undefined* scope of its applicability. The exclusive prerogative of the *res publica* – the supreme level of sovereignty which Althusius calls the *universitas* – is to be able to bring within its jurisdiction *any object* by *declaring* it to be of public interest, whereas the associations on the lower rungs remain *determined* by their partial purposes. The *res publica* is the undefined contour that befits and is consistent with the *all-encompassing nature* of a way of living whose 'concern' can potentially be extended to all objects within its reach.

---

13 [TN] '*Récommune*' is a neologism coined by the author in his 2009 book *La Crise de trop. Reconstruction d'un monde failli* (Fayard, 2009). Echoing the etymology of 'republic' (*res publica*), it denotes the things which are common to a collective ('*commune*') and in relation to which the collective has the democratic right to make decisions.

The Variable Degrees of Capture

There is really no reason to turn this conceptual characterisation into an intellectual battleground or to interpret the undefined contours of the nation-state 'concern' as a licence for an omnipotent state to do what it likes. The authority that monopolises the *res publica* (and there will necessarily be such an authority) encompasses all the *res communes* and decides what it brings within its jurisdiction but also what it leaves out. That subsequent process of capture is contingent – nothing in the concept *per se* suggests that its contours are predetermined, and therefore differences will arise further down the line. But, before that happens, there is the encompassing of a certain human grouping by a certain authority that is characterised by its general applicability and the fact that its scope is undefined *ex ante*: it is this, and this alone, which the concept of the republic connotes.

However, an *ante* phase necessarily implies a subsequent phase, and it is by that later phase that we are able to judge the nature of the state: in other words, by the way in which it has defined its contours *ex post* through determining what it brings within its jurisdiction and what it leaves to the self-organising activities of the lower rungs. So, what will the state *concern* itself with, given that it can concern itself with everything? What 'quantity of matter' is it going to capture with its prerogatives, and what will be its scope? This is the respect in which the *form* of the totality comes into play, including the possibility of a non-totalitarian totality. The determination of its form is contingent, and if a totalitarian outcome for what we might call a republic is by no means inevitable, it nevertheless remains a permanent threat.

We are already familiar with one extreme of the spectrum available to these forms: the complete absorption of social life by the authority monopolising the *jus regni* – this is Bodin's version of sovereignty. But things at the other end of the spectrum are less clear. Anarchist thinkers believe that they are drawing a logical conclusion from the antinomy when they assert that the opposite of complete absorption is complete emancipation, and the opposite of total subordination to the centre is the elimination of the centre. As we have seen, Althusius is careful not to go that far. Since internationalism was not part of his intellectual environment, there was in his eyes nothing problematic about the idea of an endpoint to the capturing process. This seemed obvious enough to him from within the political ensemble that did constitute his intellectual environment, namely the Holy Roman Empire – and that empire was not the totality of the world. The capturing process necessarily has a centre of gravity, so to speak, and the political ensemble that it forms must necessarily close itself off to some degree under the influence of that centre. And the question of the subsequent determination of the form of political grouping hangs on the degree to which it closes itself off. Althusius knows that this will happen to *some* degree but hopes that it will be to a limited degree, which is no doubt a laudable aim.

Violence Is the Business of the Whole (Not of the Parts)

But why cannot the process be seen through to the end? What is the stumbling block? As ever, it is first and foremost a question of numbers and the effects of exceedance. The horizontal is merely an asymptote under the law of large numbers of the social which endogenously produces verticality. The general structure of the *consociatio universalis* increasingly escapes from the full control of the symbionts as it grows in size and in levels of association and as the chains of delegation stretch out. In reality, this loss of control is down to much more than a simple effect of complexification and stretching of distances. In the non-synoptic condition, numbers produce qualitative differences above and beyond the informational deficits of horizontality, which can in principle be remedied by the vertical and subject-less supplement of self-transcendence.

But it is doubtless in the requirement to regulate violence that the need for a vertical totality manifests itself most clearly, and herein lies the main obstacle to horizontality. The happy dynamic of social life that gives rise to associations and going concerns of the most varied kinds is one thing, but getting them to coexist on good terms is quite another. It is worth repeating once again that, contrary to the anarchist's waking dream, the associative principle has no intrinsic value in itself: people coming together can result in the best but also the worst of outcomes. A group of racists are just as much an association as a book club, a far-right group as much as a communist faction. The homophobic morass that was seen on the streets of France during the '*Manif pour tous*' demonstrations against same-sex marriage in 2014 was a remarkable association of associations: very network-based, as uncentralised as possible and as autonomous as anyone could wish – a small miracle à la Proudhon. Only by falling under the spell of the promise contained in the word 'cooperation' could one see in it a guarantee of the best of human nature. Cooperating means operating in concert – the question is, to what end? If this subsidiary question is forgotten, it is by no means certain that throwing every association into the same melting pot will result in the best of all possible worlds.

The idea of incompatibility and divergence – in other words, the idea that violence might ensue – does not occur easily to the champions of horizontality, if indeed it occurs to them at all. But it ought to, and a simple thought experiment can demonstrate why: imagine a racist association attacking in impeccably associative fashion a cultural association, say a Muslim one. We tend to forget it, but violence need not involve a reciprocal conflict and can consist of entirely unilateral acts of aggression. Who will deal with these aggressions? In our thought experiment, a third-party association is the only available solution – an anti-racist association, but one which will have to use force to achieve its ends and so run the risk of bringing a racist sister association into the picture. Aware of the potential for divergence, there is bound to be someone who declares that it is a matter for the whole community to deal with. And that person will have invented the state, which is to say the general state: a centre that stands above the parties and is endowed with force. And this is none other than the *imperium*, that right which is defined by the power of the multitude – the force of the collective. Calling it a popular militia, a national guard or whatever else will not alter the true nature of the body specifically tasked with containing racist, homophobic or criminal associations: it will be an expression of the common desire of the totality of going concerns to live in peace and thus to mutually guarantee themselves that peace, knowing that discord – divergence on account of affective inconstancy, as Spinoza would put it – can always resurface.

In truth, the 'specialist body' only intervenes on the margins to compensate for failures to regulate violence. Most of the time, violence is regulated in a very different way: through the affective power of the multitude defending its own axiological productions, drawing its own boundaries between good and evil and ensuring that its constituent parts adhere to those boundaries by virtue of the very affects that give rise to those productions. This self-affecting of the multitude, which produces the affect of compliance that Spinoza calls *obsequium*, is not reducible to any contractual rationalism or free expression of associative reason – it is the effect of the power of all, and that is what the general state is. We have no choice but to accommodate this idea too: even in anarchist communities, there will be the *obsequium* or affect of compliance, whose nature we can specify more clearly still: it is a *normalising* affect. This will seem heinous to those who set their entire store by 'escaping from norms' and who fail to realise that every form of collective living, theirs included, *is* a norm. How much intellectual prowess does it require to realise that it is simply a *different* norm to the one from which they wish to escape (often for very sound reasons)? Norms are social productions, and affiliation to them is the consequence of the power of the multitude – the multitude as a totality that encompasses a certain grouping of people.

Coherence and Totality

There comes a point, then, when a totality is reached: all of the constituent associations establish themselves in a *finite* ensemble which expresses their common desire for a certain way of living in peace. This ensemble sets out the conditions for the compossibility of its parts – in other words the conditions for peace that will allow it to persevere in its being as an ensemble. There is nothing spontaneous about this compossibility and it is by no means intrinsic to the simple act of association. Rather, it is something that must be produced – a fact that has given rise to all manner of logical confusion among those who believe that the result will necessarily be Bodin's sovereignty and 'exogenous' capture by an all-encompassing state. They deduce that the way to resist this is through the contractual network of associations, which is (mildly) surprising, in that it echoes that most outlandish of economic theories which conceives of institutional orders as structured exclusively by rational contracts. From this it is clear that the refusal to conceptualise the social as exceedance and verticality extends far and wide and can create some rather unlikely affinities.

It can never be said too often: the production of compossibility can result in a wide variety of forms, but what they all necessarily have in common is a vertical dynamic at work, which is to say the action of common affects. And it is this permanent presence of the vertical, characteristic of all non-synoptic groupings, which poses the thorny problem of capture. For the reasons already outlined, Althusius has no problem with the notion of finite groupings and shows no inclination to speculate on the possibility of the unification of humanity. He seems equally comfortable with the centralising conditions required for the regulation of violence within what, rather than a republic, he calls the public *consociatio* – the *consociatio* of all the *consociationes*. He is, therefore, lucid in recognising that, to a certain degree, groupings necessarily assume a defined form under the influence of a particular centre of gravity: 'In fact, a plurality or a multitude cannot administer and govern properly, appropriately and usefully the wide variety of public affairs and the various bodies of the province without the divisions arising from discord and the dissension of opinions – quite the contrary. This is why it is necessary to invest a director and governor who is able to ensure that those bodies, as well as individuals, observe their duties. There is no people where there is no governor.'[14]

Less blinkered on this subject than anarchist thinkers, of whom he is, in many respects, the distant precursor, Althusius nevertheless already reveals a tendency to trust in the promises of symbiotic good will. Good will may perhaps not resolve every problem, and some discord will still need to be minimised, but very little in his view: the *communicatio* will do most of the necessary work. As Gaëlle Demelemestre notes: 'The unit of the collectivity will come about through the *communicatio*, that is the pooling of functions, goods and rights, and so falls within the realm of politics because this pooling is not a foregone conclusion.'[15] It is indeed true that the unit is 'not a foregone conclusion', but is that any less true of the symbiotic good will of the *communicatio*? After all, what is the *communicatio* (beyond the trivial fact that individuals spontaneously communicate with one another) if not a happy inclination to cooperate by the 'pooling of functions, goods and rights'? The *communicatio* thus invokes a principle that in a sense declares the problem to be resolved in advance.

---

14 Althusius, *Politica methodice digesta*, VIII, § 52, quoted by Demelemestre, *Introduction à la* Politica methodice digesta, p. 74.

15 Demelemestre, *Les deux souverainetés*, p. 184.

The Dilemmas of the Totality (Not Too Much nor Too Little)

Gaëlle Demelemestre nevertheless examines with considerable candour the historical destiny of the political entity that inspired Althusius's thinking, namely the Holy Roman Empire. She is clear on its shortcomings in terms of achieving an overall coherence, highlighting the primary balancing act that any political form must pull off if it is pursuing a project of ascending construction and subsidiarity in the pyramid of mandates: not too much nor too little. In other words, the challenge of endowing the top level with sufficient power to be effective, but not to the point of transforming it into a power that subjugates the lower levels. Bodin's form of sovereignty does not encounter such problems since it merely breaks the butterfly on the wheel. Everything is held wonderfully together and in place, but social life vanishes as a result. And yet, as Demelemestre demonstrates, it is precisely because the imperial centre of gravity (conceived of purely as an arbitration authority lacking its own powers and implicitly reliant on conciliatory good will) is not sufficiently powerful to contain powers at the lower level when they start to acquire the size and coherence of nations that aspirations to autonomy, or more precisely to emancipation, emerge. It was on account of this lack of power that the imperial centre of gravity, no longer able to accommodate its internal divergences, went into terminal decline.

Everything, everywhere, is always a question of power and the balance of power, particularly when it is a case of trying to hold together parts that are inclined to cede to their centrifugal tendencies. The English language has a word, lacking in French, to express that additional element of force without which the law, which is intrinsically weak, is doomed to remain a dead letter. Even to a French ear, its meaning is immediately clear: *enforcement*. It is such an eloquent term that one would like to import it, unchanged, into the French language, as it conveys precisely that 'something extra' which Spinoza tells us has to be invested in a promise or pact for this to have a chance of being honoured, should the contingent convergence that gave birth to it evaporate. Enforcement is a power but of what kind, and where does it come from? The answer is, from the only reservoir of power the multitude possesses, namely the multitude itself. The multitude is the sole source of the mechanisms that hold it to its own norms – that is what integral immanence means.

However, Althusius writes that the *consociatio* is instituted 'through an express or tacit pact through [which] the symbionts oblige each other to communicate mutually the things that are useful and necessary for normal and communal social life'.[16] Is this statement valid, or rather, to what degree is it valid? We can safely grant that it is valid for local *consociationes*, though subject to the caveat formulated by Spinoza: if it is reliant on the contractual good will of the symbionts, which is to say the convergence of their interests (desires), and it lacks that 'something extra invested in the promise', the 'express or tacit' pact will only last for as long as the contingent convergence lasts. Some might be tempted to respond: so what? *Consociationes* form and dissolve as is the way with associative entities, but surely this is the way of things in general? They are born, they live and they die. What is so remarkable about that? This 'philosophy' of impermanence naturally fits very well with the liberal ethos, which hates nothing more than the idea of fixity and is determined to hold on to the notion of reversibility. But macroscopic political formations cannot indulge in this quiescent observing of things forming and unravelling since they contain within themselves a striving for perseverance, which means a need to stabilise affective divergences and to regulate violence. For, while it is entirely possible, and even advantageous, to tolerate a certain degree of divergence, that divergence cannot be allowed to overstep a certain critical threshold that threatens to dismember the community. As with all things in the world, a way of living which has achieved coherence is a finite mode which *strives* to persevere in its being, though it is of course essential to appreciate that this striving for perseverance – the conatus – does not in any way imply that there is a conscious authority 'in charge of perseverance'. In the case of all bodies, human or political, the striving is an affair of the body itself: of the body as a body whose individuality is recognised precisely because its power is directed first and foremost at continuing to exist and resisting anything that could destroy or diminish it. It is a typical error of anthropomorphic thinking to conceive of the striving for perseverance exclusively in terms of the human body, and thus to attribute that striving to a conscious effort. In fact, the error is twofold since even in the case of the human body, the striving is done by the body *itself* and certainly not by its 'consciousness' or 'will'.

---

16 Althusius, *Politica methodice digesta*, I, § 2, quoted by Demelemestre, *Les deux souverainetés*, p. 187.

In any case, perseverance requires that the body – a locus of oppositions,[17] meaning that the body is necessarily *subject to forces* – contains the centrifugal forces and prevents them from crossing the critical threshold that will signal its decomposition. We might ask ourselves, for example: would a communist community look on with equanimity and tolerance as a faction of neo-entrepreneurs formed, acting aggressively to re-establish the ethos of capitalism? If not, which of the specific *consociationes* should take it upon itself to put an end to the venture? Would it not be incumbent on the *consociatio* of *consociationes*, the public *consociatio* which Althusius calls the *universitas*? In other words, the gravitational pole which is in itself the affirmation of the communal way of living? No doubt, this overall way of living first expresses itself at the level of the parts. But, by virtue of its very definition, if it is a communal way of living and not simply a soup of diverse local commons coexisting on the basis of uncertain ties, decomposing and recomposing at random, then it is a commons of the higher level. That is the tautology of a totality. The assertion of the commons by the constituent parts only makes sense because the commons exists and asserts itself as a commons above and beyond its parts.

Though it may be valid (and even that is questionable) for particular *consociationes*, the horizontality of the 'express or tacit pact' cannot underpin the public *consociatio*, or at least not without condemning it to an incoherent and transitory existence doomed to decomposition. The cellular life, so to speak, of *consociationes*, characterised by splitting and absorption, sudden genesis and degeneration (or brutal explosions), cannot sustain its own framework. Or else, we have to imagine that there is no framework at all and that the world is a boundless plane of *consociationes* of every kind, highly fissile and heterogeneous, and often highly divergent and antagonistic. The likely result would be chaos, from which some groupings would doubtless attempt to extricate themselves in the hope of preserving themselves more successfully – in other words, of achieving a certain internal coherence that would enable them to persevere.

---

17 Bove, 'De la prudence des corps. Du physique au politique'.

Capture and Dispossession

It is the *potentia multitudinis*, the verticality of immanent transcendence, which underpins this coherence, and it is *for this very reason* that ensembles which endure are necessarily exposed to the risk of institutional capture. The *potentia multitudinis* is the very stuff of capture, the 'thing' to be captured: that incommensurable collective power which individuals seeking 'authority' attempt to capture in order to supplement their own personal power. There will always be such individuals, and one could characterise the institutionalising process itself as capture. The origin of the authority of institutions – their normative and tangible power to make us behave a certain way and do certain things as dictated by their norms – is none other than the power of the multitude, which they capture by crystallising it, so to speak: institutions are crystallisations of the *potentia multitudinis*. They are also the sign that the multitude has entered the realm of mediated self-affections – one might say that the era of innocent, unmediated self-affections has drawn to a close. Exceedance already leaves the multitude bemused by its own productions, since none of its parts can claim to be directing its collective productivity. Imagine, then, what happens when exceedance becomes intensely mediated by the proliferation of institutions, and the degree to which this increasing mediation renders its own productions unrecognisable to the multitude. In the realm of mediated self-affections, the multitude becomes utterly blind to itself. It recognises itself so little in its productions that it needs truly clear-sighted individuals to help it remove the scales from its eyes. La Boétie was one of the first to write about the primary capturing and mediating entity, namely the state: 'Where would it have got all these eyes to spy on you, if you had not provided them? Where does it get all these hands to strike you, if not from you? How is it that it has no power except through you?'[18] One might generalise the question: how does any institution get you to do what it wants you to do, if not through you?

To draw attention, as La Boétie and Spinoza do, to the immanence of immanent transcendence is to short-circuit the system: their insights rip away the veil of the intermediaries to connect productions directly with those whose actually produce them – a necessary first step in

---

18 La Boétie, *Discours de la servitude volontaire*, p. 30.

getting the multitude to perceive that it is subjugating itself at its own expense. Whether it then emancipates itself after perceiving this is another question entirely – a question that has been explored with admirable tenacity by all the leading philosophers of emancipation.

It was the major focus of Marx from the very outset as he drew on the theories of Feuerbach. Questioning the optimism of the Enlightenment and the notion of having full control over politics courtesy of the transparency of the contract, Marx (who, in this respect, was a precursor of the sociological perspective) not only analysed social relations in their social dimension, as opposed to through the modern atomised and individualistic lens, but also saw them as an endogenous production of an impersonal process that he called history. It is the history that people make without realising that they are doing so, succumbing for example to the lure of market values and becoming trapped in a world where reality is constantly warped and relations between people are misconstrued as a relationship between people and things. But the canonical lure is religion, and it is Marx's analysis of religion that provides the template for his later analysis of capital by analogy. How can people have become so alienated as to enslave themselves to an entity which they have themselves created and projected above themselves? How is such a perfect case of voluntary servitude even possible – moreover, through the sole force of collective imagination? Though he thoroughly reworks the answer, Marx retains Feuerbach's question and generalises it into the political question par excellence, which is that of sovereignty. More specifically, it is the question of how collectivities of people can fully appropriate their own destiny. Sovereignty is not merely about people making history (for they will do that anyway, regardless) – it is about people making history as they had intended and imagined it. Emancipation, as Marx formulates it, is fundamentally an exercise in reappropriation, but of what, exactly? It is less the collective power itself which is immanent to the multitude and will always exercise itself; rather, it is a certain regime within which that collective power can express itself, the reappropriation in question being more akin to a conquest. The maxim of this new regime could be 'prevent power from slipping away' – if it is not possible to reappropriate the power itself,[19] then at least one should strive to make those who exercise it fully

---

19 See Chapter 5 above, and Conclusion below.

conscious of that fact, such that their power is transparent to them once again. Or, perhaps, instead of saying 'once again', we ought to say *finally*. That is what changing the world, as opposed to merely interpreting it, means: stopping our own collective power from slipping away from us, organising our full, conscious and shared reappropriation of it, and making it truly consonant with our desires.

The Unending Process of Reappropriation (Dreams of Transparency)

However, there is a sophism inherent in much of the thinking about emancipation which involves conceptualising the collective as a simple extension of the individual, society being thought of as merely a human being writ large. Needless to say, this results in a failure to see that a large grouping of individuals is more than a magnified individual and that the whole is more than its parts, even if it is 'representative' and scaled up to the dimensions of the whole. We have here the modern, free and autonomous subject projecting an idealised notion of the sovereignty of collectivities, and also the individual aspiration to total self-control, which, it is believed, can be exactly replicated at the level of the collective. For the sake of a fortiori argumentation, let us grant the notion of the free and autonomous individual (though individuals are anything but, in fact). It by no means follows from this premise that a collectivity formed by many such individuals will enjoy the same autonomy, in the sense of having perfect transparency regarding its own deliberations and actions. This sophism arises from a misunderstanding of how composition works, which results in a failure to see that a collectivity is more than just an aggregation and that its formation is more than a simple matter of adding up. Rather, it is a process that gives rise to something additional. Liberal and atomistic thinkers are bound to systematically overlook the qualitative difference produced by the process of composition and to fail to appreciate that properties absent at the microscopic level can emerge at the macroscopic level, and conversely that the sovereign individual who is transparent to themselves (if such an individual exists) can partially be abolished by the exceedance that arises out of the composition process. 'Exceedance' is the name for this qualitative difference which makes it impossible to reduce composition to a simple homothetic extension. So, what emerges in the transition from the individual subject to a body composed of subjects? The exerting of the effects of capture on the multitude itself. And what is lost? The simplicity of transparency and unmediated self-control – in other words, sovereignty in all its plenitude.

Though, as we have seen, sovereignty is itself a slippery category. Even in the analyses of classical political philosophy, it had to be broken down into its various forms. For Bodin, this meant absolutist, centralising and 'national' (more precisely governmental) sovereignty, which we associate with the right. For Althusius, it was something to be evenly distributed, as immanent as possible, ascending and popular, involving the delegation of mandates and subsidiarity – all things we associate with the left. And now it demands to be analysed according to a different conceptual scheme again: either in terms of the transparent control of the collective 'subject' over its own existence, or in terms of its exact opposite, namely as *imperium* and exceedance – the sovereignty of the impersonal multitude over all of its constituent parts. Sovereignty as self-mastery or sovereignty as capture – it is remarkable how the same idea can give rise to such a stark antinomy. The modern multitude lays claim to the first form of sovereignty, which the second form prevents it from ever achieving completely. It postulates the modern ideal of itself as subject and finds itself to be the predicate (of itself, moreover).

However, only faulty logic would lead us to conclude that the opposite of 'the multitude can do everything' is 'the multitude can do nothing', that the opposite of 'the multitude is *fully* a subject' is that 'the multitude is *only* a predicate'. Moving beyond that ultimate state of heteronomy, namely the submission to the theological-political, was no illusion. Liberating ourselves intellectually and politically from all the pontificates, and the servitude organised in the name of connecting with the divine, did indeed, as Kant argued, mark 'man's release from his self-incurred tutelage' and his entry into the condition of political subject.[20] But it is one thing to enter into that condition and another to accomplish the transition *in full*. And it is yet another thing to strive, *despite everything*, to achieve that complete transition.

---

20 Immanuel Kant, *What Is Enlightenment?*, in Lewis White Beck, *Kant: On History*, Bobbs-Merrill, 1963.

But the illusion of transparency is not easily dispelled. It is disconcerting, for example, to see Negri, one of the most accomplished commentators on Spinoza, lose his way and suggest that 'the democracy of the multitude is as an open-source society, that is, a society whose source code is revealed so that we can all work collaboratively to solve its bugs and create new, better social programs.'[21] It is not just the modern tech-speak, the semi-managerial and vaguely Silicon Valley talk of open source, solving bugs and better social programmes, that disconcerts, but the fundamental misunderstanding of the core message of the *Political Treatise*: that the power of the multitude is the driver of immanent transcendence, and that the exceedance of the social produced by all the individual powers renders it immensely difficult (impossible, in fact) for the multitude to become entirely transparent to itself. The open-source society does not exist. But, again, it would be faulty logic to suppose that this means we must abandon ourselves to the 'mainframe' state (if we really must adopt IT metaphors). What it does mean is that we need to be conscious of what our striving to reappropriate our own existences is capable of achieving, and above all what it is not capable of achieving. But the idea that it might have its limits should not discourage us in any way from stubbornly pursuing our goal. The fact that the pursuit may be never-ending is the best reason to persevere with it.

Capture, or, The Phoenix Rising

Interpreted in rather strict terms, complete accession to political subjecthood is thus a never-ending enterprise, which is, however, no argument for renouncing the endeavour. It merely means taking from the Enlightenment that which is positive and being clearer about what we must continuously strive against, and not least capture. For capture prospers naturally in the vertical element – one need only look at the fate of all large associations to be convinced of this. Hierarchisation and institutionalisation are the common destinies of such groupings. And this is something that emerges very quickly, especially if there is a prevailing ethos of the division of labour – this is the most 'spontaneous'

---

21 Michael Hardt and Antonio Negri, *Multitude: War and Democracy in the Age of Empire*, Penguin, 2004, p. 340.

correlate of number in a society which has already been accustomed to dividing labour for centuries. But the division of labour marks the start of capture and of a separate ruling class, as Marx did not fail to notice. First and foremost, it divides by separating the orchestration of labour from its execution and breaks the symmetry by immediately introducing coordination and oversight functions with exclusive access to the totality of information, which others possess only partially. Encouraged by their privileged access to information and ability to adopt an overarching perspective that is superior to localised viewpoints, those who are supposedly tasked with orchestrating end up giving orders.

In this respect, the scepticism of Deleuze regarding the future of minority groups is well known: lines of flight that forever lead back to the point of departure. The problem is that there are ways of 'succeeding' for these lines of flight that represent an irremediable failure. The molecular 're-molarises', the smooth becomes striated once again, and the flight *organises itself*, thereby dealing itself a fatal blow.[22] And everything (always) has to begin all over again. For example, what is a union at the outset? It is ten people sitting around a table one evening deciding to engage in a joint fraternal struggle. What is a union that has 'succeeded'? An organisation with a headquarters on the outskirts of Paris employing hundreds of thousands of people which calls itself a confederation, but a confederation with no apparent link, however distant, to anarcho-syndicalist notions of unionism and whose leaders can become divorced from their own grassroots. What could splitting hope to produce? In the worst-case scenario, entire blocs of ten thousand people who promptly come together in a new 'confederation' somewhere else which is made of the same 'confederal' cloth; in the best-case scenario, ten people sitting around a table again – waiting for another ten to turn up.

We have already discussed the perfect antidote, or at least the necessary precondition, to inhibiting capture: a refusal to grow and a determination to remain limited in number and thereby conserve the synoptic condition. We know that there are desires to master and impulses to capture – gurus and capturers – even in the smallest of groups. But, although they may not be able to resist entirely, small numbers at least have the virtue of

---

22 [TN] The terms used in this sentence are borrowed from Gilles Deleuze and Félix Guattari. See, for example, *Anti-Oedipus* (1972) and *A Thousand Plateaus* (1980).

making it *less certain* that gradients of power and hierarchies will arise from the functional division of labour, and that is already an achievement of sorts.

The Paris Commune – A Case of Too Little Time?

But what are we to say about large groups? The history of struggles involving large numbers affords a generic scheme of capture. The Commune, for example, tragically experienced contradictory internal tensions that were heightened by the fact that it was engaged in a struggle to the death. As if it set out to exemplify the aporia of horizontal perseverance, it attracted criticism from completely opposing camps: for some, it had failed to centralise enough to ensure its own survival, while, for others, it had not kept its promise to establish itself as an accessible authority on the same plane as the people. Lissagaray is highly critical of the lack of proper organisation and the absence of a central command with the authority to effectively coordinate the war effort,[23] seeing its refusal or inability to centralise itself adequately as the cause of its downfall. Bakunin takes the opposite tack: though the Commune did not actively betray its principles, it was nevertheless swept along by events and de facto abandoned the essence of its endeavour: to experiment with non-state forms of politics. 'They [the Communards] had to set up a revolutionary government and army against the government and army of Versailles; in order to fight the monarchist and clerical reaction they were compelled to organize themselves in a Jacobin manner, forgetting or sacrificing the first conditions of revolutionary socialism.'[24] It is worth dwelling on why they were so 'compelled' and what exactly the nature of this compulsion was. Bakunin answers that it was circumstantial: as the Jacobins were the bigger grouping, the Commune had no choice but to adopt a Jacobin character. Under these circumstances, it seems like a miracle that the uprising did not completely succumb to the temptation of centralisation.

---

23 Prosper-Olivier Lissagaray, *The History of the Paris Commune of 1871*, trans. Eleanor Marx, Verso, 2012.

24 Mikhail Bakunin, *The Paris Commune and the Idea of the State*, cited in *Bakunin on Anarchy*, trans. and ed. Sam Dolgoff, Vintage Books, 1971.

But we could turn the question on its head: was it really a miracle, or was there simply not enough time for the inevitable process of centralisation to be played out in full? Marx too was inclined to believe that the Commune had invented a novel form of politics and that the notion of the state withering away was finally being enacted in practice. We are familiar with the divergent interpretations by Communists and anarchists of Marx's *The Civil War in France*, the pamphlet that he published on the Paris Commune in 1871. The text also pointed up the differences between Marx and Bakunin, the latter considering it to be an interesting but incoherent deviation from certain principles, whereas Marx himself regarded it as the ultimate formulation of his political vision of Communism. It was certainly a strange moment when, above and beyond the internal rifts, two key figures in emancipation thought not only shared the same fascination for the event but also reached the same conclusion as to what had been lacking and had thus prevented the Commune from making good on its promise, namely time. Marx regretfully speaks of 'a rough sketch of national organization, which the Commune had no time to develop' and is forced to use the conditional to imagine how the 'Communal Constitution would have restored to the social body all the forces hitherto absorbed by the state parasite feeding upon, and clogging the free movement of, society'.[25] Bakunin, who is in full agreement with Marx here, takes up the same point: 'The Paris Commune lasted too short a time, and its internal development was too hampered by the mortal struggle it had to engage in against the Versailles reaction'.[26] Too much adversity and too little time, otherwise . . .

However, one can argue the exact opposite (though admittedly this remains no more than a plausible conjecture): even if the Commune had 'had the time', it might have been less likely to see through to fruition its programme to emancipate itself from the state, since it would have passed through all the stages of recomposing a state – this would doubtless have assumed new forms, but the overall scheme of the general state would have been the same, involving as it does verticality and *institutions*. Contrary to the hopes of Marx and Bakunin, what the lack of time may have prevented the Commune from exhibiting was the endogenous force of the mechanisms of capture, the power of institutionalising dynamics

25 Karl Marx, *The Civil War in France*, 1871, marxists.org.
26 Bakunin, *The Paris Commune*.

and the division of labour, which constantly establish authorities that are elevated and separate.

The State as Revenant (out by the Front Door, in by the Back)

Once it crosses a certain threshold, the complexity of social life makes it impossible in practice for everybody to take care of everything on an equal footing, and specialisation carries certain consequences, including separation. Distancing is inherent to delegation and is also proportional to the size of a group, which determines both its complexity and the degree to which it falls short of the synoptic condition. Wisdom is always an option for 'small' going concerns, which is to say the wisdom not to grow. But, by definition, this impulse to voluntary self-containment does not obtain in the case of a social totality – the public *consociatio* – which is formed by private *consociationes* coming together to persevere jointly in their being. Subsidiarity is a genuine restraining factor, but its powers are limited. A totality cannot form without a centre of gravity in relation to which the ensemble recognises itself as a totality, and it is this centre which assumes responsibility for the common 'concern' at a higher level – this common concern being the literal meaning of 'republic': all those things that are declared to be in the public interest. The name we have given to the fact that such totalities form, expressed metonymically as the effect of a centre of gravity, is the 'general state'. And, by definition, it is not possible to emancipate oneself from that state.

It is therefore no surprise that it constantly re-emerges, forcing anarchist thinkers to acknowledge its existence, albeit with the greatest reluctance. They have invested so much in the notion of emancipation from the 'state' – which they assimilate to a general category, although what they actually mean is one particular configuration, the modern bourgeois state – that they struggle to accept that, even if the 'state' is ousted, it will come back, and in fact can never go away completely. With scrupulous intellectual honesty, Daniel Guérin does not disguise the inconsistencies, even incoherence, of the conceptualisations of the 'state' that lead Bakunin, for example, to declare, 'I do not hesitate to say that the State is an evil'[27] and

---

27 Bakunin, *The Immorality of the State*, in *The Political Philosophy of Bakunin*, ed. G. P. Maximoff, The Free Press, 1953.

'the State must be entirely demolished', and then to write, just a few lines later: 'Thus, upon overthrowing the established government, the communes must reorganize themselves in a revolutionary manner, electing the administrators and revolutionary tribunals'.[28] He sees the commune as the basic unit of a future federation: 'The commune elects all functionaries, law-makers, and judges. It administers the communal property and finances'.[29] In Bakunin's writings on an international revolutionary brotherhood, one notices the surreptitious reintroduction of all the classic state categories: parliament, taxes, administrations and laws. It is a state in federal form, but a state nonetheless: 'all organizations must proceed by way of federation from the base to the summit, from the commune to the coordinating association of the country or nation'.[30]

However, perhaps what is most revealing is what is only half-said – a hedging that may have seemed appropriate when addressing the most sensitive point of all: the justice system and repression, which is to say the institutionalised violence that regulates spontaneous violence. According to the standard perception, the state is that regulating authority, but anarchist thinkers instinctively resist this idea and are quite incapable of countenancing it after having rejected it so emphatically. And yet they are irresistibly drawn back to the issue in an attempt to vindicate their own political vision, whereupon they fall into self-contradiction. As they refuse to use the word 'state', the only other way of designating, or rather referring to, the authority that regulates violence is 'society'. It is 'society' that is the counterpoint to 'absolute freedom', for of course everything begins with freedom. It must be 'absolute and complete, freedom to come and go, to voice all opinions' (who would not agree with Bakunin here?) and 'to be lazy or active, moral or immoral' (the fun part of anarchism). But this also means the 'absolute freedom to organize associations even for allegedly immoral purposes including even those associations which advocate the undermining (or destruction) of individual and public freedom'.[31] Once one has posited such an intransigent political idea of liberty, no compromise or accommodation can be permitted. And yet the caveat is not long in

---

28 Bakunin, *National Catechism* (1866), in *Bakunin on Anarchy*.
29 Bakunin, *Revolutionary Catechism* (1866), in *Bakunin on Anarchy*.
30 Ibid.
31 Ibid.

coming. 'Society cannot, however, leave itself completely defenceless against vicious and parasitic individuals.'[32] What becomes of the determined embrace of laziness and immorality in the name of liberty once the hunt for 'parasitic individuals' begins? What remains of the freedom that brooks no compromise and is fully granted even to those who advocate the destruction of freedom as a way of life, when it comes to dealing with the 'vicious'? And what do terms like 'parasitic' and 'vicious' even mean under such circumstances? The only thing they can mean is that which the anarchists begin by denying the existence of: affective divergences and the familiar differences of opinion. And, suddenly, what had been chased out of the front door returns through the back, since such forms of violence will be sanctioned by law, which is to say by the state: 'Persons who violate voluntary agreements, steal, inflict bodily harm, or above all, violate the freedom of any individual, native or foreigner, will be penalised according to the laws of society.'[33] Property, law, penalise: this is a terrible resurgence, and the terrible epitome, of all that we had thought banished, namely the state. The state is the ghost that is always returning – the state is the ultimate revenant.

But Bakunin's unease with using the word 'state' (though with all these laws and penalties, how could it be anything else?) is implicitly perhaps the most revealing and uncomfortable admission of all. He chooses instead to use the word 'society': it is society that cannot leave itself defenceless and it is the laws of society that will penalise individuals. And, of course, this is true – *in the final analysis*, society is indeed the agent of enforcement. Who are the 'parasitical' and the 'vicious' who have violated agreements if not the individuals who have failed to respect the pact of symbionts? Who are the individuals who must be forced back into the fold because they seemingly do not want to return of their own accord? But society thus conceived, as a power that holds society's members to their pact when they cannot adhere to it on their own, is the general state. And, for all his refusal to give things their proper names, this is the admission that Bakunin implicitly and thoroughly unwillingly makes: take away the 'state' – the modern bourgeois state – and what you are left with is the general state: the *imperium*, the power of the multitude, and the sovereignty of the multitude over each of its parts.

---

32 Ibid.
33 Ibid.

L'État . . . C'est Nous!

And yet the denial of exceedance continues to nurture the fantasy of transparency, which is a kind of dream of reconciliation or at least a teleological notion of regaining complete self-control: here is the horizon of horizontal thinking. But, of course, by its very nature, the horizon recedes as one walks towards it . . . This fact does not sit well with defenders of horizontality whose project is fundamentally one of *reunion* – the multitude 'reuniting' with its power; awareness and self-control 'reuniting' with action. They do not want to countenance the phenomenon that will constantly hinder their forward march, namely the inevitability of verticality in the non-synoptic condition. It is hardly surprising, then, that horizontalist thinkers should all fall into the same paralogism of the 'exogenous state': that the state is something external, an oppressive Other that subjugates us. 'It' is different to 'us' and 'it' is against 'us'. This is to spectacularly miss the point. There is no doubt that the modern bourgeois state does subjugate and that it does involve capture – we see the overwhelming evidence with our own eyes. But the question we have to ask is: what is being captured, and by whom or what? There can only be capture if there is 'something' to be captured. But the only power that can be captured is that of the multitude, in other words our own. The state is therefore not an 'it', or the 'he' who declares *'l'État, c'est moi'*.[34] On the contrary, *l'État, c'est nous! We* are the state. But 'we' are strangers to ourselves in the opacity of exceedance and so suddenly the equation becomes rather more complicated. We can certainly aspire to rid ourselves of 'it' or of 'him', but getting rid of ourselves is likely to prove trickier . . . This is the sense in which the state – the general state – is a phoenix: it is of *endogenous* extraction. There is nothing mysterious about its rebirth, since the state only exists through us. Althusius only grasped half the picture: yes, the starting point is social life and the plane of immanence. But the image of a linearly ascending structure of associations and delegations is misleading, since it is essentially an unwarranted projection and extrapolation of the synoptic condition, which is to say the transparency that comes with small numbers. The geometry of immanent transcendence is altogether more complex: the plane of

---

34 [TN] A famous declaration allegedly made by Louis XIV.

immanence is in fact a sheet that can be folded and scrunched such that it is elevated above its initial plane and thus rises over itself – like the Hokusai wave that we have already mentioned. For a *comprehensive* description of the state, we need to look to La Boétie and Spinoza. They show us not only the transcendent fold engendered by immanence but also the immanent origins, in the final analysis, of everything that presents itself to our eyes as transcendence.

In a convergence that is no accident, both anarchist and libertarian thinkers fall into the paralogism of the 'exogenous state'. As with Bakunin and Proudhon, the failure to correctly distinguish the endogenous and the exogenous is the blind spot in Hayek's thinking as he sets out to establish that constructivist attempts to invent the social order are doomed to failure, championing instead the notion of 'spontaneous order'. But his whole edifice is undermined once we realise that the state institution falls squarely into the category of a spontaneous order. For if the state is exogenous (and in Hayek, it is the epitome of the exogenous), where does it come from? Has it fallen from the sky? And if not, how do we account for the fact that it exists? Might it be the product of a constructivist endeavour that preceded it – a sort of meta-state which would itself have had to be engendered by something prior to it, and so on ad infinitum? The only way out of this web of absurdities is to recon-cile oneself to the idea that the state is a 'spontaneous' endogenous prod-uct of history, that temporal unfolding of the power of the multitude exercising itself. We know that the state has a history, and like all insti-tutional histories, that history is the product of the endogenous playing itself out. Unfortunately for him, Hayek's cherished 'spontaneous order' is a social order that spontaneously engenders the state. The state is a product of the multitude, and the multitude cedes its own power to a state that deceptively appears to be separate from it – a state that is falsely perceived as exogenous.

However, as Spinoza notes, 'falsity cannot consist in absolute privation . . . nor again in absolute ignorance, for to be ignorant and to err are different. Therefore it consists in that privation of knowledge which inadequate knowledge, that is, inadequate and confused ideas, involves.'[35] He goes on to give an example: 'When we gaze at the sun, we see it as some two hundred feet distant from us', whereas 'the sun is more

---

35 *Ethics*, II, 35, proof, p. 86.

than six hundred times the diameter of the earth distant from us.'[36] Spinoza stresses that 'the error does not consist in simply seeing the sun in this way', since it is a function of our bodily structure that we see the sun thus and our perception, though false, is determined. The error arises from our ignorance both of the true distance and of the cause of our seeing it as we do. What applies to the distance of the sun applies equally to the state and its apparent separation. It is a privation of knowledge that prevents us from recognising the state as our own oeuvre – and this is precisely the deficit that La Boétie urges us to compensate for by finally recognising that 'its' eyes are our eyes and that 'its' arms are our arms. Although they are in error, we might assert (at the price of a slight abuse of language) that our imaginations do not lie to us: we objectively experience the state as separate and oppressive since, *to a certain degree or from a certain point of view*, it is. That is the point of view of the parts that we are – a point of view that cannot be that of the whole. Among state subjects, the 'local' affects of fear or hatred (or joy, for some) that arise from life under the state norm preclude us from seeing the bigger picture, namely that the source of all these productions is the power of the multitude which we form. *We* are the state, and yet we do not recognise it as being ours. And we will be unable to conceptualise what it is possible to do with the state unless we accommodate this internal tension within our thinking.

---

36 *Ethics*, II, 35, scholium, pp. 86–7.

8

An Anthropology of Horizontality

The state is our oeuvre, and our oeuvre is escaping from us – at least partially. The fact that the vertical can never be eradicated, since the multitude necessarily exercises its powers and engenders the *imperium*, does not rule out the possibility of resisting capture, and still less does it mean that there is no scope for extricating the multitude from its current state. There is clearly ample scope for doing so. However, anarchist thinkers are mistaken if they suppose that they can pull off a radical leap that takes them beyond the state (as we have seen, even they are reluctantly obliged to acknowledge that the state will always come back). But they are not mistaken when they say, for example, that the central state and the federal state are not the same thing. And they are not mistaken either if, after perceiving the effects of institutionalisation, specialisation and division of labour that arise from the non-synoptic condition of large numbers, they are on their guard against the mechanisms of capture and resolve from the outset to resist them (even if they cannot hope to neutralise them entirely). In this respect, they are better armed than anyone else thanks to their anti-authoritarian mind-set and the matchless political and intellectual prescience of forebears such as Proudhon and Bakunin, who anticipated the fate of 'communist' (socialist) states almost half a century in advance: 'We are the natural enemies of such revolutionaries, the would-be dictators, regulators, and trustees of the revolution, who . . . already dream of creating new revolutionary states, as fully centralized and even more despotic than the states we now have. These men are so accustomed to the order created by an authority, and feel so great a horror of what seems to them to be disorder but is simply the frank and natural expression of the life of the people, that even before a good, salutary disorder has been produced by the revolution they dream of muzzling it by the act of some authority that will be revolutionary in name only, and will only be a new reaction in that it will again condemn the masses to being governed by decrees, to obedience, to immobility, to death; in other words, to slavery and exploitation by a new pseudo-revolutionary aristocracy.[1] Need anything more be said?

Is Man Good or Evil? The Futile Anthropological Antinomy

However, prescience is often selective and the same mind-set that sees certain things extremely lucidly can be blind to others. Anarchist thinkers are wilfully blind to verticality and to violence – or if they do deign to address violence, it is to deny it. These two blind spots are in fact two sides of the same coin, since the solution to violence, or rather the only way to regulate it, is through the vertical. Indeed, sensing that the two are linked, anarchist thinkers have always gone out of their way to deny violence, in the belief that this is also a means of emancipating themselves from verticality. This is why the anthropological path is so well trodden in contemporary anarchist thinking; it is no coincidence that the leading anarchist intellectuals of today are anthropologists, such as David Graeber, James C. Scott, Marshall Sahlins and Pierre Clastres. It is as though we had to wait for the division of labour to work its effects in the scientific world and establish anthropology as a separate discipline before a very characteristic theoretical strategy could be developed. This consists of reducing the political problem of verticality to the anthropological question of violence, dealing with the latter, and concluding that one has also dealt with the former. This was not a strategy that spontaneously occurred to anarchist thinkers of the nineteenth century. Their contemporary heirs will quite legitimately retort that they are merely

---

1 Bakunin, 'The Program of the International Brotherhood', cited in *Bakunin on Anarchy*.

tackling the state on its own ground and turning its own central argument against it, and it is certainly true that the intellectual champions of the state have long since staked out that ground. It was Hobbes, in the seventeenth century, who planted the major argument: man is a wolf to his fellow man, violence is an ever-present threat, and only the superior power of the Leviathan can put an end to the war of all against all. In a move that seems perfectly logical, anarchist thinkers have sought to reclaim that ground by proposing an alternative anthropology.

But the problem with overly radical polarisations and antinomies is that they are logical in appearance only and are, in reality, rather deficient in logic. For example, the opposite of 'everything is A' is not 'nothing is A', but 'not everything is A'. And the opposite of 'man is a wolf to his fellow man' is not 'man is a god to his fellow man', but rather 'man is not exclusively a wolf (and not exclusively a god)'. *Homo homini lupus* et *deu*[2] – this is Spinoza's logic and it is the correct logic. It seems like such a minor point, and yet the ramifications are enormous: a simple coordinating conjunction signals a completely different anthropological and political outlook. Spinoza can thus say that men do not agree in nature and 'they can be contrary to one another' when they are assailed by the passions, *and* he can say that daily experience affords 'so many convincing examples as to give rise to the common saying: "Man is a God to man"'.[3] Wondering why certain thinkers find it so difficult to adopt Spinoza's elementary conjunction and seem determined to wander astray in the false logic of all or nothing, one might hazard the conjecture that the debate is distorted by the terms in which it is couched. For, ultimately, the controversy centres on human nature, and the tendency has always been to interpret human nature univocally and monolithically: man is good or man is bad. It must be one or the other, exclusively and universally.

The social sciences for a long time (and for good reason) avoided returning to the question of 'human nature', for its seemingly monolithic character appeared to preclude the possibility of accounting for the sheer historical and geographical variety of the human customs and social arrangements they sought to elucidate; there was a fear that all

---

2 My emphasis.

3 *Ethics*, VI, 34, p. 170; *Ethics*, VI, 35, scholium, p. 172

this variety would be brutally reduced to an essentialist, one-size-fits-all category. But again, what is chased out of the front door has a habit of reappearing via the back, and in fact it is rare in the social sciences to come across theories that do not implicitly (and whether consciously or not) contain a certain notion of what human nature is. For example, is the claim of neoclassical economic theory – that man is in all things a rational and calculating being – not at the same time a theory of human nature? And cannot the same be said of the opposing theory of Mauss, that man is essentially a gift-giver? And the list goes on. We can say that the impulse to 'leave well alone' is fairly rapidly overcome and so, as often, the best option is surely to abandon denial and look the problem squarely in the face. Otherwise, it is likely to proliferate beyond all intellectual control. And sidestepping it is still less of an option when one is attempting to conceptualise the state. Indeed, it is no coincidence that political philosophies that address this subject are built according to an implicit anthropological blueprint which is also what sets them apart. For example, it is because the being that inhabits the *communicatio* of Althusius is different in every respect from the wolf that stalks the Hobbesian universe that the two philosophies envision two such radically different political landscapes.

One Human Nature and One Thousand Ways of Being Human

But how do we address the question of human nature without adopting a univocal stance that slides into essentialism? Spinoza's answer to this is straightforward: through the multiplicity of elements involved and their combinatorial possibilities, and the indeterminacy that results a priori from the countless composite bodies which this can engender. He develops a monist conception of the divine substance, but stresses that its modal expressions are infinite. And this acknowledgement of multiplicity means that he does not fall into the error of claiming that the human mode is a univocal substance. But, if 'all men share in one and the same nature', what is its content?[4] Broadly speaking, Parts III

---

4 *PT*, VII, 27, p. 90. It is fair to point out that the word 'content' is being made to do a lot of work here. 'Human nature' and the 'essence of man' are highly problematic notions in Spinoza, at least when one considers not the (singular) essence of a particular individual but the (specific) essence of humans in general. Julien Busse (*Le problème de*

and IV of the *Ethics* supply the answer in the course of the exposition of the elementary mechanisms of affective life. What Spinoza makes clear is that man is a being of desire: 'Now desire is the very essence, or nature, of each individual in so far as that is conceived as determined by some given state of its constitution to do something.'[5] As soon as an individual acts, having been affected by an affection of some kind, they manifest their desiring nature. How, *in very general terms*, the causal chain of affections, affects, desires and bodily movements operates is set out methodically (geometrically) in Part III and the first half of Part IV. In other words, Spinoza deduces the elementary character of affective mechanisms; but what do we mean by 'elementary' in this context? The fact is that an elementary affective mechanism is most of the time too raw and too divorced from the complexity of real life, hence too 'abstract', 'pure' or 'purified', to be concretely observed as such. Its primary status is to be one of the basic building blocks which in combination are

---

l'essence de l'homme chez Spinoza, Publications de la Sorbonne, 2009) offers a highly original perspective on this issue: noting like many commentators the remarkable absence of a formal definition of the 'essence of man', he attempts to explain this absence rather than trying to piece together Spinoza's view from various textual sources, as if the lack of a definition were an oversight. Busse instead points to Spinoza's consistent and unwavering nominalism and rejection of universals. There is not room here to go into the details of his persuasive argument, except to say that strictly speaking it is wrong, or at least problematic, to talk about the 'essence of man' without further qualification in Spinoza. Does the same apply to 'human nature', which we tend to assimilate to the 'essence of man'? Busse demonstrates that, contrary to what a cursory reading might suggest, these two notions are distinct. Moreover, although 'human nature' is mentioned some fifty times in the *Ethics*, it is not defined either. Does the absence of a definition preclude us from using the notion? No; firstly because it can be legitimate to use it in certain contexts or certain senses, such as when we are analysing relations within communities and customs. And secondly, because even without a formal definition we can make use of the notion through its *content*: 'What endows the concept of "human nature" with empirical content is not a series of properties or natural faculties that are present in each individual, but the existence of a series of common activities governed by common laws', writes Busse (p. 36). In short, the most appropriate way to make sense of the idea of human nature is to conceptualise it as a 'structure of activity' (p. 93 *sq.*). Other commentators who have afforded important insights into this question of the essence of man include Alexandre Matheron ('L'anthropologie spinoziste?' in *Études sur Spinoza et les philosophies de l'âge classique,*) and Ariel Suhamy, 'Comment définir l'homme? La communauté du souverain bien dans Éthique, IV, 36 et scolie', in Chantal Jaquet, Pascal Sévérac and Ariel Suhamy (eds), *Fortitude et servitude. Lectures de l'Éthique IV de Spinoza,* Éditions Kimé, 2003.

    5 *Ethics*, III, 56, proof, p. 137.

capable of engendering concrete affects. An example of this is afforded by *Ethics*, III, 27, which is a proposition of great importance in that it sets out one of the (elementary) mechanisms of how we are affected by things, namely imitation. 'From the fact that we imagine a thing like ourselves, towards which we have felt no affect, to be affected by an affect, we are thereby affected by a similar affect.'[6] And it is the phrase 'towards which we have felt no affect' that signals the pure, abstract and elementary character of the mechanism, for in actual daily life it is impossible to come across another human being ('a thing like ourselves') towards whom we would feel no affect. Even if that person is a stranger, we would nevertheless spontaneously form images of them on the basis of familiar social qualities such as gender, ethnicity, class, etc. And these are themselves a driver of affects and variations in our spontaneous reactions: depending on whether (as a white man myself) I meet a man or a woman or a white person or a black person, I will immediately be affected in a certain way under the effect of all the social preconceptions of gender and ethnicity that have been folded into me, and of course under the effect of my idiosyncratic modulation of those folds – am I (have I been shaped into) a sexist or racist person, for example? So, even if I have never met somebody before, and prior to any kind of interaction with them, my encounter with them will immediately affect me, attesting to the fact that there is no such thing as a *pure* bilateral or interpersonal interaction. Our encounters are always social encounters. Because it is impossible for us to encounter 'a thing like ourselves, towards which we have felt no affect', the elementary mechanism of imitation set out in Proposition 27 is, in its purity and abstraction, unobservable as such in actual daily life. What can be observed, however, are the multiple modulations *in social situations* of this elementary mechanism of imitation through all the supplementary determinations generated by the familiar social qualities inevitably attached to any 'thing like ourselves'. In other words, actual emulation is always complex emulation: the product of combinations of the elementary mechanism of imitation set out in *Ethics*, III, 27 and the many other affective, interpersonal and social determinations that arise in actual situations.

It is the elementary character of the 'laws of affective life' deduced in the *Ethics*, Parts III and IV, that qualifies them as constituting human

6 *Ethics*, pp. 118–19.

nature ('all men share in one and the same nature') and confers on that nature an appropriate level both of specificity and generality: not too general (otherwise the term would cease to have any meaning) but general enough not to confine human nature in a straitjacket of overly specific contents. The elementary, multiplicity and combination: these are the traits of this appropriate level of generality within which infinite variations are possible. One might describe it as a generative generality. And the defining characteristic of human nature which thereby emerges is that it is fundamentally *under-determined*. In other words, if there is something that can legitimately be called human nature in Spinoza, there is nothing concrete or specific that we can say about it. It is formulated at a level of generality that precludes it from being *directly* applied to actual human behaviour, meaning that it has no empirical referent. Put another way, even if there is such a thing as human nature in Spinoza, to apply it directly, *without intermediate steps*, to concrete situations would be an obvious error.

We can only move from an under-determined human nature to fully determined actual behaviours by adding into the mix a whole series of additional but contingent determinations – and this is a decisive addition that can only come from social formations where individual behaviours are engendered in concrete situations. What we call history is the temporal (and spatial) playing out of the combinatorial possibilities of this human nature. It is in the course of history that the concrete combinations occur and the affective lives of people assume a distinct form. The under-determined generality of human nature expresses itself historically in customs and institutions – contingent historical productions whose extraordinary variety makes it quite impossible to imprison human nature in a fixed category. On the contrary, there is enormous scope for creativity in the virtually infinite combinatorial possibilities. It is therefore indeed *the same* human nature that engenders societies where the sacrificial murder of children is an entirely legitimate ritual practice, and societies where the physical integrity of individuals, especially children, is sacrosanct. That nature emerges from its under-determined state through the self-affecting of the multitude (of multitudes). Human groups, recombining in original forms the elementary mechanisms of affective life, fashion themselves. This is what the 'self-affecting of the multitude' means: it is their common *customs*, their codes of behaviour, their values and their systems of meaning which give full and specific expressions to human nature, which can thus differ radically from one time and place to another.

Variations on the Theme of Solidarity

In the light of this combinatorial variety, it is clear that notions of a 'good' versus 'evil' human nature are a poor tool indeed for analysing concrete affective formations, and will preclude any proper understanding of the problem of violence. With all the detachment that his geometrical analysis permits, Spinoza says virtually all there is to be said on the subject in two lines: 'In so far as men are assailed by affects that are passive, they can be contrary to one another.'[7] They *can* be contrary to one another, meaning that they are not necessarily so but that it can happen ... It is difficult to understand why defenders of a univocal human nature should struggle to accommodate these two simple ideas: sometimes they are contrary to one another, and sometimes they are not. And it is a shame that they struggle with this, because they then inevitably overlook the only question of interest: *under what conditions do people converge more than they diverge?*

This is a question that ethnologists are well placed to throw light on since, in their research, they systematically take account of how external conditions, resource constraints in particular, determine the form of, and modifications to, interactions within tribal communities. In a somewhat paradoxical turn of events, it is Marshall Sahlins, a central figure in anarchist anthropology for having contested the Hobbesian view of human nature (considered to justify state authority),[8] who in his major work *Stone Age Economics* reveals the extent to which the emergence of cooperative and mutually supporting (or individualistic and selfish) behaviours is regulated by the abundance or scarcity of resources, thus demonstrating that both these opposing modalities of behaviour are possible and that both are contingent.[9] Moreover, neither is a definitive expression of human nature. The activation pattern of these opposing

---

7 *Ethics*, IV, 34, p. 170.

8 Marshall Sahlins, *The Western Illusion of Human Nature*, Prickly Paradigm Press, 2008.

9 Marshall Sahlins, *Stone Age Economics*, Routledge Press Classics, 2017.

modalities is far from simple and indeed is non-linear. Individualistic and selfish behaviours are liberated at the two extremes of the spectrum of scarcity: when there is relative abundance, individuals believe that they can get by on their own and feel less beholden to the demands of cooperative solidarity; when there is great scarcity, the extreme challenges of survival reactivate a selfish, self-preserving impulse that can bring the group to the very threshold of disintegration. Ultimately, it is intermediate situations, where a certain pressure on resources makes it difficult for individuals to get by in isolation and yet they are well within the survival threshold, that are most conducive to the emergence of cooperative behaviours and to a collective reproduction organised along social and mutually supportive lines. Bernard Formoso, discussing *The Art of Not Being Governed* by James C. Scott, also raises questions about the author's anarchist views by highlighting formally similar mechanisms.[10] The egalitarian, cooperative and anti-hierarchy norms are undermined when individuals from the mountain forests of Southeast Asia (Zomia) have differing degrees of access to the lowland market, prompting acts of individualistic opportunism. Cooperation or non-cooperation is not therefore a question of 'human nature' but of external conditions and how they favour one suite of behaviours over another.

Experiences of Convergence and Divergence

All of that said, we do not really need anthropology to convince ourselves of the fact of affective duality, the equal chances of convergence and divergence, or the impossibility of precluding divergence altogether, divergence being so frequently observed in everyday life (and yet still obstinately denied by horizontalist thinkers). No one, surely, who has ever been involved in an experiment in communal living has not experienced first-hand the precariousness of these collective groupings, even when set up with the best will in the world. The reason is that good will alone is not enough, and indeed this is the nature of human condition as

---

10 James C. Scott, *The Art of Not Being Governed: An Anarchist History of Upland Southeast Asia*, Yale University Press, 2009; Bernard Formoso, 'Les sociétés libertaires existent-elles?' *L'Homme*, no. 209 (January–March 2014).

Spinoza conceives it: our servitude to the passions means that affects dominate the (illusory) decrees of the mind.[11] Whether the assemblage holds together or falls apart will, in the final analysis, depend on the interplay of its constituent individual affects.

And there is, of course, a genuine possibility of it holding together: 'man' is not merely a *lupus* and is just as capable of centripetal as centrifugal affects. As we have seen, the affects produced by material need are likely to be collective and cooperative in character. If man is as much *deus* as *lupus*, it is primarily out of self-interest and the need to procure the resources for his own self-preservation. But this is not the only driver, since assemblages of different powers can underpin intensely joyful affects. To paraphrase Marx, when an individual is well fed and possesses clothes, a roof over their head and a few other essentials, there is scope for engaging in activities that have less to do with material needs. And there is pleasure to be had from engaging in those activities jointly and experiencing the heightened power that results from group formation, as anyone who has been involved in a choir, a team sport, a stage production or more generally the pursuit of a common pleasure will confirm. It is perhaps on those occasions (despite not being exempt from servitude to the passions) that we are most acutely aware that 'nothing is more advantageous to man than man'.

However, common desires are no guarantee of immunity to dissensions. Nothing in convergent desires precludes continuing affective divergence, as is well known by those who have embarked on a common enterprise and discovered how fragile the apparent initial harmony was – and this is simply because the initial desire that brought people together rarely exists on its own and can enter into conflict with other individual desires that are not shared to the same extent and are less compatible. This can take the form of disagreements on how to proceed or on the ultimate goal (such divergences having initially been downplayed), or can involve an impulse to capture and dominate, something horizontality by its nature will struggle to contain. Partners quarrel, troupes fall apart, and collective adventures end (badly), though others don't and can give rise to much shared joy – it really depends. This is the inherent contingency and fragility of the horizontal collective.

---

11 *Ethics*, IV, 14, p. 161.

Selective Anthropologies

This is merely another way of framing the fundamental ambivalence of the passions in the productions of human nature, some of which are 'social' (centripetal) and some of which are not. We must take them all into account, rather than selecting only those that serve our purpose. But selective sifting is a characteristic practice among thinkers who come down emphatically on one side of the argument. Defenders of the Bodin–Hobbes model of sovereignty wish only to see the wolf, all the better to justify the state's absolute control over society. And champions of horizontality only want to acknowledge the noble passions, since these are the anthropological precondition for the type of political community of which they dream – and since such a community is only possible if this precondition is met, they declare it met . . . A substantial proportion of anarchist anthropology is thus a somewhat fraudulent exercise in trying to exorcise the ghost of the Hobbesian wolf by emphasising (legitimately enough) that man is *also* capable of demonstrable reciprocity, but then surreptitiously deleting the 'also' and constructing an affective landscape where only cooperation and altruism are to be found.

This anthropology then takes its reconstruction a step further: the Hobbesian wolf, rejected as a characterisation of the essence of man, is instead identified with the state itself, in a move reminiscent of Rousseau's in the *Second Discourse*: man in the state of nature knows no passions, as these come to him only through society.[12] Far from violent passions in any way justifying the existence of the state, the argument runs that what fosters evil passions is living within a state. It is not because man is naturally violent that the state is necessary, it is the existence of the state that makes man violent; the state falsely presents itself as the solution to the problem of violence, whereas in reality it is the source of that problem. It naturally follows, then, that the state must be suppressed in order to restore man to his natural state of goodness.

The height of such theoretical misfiring is perhaps attained by Kropotkin, who, in his own way, adopts this inverted scheme of things

---

12 In fact, Rousseau does accord two fundamental passions to man in the state of nature: compassion and self-respect.

in a sort of positive version of Spencerism. Whereas it is most common to see (wrong-headed) applications of evolutionary theory to society which positively embrace the competitive character of the survival of the fittest, Kropotkin opts to see only cooperation in the animal world.[13] Among social animals such as ants, bees and monkeys, we observe the curbing of selfish opportunism and frequent acts of cooperation and devotion to the group: 'The idea of good and evil has thus nothing to do with religion or a mystic conscience. It is a natural need of animal races';[14] 'equality in mutual relations with the solidarity arising from it, this is the most powerful weapon of the animal world in the struggle for existence'.[15] Exemplified in the animal world, morality is thus a property inscribed into nature and man is a fortiori the happy heir to it.

Moments of Lucidity

Not all anarchist thought descends to these levels of fantastical reconstruction. At times it can even be lucid when analysing human behaviour, though at the price of tensions analogous to those engendered by the question of the state – tensions that stem from the desire to retain something even after perceiving its inherent contradictions. Just as with Bakunin and the inevitable return of the state after it had been banished, so more lucid anthropological exercises come back to earth after indulging in some of their more improbable speculations. Proudhon overcomes his early naivety and 'subjects workers' associations to harsh criticism'.[16] 'All the abuses of capitalist societies "were exaggerated still further in these supposedly fraternal associations". They had been torn apart by discord, rivalries, defections and betrayals'.[17] This criticism is harsh indeed, but necessary, for it sets into sharp relief the

---

13 As Patrick Tort has stressed, the correct word for this intellectual current is Spencerism, not Darwinism.

14 Peter Kropotkin, 'Anarchist Morality', in *Fugitive Writings*, ed. and intro. George Woodcock, Black Rose Books, 1993, p. 135.

15 Ibid.

16 The comment is by Daniel Guérin, *L'Anarchisme*, 'Essais', Folio, 2012, p. 68.

17 Ibid. The internal quote is from Proudhon, *Manuel du spéculateur à la Bourse*, Garnier Frères, 1854, p. 319.

(anthropological) problem of horizontalism: 'horizontal' man is not immediately to hand. To a large extent, he still has to be produced. Local horizontal (and experimental) political arrangements inherit individuals as they currently are, formed by the society and the history of the society in which they live, which happens to be a capitalist society. These are individuals whose folds are familiar to thinkers like Diego Abad de Santillán, for example: 'The capitalist system has not prepared human beings [for anarcho-communism]: far from developing social instincts in them and a sense of solidarity, it tends on the contrary, and in every respect, to banish and emasculate feelings.'[18]

Marcel Mauss, who defines himself as a 'socialist', also perceives the problem: 'Socialist action . . . will tend to give rise in the minds of individuals and in all social groups to a new way of seeing, thinking and acting.'[19] However, Mauss's confident use of the future tense ('will tend') gives way to the altogether more problematic prescriptive register: 'Socialist action *must* substitute the socialist mind-set for other mind-sets. It *must* engender in both the individual and the group these new ways of living of the society of the future: a new way of conducting oneself in the face of facts, a new law, a new social hierarchy, a new scale of values, and a new moral system of reward and punishment.'[20] This 'must' effectively confirms that the socialist mind-set is still to be produced, which is to say that it does not yet exist. It also indicates how dangerous it would be to put the cart before the horse, and the lengthy practical effort that this production will require. For these social and moral engineers 'must not supersede morals with laws, nor criticise in the name of a universal morality . . . the technical, economic and mental habits of the people. These can only be corrected by substituting in their place other habits inspired by other ideas and other feelings.'[21] The advent of the socialist mind-set, on which hangs the very possibility of socialism, requires a lengthy process of revising our habits. Four centuries ago, Althusius was also aware of the preconditions for a new way of living and he did not fail to mention that, in order for people to enter into the

---

18 Guérin, *L'Anarchisme*, p. 73.

19 Marcel Mauss, 'L'action socialiste', in *Écrits politiques*, Fayard, 1997, cited in Dardot and Laval, *Commun*, p. 397.

20 Ibid., my emphasis.

21 Ibid.

consociatio as if into a private pact, it would 'require their accord and *a certain state of mind'.*[22]

Nobody can consent to the perilous leap that presupposes that the 'state of mind' or 'socialist mind-set' already exists. The truth is that they do not, or rather they exist only partially, constantly coexisting with affective motions which are far less cooperative. And nothing can guarantee in advance that they will be the exclusive, or even the primary, motions. Horizontal collectives are, therefore, at the mercy of the contingent relations that will be established between antagonistic affective forces – the cooperative and non-cooperative forces. But you cannot build an overarching political form on such unpredictable foundations.

The Case for Critical Anthropological Realism

As a rule, conservative anthropological realists stop here, pleased to have managed to justify their hatred of change and deducing from their fraudulent analysis (which invests the current state of affairs with a certain inevitability) a reason for acquiescing in the current order of things. 'Face up to the evidence: with people "the way they are", it can never work.' In other words, it can only ever work as it does now. If Spinoza's distinct conception of human nature has a strategic value, it is here that it emerges. For what we termed the 'appropriate generality' (the under-determination), which is given more specific forms by the endless combinatorial possibilities, is the same thing that gives Spinoza's human nature its infinite plasticity.

The question then becomes: how do we practise anthropological realism (without making up any old story)? For practise it we must, since the question of convergence cannot be assumed to be self-evident or to be resolvable by appeals to principle. In short, how do we practise anthropological realism without falling into the powerful (and false) lure of conservative realism?

Anthropological realism is first and foremost a stance that directly addresses the issue of divergence, which is to say of violence, without seeking to reduce human nature to this phenomenon. Violence is a

---

22 Quoted by Demelemestre, *Introduction à la* Politica methodice digesta, p. 69, my emphasis.

possibility in the life of the passions and is to some degree present in *all* the expressions, however different, of human nature, and any political project that closes its eyes to this fact is doomed to theoretical vacuity and practical disaster. The starting point of this anthropological realism is surely to avoid the philosophers' error which, in Spinoza's famous formulation, is to 'conceive men not as they are, but as they would like them to be',[23] while noting that it is not a question of 'man' but of *men and women* located within determined social and moral formations, and that if they are such and such a way in this place and time, nothing in principle excludes the possibility that they can be another way elsewhere or at a later point.

It is thus this constantly open possibility (and often observable fact) of *difference* that underpins a *critical* anthropological realism. It is critical precisely to avoid the slippery slope of conservatism, which is generally seeking to state *definitively* what 'man' is – a discourse of closure claiming to establish once and for all what people can do and 'what they will never be able to do', and which predictably defines their capacities to be such that they could never do anything outside the contemporary social order. The whole theoretical force of the Spinozan stance lies in its under-determination of human nature, which always requires an additional input that only history can furnish and thus is open to all the inventions that history can produce. The fact that what constitutes human nature is the combination of elements means that what defines man (or rather people) is first and foremost a *capacity for modification*. And herein lies the essential difference between conservative and critical anthropological realism: whereas the former seeks to deliver verdicts on the fixity and essentialism of human nature and thereby to argue that the current state of affairs cannot be superseded, the latter is centred on notions of under-determination, the capacity for combinatorial invention, and the possibility in principle of modification.

The Possibility of Modification

Do we really need to stress again the extraordinary variety of configurations in which human nature has expressed itself down the ages and

---

23 *PT*, I, 1, p. 33.

across the planet? And the extraordinary variety that the future necessarily holds too? This is where all the power of the ontology of finite modes becomes evident: because they are not substances, finite modes only exist in relation to each other, and in the case of humans this primarily means those that are like ourselves, since nothing is more advantageous to us. By virtue of their very finitude, the existence of finite modes is necessarily relational. And on account of the complexity of the human body, says Spinoza, these relations and the mutual affections that result have the power to modify those relations. To modify them 'simply' through the experiencing of affects, which are *variations* (variations in the body's power to act and concomitantly of the mind's power to think).[24] And to modify them 'profoundly' when these affects leave enduring traces, and it is then their affective complexion itself (their *ingenium*, to use Spinoza's term) that is modified. And this 'profound' modification involves a modification of the way in which 'simple' modifications are produced: if my complexion is modified, I no longer react in the same way, being more affected by the same things than I was before. The *ingenium* is therefore the structure that embodies my habits – my habits of feeling, judging, thinking, and seeing when I am engaging with the external world. And these habits, which determine my modifications in the weak sense (my affects), can themselves be modified in the strong sense, and I am thereby modified in my way of being affected.

And this is the advantage of adopting Spinoza's perspective on human nature. It is the under-determined matrix from which modifiable *ingenia* are engendered: complexions whose folds are first formed by the effects of socialisation in our early years but become complemented and confirmed, smoothed out or reinforced, in the course of our path through life, punctuated as it is by affections that mark us (that modify us in the 'strong' sense). Some of those affections will be common to our group, while others will be more personal and idiosyncratic. The point about modes is that they are modifiable. The whole power of Spinoza's theory lies in this statement, which should permanently inoculate us against ill-conceived attempts to define a fixed essence of man. We might even say, in a non-Derridean sense but adopting Derrida's spelling, that the Spinozan theory of modes is a philosophy of 'différance'.

---

24 *Ethics*, III, definition 3, p. 103.

The human mode never ceases to differ and defer. It differs and defers necessarily, since our paths through life are open-ended and we can always potentially be exposed to encounters that mark us (encounters with people, images, situations, events) and result in a deep restructuring of our *ingenium*. No doubt such encounters are fairly rare in life, most of our experiences replicating previous experiences and thereby reinforcing (hardening, even) the folds that the *ingenium* has already acquired. But nothing excludes the possibility that, one day, a powerful affection (one that is literally extra-ordinary) will occur whose power to modify is unpredictable.

The revolutionary event is one such powerful, and powerfully modifying, affection. Those who stubbornly deny the possibility of insurrection by extrapolating from 'how people are' now are mistaken, since tomorrow those people will not be the same. They will no longer be as they were yesterday, for the event has modified them. The event, or at least the insurrectional event, is not a mysterious power. It is a mutual affection that occurs at a critical point in the collective affective situation. There is a long history of individual affective balances reaching the threshold of indignation – this is the seditious affect, according to Spinoza.[25] The insurrectional moment is a crystallisation which, through mutual affections, pushes those individual balances over the threshold, and so involves much more than being simply affected or modified in the 'weak' sense. One recognises the insurrectional event by the scale of the modifications it is capable of inducing and by the abruptness with which it induces them: our desires and our representations of the world, as well as our customs and habits, are profoundly reconfigured and suddenly take on a new complexion and new orientations. And the human modes affected by the event are modified in the 'strong' sense, sometimes so greatly that those affected are astonished at their own metamorphosis. During the Commune, the painter Gustave Courbet was certainly taken aback: 'Paris is a true paradise: no police, no stupid behaviour, no abuses of any kind, no quarrels. Paris is running smoothly all by itself.'[26] And yet no one would have bet on such a Paris on 17 March.

---

25 *PT*, III, 9, p. 52.

26 Cited by the Invisible Committee in *À nos amis* [*To Our Friends*], La Fabrique, 2014, p. 235.

The Paralogism of the Insurrectional Moment

However, there is little point in correcting an error if we then fall into another one. Asserting, in opposition to conservative realists, that modes are modifiable and moreover that they can be modified 'profoundly', introduces remarkable possibilities in principle but leaves questions of 'detail' entirely open, such as under what conditions, in which directions, at what speed, and with what level of irreversibility modes can be modified. Amid his surprise and delight, Courbet is assailed by a slight doubt as he adds: 'If only it could always remain like this.' There is in that 'if only' caveat a dread of disillusionment, and an instruction to himself not to get carried away. There is no guarantee that Paris will continue to run smoothly all by itself, nor that it will always remain like this if things are left to unfold spontaneously.

Courbet's hesitation conveys the hidden variables – the unobserved and exceptional conditions of possibility – of unexpected harmonies. We might call the error of extrapolating to ordinary times the particularities of the exceptional moment the 'paralogism of the insurrectional moment'. That the insurrectional moment carries within it a power of modification is a fact that only conservative realism (in this case, the truncated realism that is incapable of perceiving the reality of mutual affections and their transformative potential) stubbornly refuses to acknowledge. But the insurrectional moment is one thing and the return to normality another, which necessarily raises the question of how permanent the modifications will be. Some may well be permanent, but there is no guarantee that all of them will be. Individuals may be changed for the long term, but not necessarily to the point where collective harmonies are certain to emerge. When the insurrectional moment occurs in the appropriate context, it brings with it a specific additional element: the force of the common affect, jointly deployed. The adversity experienced collectively and the desire to triumph over it afford in themselves an unmatched force of collective cohesion, while the urgency of the stakes (that can amount to life and death) relegate all other divergences to secondary status. It is only when the tension relaxes and things return to normal that those divergences will reassert themselves. As ever, the affective power balances will decide the issue. And, while it is true, as stated in the *Political Treatise*, that 'the multitude will unite and consent to be guided as if by one mind not at reason's prompting but through some common affect such as a common hope, or common fear, or desire to avenge some common injury',[27] the multitude will only stay united for as long as that common affect lasts – and the insurrectional multitude will only last for as long as adversity continues to drive its struggle. Divergent idiosyncratic affects do not disappear during the insurrectional moment: they are dominated by a common affect that surpasses them all in intensity. However, when the collective coherence engendered by the state of war begins to weaken as peace returns, the centrifugal passions recover their relative intensity and make themselves felt once more.

It is not fruitful to analyse ordinary times through the lens of the exceptional moment. The task of a political philosophy of revolution is to reflect on what happens immediately afterwards. It is true that intellectuals, professionally inclined to believe in their own singular nature, constantly and almost invariably succumb to the temptation of projecting their singularity onto the rest of the world. No doubt it requires a rather rare and special *ingenium*, such as that possessed by Bourdieu and the historians of the Annales school, to avoid this temptation of the singular and continue attending to the regular: the dullness of reproduction, the banality of the ordinary and the drudgery of daily life rather than the splendour of the event. Admittedly, the insurrectional event cannot be apprehended without taking into account its irradiating power, but the prospects of a revolution are not determined by the inaugural flare-up – on the contrary, in fact, because this is what distinguishes insurrection from revolution. The first gives us access to the second, but revolution does not consist merely of a *moment*: it involves the stabilisation of the new social relationships, which is to say of a new way of living. We should not get carried away by the romanticism of manning the barricades, for it is not possible to live in a state of permanent insurrection. The philosophy of revolution would thus do well not to bask in the exalting glow of riots and instead realise that the ordinary is the object of study to which all its efforts should be directed. Admittedly, it may be a very different ordinary, accessible only through an extraordinary infraction, but ultimately an ordinary all the same. 'If only it could always remain like this': the intellectual cause of the revolution is this new 'always'.

---

27 *PT*, VI, 1, p. 64.

The Politics of Modification

What, then, can a new way of living rely upon to stabilise itself once the intensity of the insurrectional common affect has abated? On institutions, especially educational institutions. Education is the name for the production of *ingenia* that are adapted to a certain way of living – it is a key weapon of a politics of modification, since these *ingenia* have to be *produced*. This is what Proudhon and Santillán implicitly concede when they recognise that the anarcho-communist world calls for certain affective conditions, namely a certain *type of individual* – an *ingenium* – which we cannot assume is immediately available. 'The most difficult task faced by associations was to "civilise the partners" . . . It was less a case of forming a "mass of capital" than a "fund of people"', observes Daniel Guérin, who concludes: 'Self-management therefore required a "certain education" of the self-managers. "One is not born a partner, one becomes one".'[28] Malatesta says something very similar: 'If it is to be feasible, Communism requires a highly developed and deep-seated sense of solidarity among members of the society which the revolutionary impetus might not be sufficient to produce, not least because at the outset the material conditions conducive to its development may well be lacking.'[29]

Though it sees people as they are *today*, the critical realism of Spinozan anthropology also perceives the possibility of modifying them such that they are different tomorrow. But it does not assert that this different state is an immediately available resource, nor that this possibility will definitely be realised. It acknowledges this as a problem, and indeed the political problem par excellence of the revolution, lying at the intersection of the institutional and the anthropological. For, once the modifiability of modes is acknowledged, we must address the question of what conditions are required to modify them effectively. The great force of the anthropology of modes is that it extricates us from the wholly sterile and doubly fallacious antagonism between a 'good' or 'evil' human nature. Doubly fallacious, since the first error is to imprison man in a human

---

28 Guérin, *L'Anarchisme*, p. 69. The internal quotes are from Proudhon, *Le Spéculateur de la Bourse*, Garnier Frères, 3rd edition, 1857, pp. 464–9.

29 Errico Malatesta, *Program and Organization of the International Working Men's Association*, theanarchistlibrary.org.

nature that is irredeemably fixed, and the second is to imagine that this fixed category can only be of the *pure* type of good or evil, God or wolf – a perspective that does not correspond to the reality of today and will never correspond to the reality of tomorrow. In his conception of human nature, Spinoza is careful to refrain from declaring what social-historical human beings will be like in a specific place and a specific time, since actual human beings are *ingenia*: situated affective complexions that are particular expressions of human nature and not human nature itself, which as we have seen is under-determined and will remain unarticulated and unobservable. Like everything in the world, *ingenia* are *productions*. They are productions of their time and place: historical societies produce particular types of individuals. Debates on 'human nature' per se are ultimately redundant – the only relevant question is how *ingenia* are produced.

The Common Affect of a Way of Living

Some may object that desires and complexions exist which are already attuned to horizontal post-capitalist ways of living. Does not the proliferation of contemporary social experiments attest to spontaneous affective convergences that give rise to tangible new social arrangements? Even if they manage to endure, these experiments are only ever an additional illustration of Spinoza's fundamental political insight, namely that multitudes come together under the effect of a common affect.[30] And this common affect (in this case, the common desire to live together in a non-capitalist arrangement) also needs to be powerful if it is to determine individuals (those who are sensitive to it) to extricate themselves from capitalist society. It is the power of the common affect – under whose influence the desire to stick with this way of living and to make it endure trumps other centrifugal movements – that produces this 'cold fusion', so to speak: a functional equivalent of the cohesive force engendered in the heat and passion of the insurrectional moment. This difference in metaphorical temperature is a difference in intensity. There is a

---

30 See for example Isabelle Frémeaux and John Jordan, *Les Sentiers de l'utopie*, 'Zones', La Découverte, 2011, and Collectif Mauvaise Troupe, *Constellations. Trajectoires révolutionnaires du jeune 21è siècle*, Éditions de l'Éclat, 2014.

difference of extension as well, since only the small number of people who are predisposed to these experiments are able to embark on them 'cold' – that is, the small number whose particular *ingenium* renders them affectable, sensitive to this proposition, and willing to join in as soon as the proposition is made to them. The majority will remain caught up in, and shaped by, the affective matrix of capitalism. Most of the time these experiments therefore remain isolates, destined to bring together only those already won over to the cause.

Their common conviction – which is to say their common affect, since being convinced is to add an affect to an idea or to invest an idea with an affect – is what cements their grouping. And if this grouping is to have any chance of lasting, it will only find it in the relative intensity of this common affect. The community therefore only endures if the power of the desire of its members to make it endure outweighs the power of their other individual desires, which are potentially centrifugal. These tautologies of viability are unavoidable: a collective entity only maintains itself through the common affect that sustains it, and for only as long as that affect outweighs the power of other affects. Conversely, if the affective situation of the whole is dominated by individual centrifugal affects, it will fall apart. Such is the logic of desire: if it remains horizontal, an experiment will only last if it is sufficiently dear to the hearts of those engaged in it. Duration is a question of the continuity of desire.

The Role of Politics and Anthropology in Producing *Ingenia*

But consolidating the desire of those already on the inside, inducing the desire of those on the outside and educating the new arrivals requires either a miraculously strong community, capable of attracting and integrating others on the basis of its spontaneous self-affections alone, or else the presence of specific institutions (which also involve self-affections but in mediated form) and educational institutions in particular – 'the seminary of society'. These are the most specific sites for producing *ingenia* which are adapted to a way of living – the most specific, since ultimately it is in the society as a whole, and through the work the society constantly performs on itself and all its members, that common habits and customs are engendered and desires for living are reproduced which correspond to a certain way of living (which are reproduced by this reproduction). Within the institutional system of the Zapatista state, for example, education is of considerable importance – a fact that can be overlooked due to the excessive attention paid to the properly political (in the narrow sense) structure of the councils. The schools receive a level of collective investment commensurate with their strategic importance, since their role is nothing less than to produce the habits – habits of judging and desiring – of the Zapatista citizen.[31] In other words, to produce over the long term the anthropological conditions (or we might say more simply the moral conditions) for Zapatista society to exist and endure.

However, should we not also ask what conditions are required for the production of these conditions? In other words, though man is modifiable, can he be modified to order? Can education in the broad sense modify human beings at will, or is that to suppose them more malleable than they really are? And what can be hoped for in this domain? Nurturing the desire in those who feel it already seems like a reasonable enough proposition, but can it be produced to order in those who do not feel it? Forcing the issue is an abusive modification and conditioning is a detestable one, which brings us back to the initial question: how do we go beyond a grouping of people who are already predisposed to being part of that grouping? How to smooth out the folds of the majority, which have been produced by capitalist society and have moulded individuals to the capitalist way of living?

Modification is an undertaking that is only partly political. Pasolini wrote of an anthropological revolution involving the complete colonisation of culture by the individualistic hedonism of capitalist consumerism.[32] We are interested in the possibility of an inverse revolution, but it will be a process of the same order. It would be wrong to say that politics plays no part at all – very identifiable powers are involved in working on the desires and imaginations of capitalist subjects such as business, advertising and the media, and these can be prevented *politically* from doing harm. So politics is part of the equation, but by no means the

---

31 Jérôme Baschet estimates that there are 500 schools in the five Zapatista zones, attended by 16,000 pupils. Jérôme Baschet, *Adieux au capitalisme. Autonomie, société du bien vivre et multiplicité des mondes*, 'L'horizon des possibles', La Découverte, 2014, fn. 6, p. 60.

32 Pier Paolo Pasolini, *Corsair Writings*, libcom.org.

whole story. Perhaps its role ultimately consists only in directing things on the margins, supporting or amplifying trends that have come from elsewhere and further away. The consumerist world did not simply fall from the sky, and the powers of marketing and the openings of shopping centres have little to do with the anthropological revolution of individualism, which has been brewing for several centuries and has offered these powers an affective resource that they have been only too happy to exploit.

An anthropology of horizontality, which is a prerequisite for living according to horizontal relations, is not a given but rather a challenge. Like everything else in the world, it is either produced or still to be produced. Nothing excludes the possibility of it being produced, but nothing guarantees it either. To become a continent rather than remaining an archipelago of predisposed isolates, a way of living must produce and reproduce, at the scale of the majority, *ingenia* that are attuned to it. This prerequisite is an additional illustration of the tautologies of viability, for, if this way of living fails to produce the conditions for its own existence, then, clearly, it will itself cease to be possible. An anti-capitalist way of living that fails to mitigate the self-interest its members have inherited from capitalist individualism, or to sublimate it into cooperative forms,[33] or to redirect desires away from objects of consumption, would be doomed sooner or later to dissolution or to some form of tyranny.

Revolutionary invocations of the 'new individual' have prompted many a horrified response – a reaction which is both justified and unjustified. Unjustified, in that it is the very nature of human nature to express itself in a multiplicity of forms and, since the history of cultural formations is entirely open-ended, it will express itself in future forms that will add their own inventions – their new individuals – to this long history of 'différance': human beings are not done with differing and deferring. But justified, too, in that, although people are modifiable, they are not made of wax or capable of immediately assuming any *ingenium*-modifying configuration imposed from without. It is through a lengthy process that involves both politics and anthropology, and which might be qualified as civilising

---

33 For it is always fundamentally a form of self-interest that is at play in altruistic and cooperative behaviours. See Lordon, *L'Intérêt souverain*.

without implying any notion of progress, that individuals modify themselves collectively. The political revolution of horizontality is dependent on a moral revolution, but the problem is that moral revolutions do not necessarily lead to social revolutions.

9

Reaching for the Universal
(a Political Ethics)

Modification towards the universal requires a great deal of patience. In the meantime, particular formations reign, which, in our current age, means nation states. Deriving self-esteem from the achievements of the group and a collective sense of solidarity through shared customs is the kernel of the national affect and not even the most internationalist intellectuals are immune to its lure. Do they not necessarily partake in some of its customs, given that socialisation within the nation is primary and necessary, and its effects can never be erased entirely? And do they not personally attest to the fact that there are amicable ways of living by one's customs and not turning them into partisan stances? Moreover, do they not also find opportunities to delight by proxy in national achievements to which the folds of their own *ingenium* are attuned? 'I have no problem admitting to loving my country, France', says Alain Badiou.[1] Admittedly, his France may not be the same as that of his sparring partner Alain Finkielkraut – Badiou's France is that of the 'ideals of the French Revolution, the Resistance and the Paris Commune'.[2] Badiou has also been more specific: 'I love my country, or rather I love what it is sometimes capable of.'[3] Even

---

1 Alain Badiou and Alain Finkielkraut, *L'Explication. Conversation avec Aude Lancelin* [*Confrontation: A Conversation with Aude Lancelin*], Lignes, 2010, p. 51.

2 Ibid.

3 Alain Badiou, *Abrégé de métapolitique* [*Metapolitics*], Seuil, 1998, p. 10.

internationalist intellectuals can be moved by what their country is capable of, and feel that they have an affective stake in it. Logically and understandably, internationalist intellectuals select the national achievements which strike them as the least conflictual and the most universal in scope. And yet, in each case, the universal is conveyed through a specific vehicle and it is precisely that (national) specificity which prompts our affective identification with it. In bald terms, it is an affect of national pride: the French Revolution possesses universal scope, but one cannot help feeling proud that it happened to take place in France . . .

However, it remains the case that the existence of distinct political bodies with their idiosyncratic customs does not inherently spell disaster. Although the history of nations, and not least European nations, is replete with examples of the devastation that the national principle can wreak, more recent history demonstrates that it does not always do so, or at least that contingent conditions can arise which steer us away from such an outcome – conditions conducive to meta-customs that can be described as amicable or even (though the word has been weakened by overuse) tolerant. However, we still need to outline what these conditions might be. Generically, we can say that they involve anything that may diminish our fixation on specific social arrangements and that makes us aware both of their contingency and the possibility of modification without a loss of personal of identity – in other words, anything that allows us to experience affectively the possibilities afforded in theory by the configurative plasticity of forms.

The constant efforts of rational historiographers of the nation to counter the essentialist fictions of the 'national novel' and morally compromised tales of a 'national history' are no doubt one of the prerequisites,[4] once the contributions of science to educational doctrine are allowed to play a role in the shaping of the collective imagination. The effects of these efforts will vary depending on our historical premises: whether our starting point is 'our ancestors, the Gauls', or whether we agree with Céline when he (paradoxically?) declares that France is the Finistère of Europe where all the outcasts of the continent have

---

4 See the 'Documents' section in Detienne, *L'Identité nationale, une énigme,* which offers some incriminating illustrations of this (pp. 149–60).

washed up – 'this great ragbag of deadbeats'.[5] Kristin Ross, who has researched the educational revolutions during the Commune, asks: 'In what way does education change, for example, when the community for which one has been educated is not the nation but the universal republic or the workers' republic?'[6] For, in these conditions, education does indeed change. It modifies individuals in their habits (acquired through education) of relating to the group and to what is external to it, and even leads them to reconsider the very contours of what constitutes a group. For Marcel Detienne, who has watched with consternation the compromising of principles evident in celebratory historiography,[7] a rational and teachable concept of the nation necessarily involves, not as direct content but as informing principle, a comparative approach to anthropology insofar as its goal is to 'make a group of people aware of the way others live and thus of the way they themselves live'.[8]

Contributive Citizenship as an Alternative to Essentialist Identity

Our gnoseological rapport with the nation, inscribed within a collective imagination that must strive to be as rational as possible, merits our attention since it is the antechamber of our practical rapport with the nation. And that practical rapport determines both the concrete conditions for admission into a nationality and the way we treat nationals and non-nationals respectively. What, then, can constitute a non-essentialist criterion for affiliation? This question is legitimate since, while essentialism is the surest route to conflict between specific formations, we must nevertheless account for something akin to affiliation once we grant the fact that political bodies persist as finite distinct groups. Given that a political body is only a partial enclosure – it is necessarily an 'open

---

5 'What you call the French race is nothing but this great ragbag of rheumy, flea-ridden, forlorn deadbeats like me who have washed up fleeing hunger, plague, tumours and the cold. The defeated from the four corners of the world. They couldn't go any further because of the sea. That's France, and that's the French.' *Voyage au bout de la nuit*, La Pléiade, I, p. 12.

6 Kristin Ross, *L'Imaginaire de la Commune* [*Communal Luxury: The Political Imaginary of the Paris Commune*], trans. Étienne Dobenesque, La Fabrique, 2015, p. 52.

7 Detienne, *L'Identité nationale*.

8 Clifford Geertz, *Works and Lives: The Anthropologist as Author*, Stanford University Press, 1988.

enclosure', like all finite modes – of a way of living that jointly organises its own perseverance in a certain manner, the least essentialist criterion for affiliation and the most in keeping with this abstract conception of the group is *contribution*. Affiliation is manifest in the contributive participation in the group's collective striving to persevere in its own being. And that striving to persevere is by no means limited to material prerequisites; there is also the striving to enhance the other powers that are part of the collective life of the body, be they intellectual, artistic, moral or cultural in the broad or narrow sense. In principle, and in the absence of other restrictions, affiliation and sovereignty are the preserve of those who contribute to the perseverance of the whole and are thereby entitled to be considered a part of it.

It is common to observe how essentialist conceptions of affiliation prevent people from perceiving the concrete contributions of those who are assumed not to belong and are assigned the 'status of foreigner'.[9] They are relegated to invisibility, as are their contributions. The tragic and absurd consequence of this self-perpetuating assignation is that invisibility is equated with a lack of contribution (entirely disregarding the marginalisation suffered by foreigners, some of whom are besides forced to live in clandestinity). Foreigners are thereby deprived of their entitlement to belong to the group – a genuine entitlement, since it is based on genuine contributions. And, in any case, contributions should by no means be understood solely with reference to the capitalist work ethic: the contributions which in principle entitle one to belong transcend mere material production. It is a matter of a general contribution ensuing from inclusion within a common living space; it involves participating in associations and cultural groups, gathering with friends and family, joining in everyday conversations and being part of the local fabric that weaves itself together to form the political body as a whole – in other words, an identical contribution to those who formally belong (with papers to prove it) and who claim affiliation on essentially the same grounds. All affiliation is based on a durable and integrated presence, as well as on the material activity and interpersonal relations this necessarily entails and which are, by their nature, contributive.

This contributive conception of the nation is very similar to that developed by Étienne Balibar, who contrasts 'statutory citizenship' with

---

9 Le Blanc, *Dedans, dehors*. See in particular Chapter V.

'active citizenship'[10] and sees activity, or more precisely, active and durable presence, as an index of affiliation. This can be seen in the (apparently) paradoxical struggles of 'illegal aliens' without official papers to obtain those documents – a tangible reflection of their political resources but also of their explicit desire to belong, even if belonging has its own servitudes, such as having to pay tax. Taxation is desired because it is the correlate of a desirable thing. And all this while the wealthiest members of the group, whose affiliation is supposed to be beyond reproach, devote boundless energy to avoiding that particular form of servitude . . .

The Transcendental Paradoxes of the Universal

The fact remains that the enclosure, albeit partial or 'open', encloses nonetheless. The individuated and distinct political body is not diluted into the rest of an amorphous human race, whose unification is merely a distant dream. Even when it is redefined by the contributions that necessarily result from individuals being durably integrated into the body, the notion of citizen affiliation continues to distinguish between those individuals who are part of the body and those who are not, and continues to treat them differently. Étienne Balibar emphasises the obvious point that, interpreted in its most literal sense, nationality entails discrimination. Whatever the modalities of a nation's customs and its enclosure, nothing can erase the primary distinction between inside and outside. Balibar goes further, however, to tease out the consequences (or as it turns out, the contradictions), demonstrating that the precondition for the internal equality that is characteristic, at least in theory, of modern national citizenship is the fundamental inequality between nationals and non-nationals. Affiliation is inherently based on a principle of inequality. The paradox arises when affiliation (a principle of inequality) is applied to a community that claims to be democratic – that is, founded upon the principle of equality. Internal equality is arrived at through external inequality. The condition of possibility of a democracy is the fundamentally non-democratic institution of the border: it is 'the absolutely non-democratic or "discretionary" condition

---

10 Étienne Balibar, *Nous, citoyens d'Europe? La frontière, l'État et le peuple*, La Découverte, 2001, p. 89.

of democratic institutions'.[11] The internal universality of citizenship is thus de facto a restricted universality, and, what is worse, it is predicated on the active denigration of outsiders.

Bourdieu identifies this same motif of truncated universality in relation to the state.[12] Anyone shocked by the category of universality being applied to the state, since the state as architect of the nation is the epitome of a specific configuration (the national configuration), should bear in mind the tremendous efforts to homogenise and minimise internal differences that go into constructing the nation state. It is worth remarking, incidentally, that thinkers on the radical left sometimes hesitate or oscillate between these two poles. Even as they embrace the universal, it is not unusual for them (at the obvious risk of inconsistency) to celebrate the regional and even the local. The right to live freely, which is to say according to specific customs, is championed at the most regional level, but so too is internationalism, viewed as the hallmark of universalism, which would seem to disregard regional peculiarities and even negate them. The principle of local identity is thus vigorously embraced and may potentially be crowned by the additional, evanescent, virtually cost-free identity (these are just words, after all) of 'citizen of the world'. The national-identity trope is rejected with the same vehemence as regional identities, and even regional pride, are asserted. The only territorial scale at which it is prohibited to form such attachments is at the scale of the nation. It is true that, on this scale, we have to deal with the state – an oppressive power of the first order, a power that opportunistically exploits its authority to its own ends, and a capturer of the power of the multitude and the passions aroused by identity – and we are quite right to fear what it may be tempted to do with this power. But, on the other hand, we are being asked to believe that the free and manifold declarations of local identity will of themselves engender a harmonious coexistence such that the regional will link directly with the international, skipping over the national hurdle – a dubious proposition about which enough has already been said.

The state, in Bourdieu's historical and sociological analysis, does not escape these ambivalences nor the oxymorons of a truncated universalism; at least, the modern bourgeois state does not. Bourdieu

11 Ibid., p. 174.
12 Bourdieu, *On the State*.

reminds us that its origins lie in a process of unification around the royal house and that its engineers were the jurists, whose specific interest lay in elaborating a legal framework of sufficiently general applicability. The formal structure of the law is conducive to a general application, the object being to exclude as far as possible specific exceptions to it, and, in that sense, it is a force for universalism, albeit internally. Admittedly, legal universalism is not universalism per se and that formal equality under the law of the modern bourgeois state is only distantly related to genuine equality. We have reason enough not to fall for the illusion of equality under the law which capitalist societies have a vested interest in propagating (equality not ostensibly being their abiding priority). And yet we have to recognise the advance the law represents in eliding the differences between those subject to the law, and to that extent (a limited one, granted) it does tend towards the universal – in notable contrast to societies that are structured around social ranks or castes.

Once again, we need to examine the genesis of this state of affairs in order to appreciate what habit may have blinded us to – in this case, the way in which the legal profession, in a long battle against institutional resistance, laid the groundwork for the general interests of the modern state to prevail over the specific interests and discretionary logic of the royal house,[13] which was, in a sense, the *primus inter pares* of the distinct groups within the absolutist state. It was a patrimonial state as defined by Max Weber, in which the state (or kingdom) was the *dominion* of the highly distinct and individual person of the king, but at the same time the process of undoing patrimonial ties, introducing laws and regarding the state in the abstract was already at a very advanced stage. The '*l'État, c'est moi*' of Louis XIV was like the last glimmer of a distant star that had already ceased to exist: already the state was no longer him but an *apparatus* in the process of being finalised.

Though it should be seen only as a truncated universalism, we are nevertheless justified in identifying, as Bourdieu does, a process of universalisation wherein differences between the parts of the whole were elided, including that part which happened to be the head of state. For the reasons already adduced, it was a universalising process that took place in stages and operated only within the limits of a certain

---

13 Ibid., in particular the lectures of 3 October 1991, 24 October 1991, 21 November 1991 and 28 November 1991.

jurisdiction, with the inevitable result that it reproduced (and initially produced, quite simply) a discontinuity between the inside and the outside. A (truncated) universalising process took place within, which involved ascribing a specific status to outsiders but at the same time conferring a specific character on the collective self of the nation state. State universalism can never escape the status of an oxymoron: it is forever destined to be a specific form of universalism.

Universalism Assailed by the Servitude to the Passions

From what necessity is this aporia of truncated universalism born? The necessity of the servitude to the passions. That is what governs the formation of finite distinct groupings and also what resolves its own problems with its own resources: it can only contain the passive affects of divergence, which is to say the violence that is a permanent possibility, by countering them with other passive affects of a special type, namely the common affects of the *potentia multitudinis* channelled into institutions.[14] It is the combined affects of the power of the multitude which are captured by the institutional apparatus of the state and which endow that apparatus with its force. Persuading individuals to live according to the norms of an institution, that is, getting them to do one thing rather than another, represents a successful orientation of the conatus of those individuals and means that they have been affected appropriately in relation to the norms of that institution. Guiding behaviours such that they conform to norms is a question of affects (by which all actions are determined), and in the case of institutional norms it is a question of the power to affect – a power invested in institutions which is drawn solely from the power of the multitude. Indeed, one can say that institutions are the *potentia multitudinis* captured and thus, in a sense, the crystallisation of the common affect. Passive affects against other passive affects, crystallised common affects versus divergent individual effects: this is the law of collective coherence under the regime of the servitude to the passions.

But what is the scope for achieving authentic universalism under such conditions? It is not zero, but the process will be a lengthy and in

---

14 On this point, see Lordon, *La Société des affects.*

truth asymptotic one. One may, if one wishes, define the universal as the complete emancipation from any specific category – an appeal to the generic humanity of individuals above and beyond any distinctive properties. But this would mean conceiving of it as a release from the servitude to the passions, since that is the regime under which all these distinctive properties are born. As soon as the problem is reformulated in those terms, one can immediately appreciate how unlikely such a resolution is, however desirable it might be.

Proposition IV, 37, which contrasts politics guided by the passions and politics guided by reason, is a rare occasion in the *Ethics* where Spinoza resorts to two scholia. The question he essentially examines is how it comes about that a man should want others to pursue the same good as himself, should desire for others what he himself desires, and desire that others enjoy what he himself enjoys, thereby guarding collective life against the threat of being torn apart by antagonistic tensions. There are two possible answers to this question, and Spinoza duly examines them in the two scholia. One explores the possibility of desires coinciding under the regime of passive affects. It is true that we are led to desire others to desire what we ourselves desire, since the desire of others holds up a mirror to our own desire and confirms its validity. Why would we desire others to desire what we ourselves desire? To acquire greater certainty regarding the quality of our own object of desire, and thereby desire it more resolutely. But such a path taken by passive affects is always precarious, since 'he who from emotion alone endeavours that others love what he himself loves and live according to his way of thinking acts only by impulse, and therefore incurs dislike.'[15] And there is the additional risk of succeeding too well and provoking envious rivalry by inducing this desire, 'since the highest good sought by men under the sway of affects is often such that only one man can possess it, the result is that men who love it are at odds with themselves; and, while they rejoice to sing the praises of the object of their love, they are afraid of being believed.'[16] Only one thing can be desired while *unreservedly* desiring that others desire it too, and that is reason. Not only does the desire of others not detract in any way from one's own desire (for reason is a non-rival good: one individual enjoying it does not

---

15 *Ethics*, IV, 37, scholium 1, p. 174.
16 Ibid.

prevent anyone else from enjoying it) but it positively adds to it. For nothing is more advantageous to a man guided by reason than another who is harmony with him, and thus the greater the number of people who are guided by reason, the better it is for mankind as a whole.[17]

However, reason is hypothetical, or more precisely the degree to which we can attain it is hypothetical. And overestimating that degree carries with it serious political dangers. What degree of reason can we attribute to the behaviour of individuals? A limited degree, is Spinoza's categorical answer, though, like everything else, it is modifiable. Indeed, this is why he took the trouble to write his *Ethics*: less to set out a well-defined path than to indicate a general direction and its omega point – that point which humans should strive to reach, even if they can never entirely do so. The reason why it will remain beyond their reach is that complete emancipation from the servitude to the passions and a shift to life under the regime of adequate causes supposes emancipation from all external causes, such that one only responds to the necessity of one's own essence.[18] But this cannot happen, since 'it is impossible for a man not to be part of Nature and not to undergo changes other than those which can be understood solely through his own nature and of which he is the adequate cause.'[19] By definition, as finite modes we will always to some degree be subject to the effect of external causes, and to that same degree prey to passive affects.[20] This should not prompt any sense of resignation in us: inability to reach the very end of the path is no reason not to go a long way down it, not least because it is the path of empowerment. In this sense, the universalism of reason, which is also

---

17 *Ethics*, IV, 18, scholium.

18 'I call that an adequate cause whose effect can be clearly and distinctly perceived through the said cause' (*Ethics*, III, definition 1, p. 103); 'I say that we are active when something takes place, in us or externally to us, of which we are the adequate cause; that is, when from our nature there follows in us or externally to us something which can be clearly and distinctly understood through our nature alone' (*Ethics*, III, definition 2, p. 103).

19 *Ethics* IV, 4, p. 156.

20 In fact, we need to be a little more cautious and nuance this assertion. Pascal Sévérac has shown that, in itself, the dependence on external causes in no way contradicts the possibility of active (in the Spinozan sense) affects. As he explains, it is possible to be active although affected by an external thing provided that the laws of its nature, according to which it operates in us, are identical to the laws of our own nature. On this challenging topic, which we do not have the space to tackle here, see Pascal Sévérac, *Le Devenir-actif chez Spinoza*, Honoré Champion, 2005, pp. 87–95.

that of politics, is a genuine goal that is worth striving towards, even if ultimately it will remain out of our reach. There is no paradox here: Spinoza does not promise us the ultimate degree of blessedness (or, which is the same thing, wisdom or freedom), and in fact he explicitly promises the opposite. But, at the same time, he alerts us to the gradations of power and, rejecting the logic of all or nothing, tells us that we are capable of increasing our power – of increasing the proportion of actions that we accomplish under the guidance of active affects, the proportion of adequate cause in our physical motions, and the proportion of reason in our mental activities. And he also tells us that we are capable of diminishing their opposites: the passive affects of inadequate cause, of imagination, and of knowledge of the first kind. Admittedly, we cannot have *everything* but we can have more.

Living beyond the Law?

Which can, of course, be stated the other way around: we can have more but we cannot have *everything*. And yet we would need to have *everything* to accede to a politics beyond the law. Understood in strict terms, the horizon where life is lived beyond the law, as Ivan Segré points out, is that of life guided by reason.[21] What separates us from it – and we will always be separated from it to some degree – is the extent to which we continue to live in servitude to the passions. And it is precisely to that extent that we need the general state, the law and institutions. At this point, it is worth citing Spinoza at length: 'Now if men lived by the guidance of reason, every man would possess this right of his (Cor. 1,Pr.35,IV) without any harm to another. But since men are subject to affects (Cor. Pr.4,IV) which far surpass the power or virtue of men (Pr.6,IV), they are therefore often pulled in different directions (Pr.33,IV) and are contrary to one another (Pr.34,IV), while needing each other's help (Cor.Pr.4,IV). Therefore, in order that men may live in harmony and help one another, it is necessary for them to give up their natural right and to create a feeling of mutual confidence that they will refrain from any action that

---

21 Ivan Segré, *Spinoza: The Ethics of an Outlaw*, trans. David Broder, Bloomsbury, 2017. But see also *Judaïsme et révolution*, La Fabrique, 2014, by the same author for further discussion.

may be harmful to another. The way to bring this about, (that men who are necessarily subject to passive affects (Cor.Pr.4,IV) and are inconstant and variable (Pr.33,IV) should establish a mutual confidence and should trust one another) is obvious from Pr.7,IV and Pr.39,III. There it was demonstrated that no affect can be checked except by a stronger affect contrary to the affect which is to be checked, and that every man refrains from inflicting injury through fear of greater injury. On these terms, then, society can be established, provided that it claims for itself the right that every man has of avenging himself and deciding what is good and what is evil; and, furthermore, if it has the power to prescribe common rules of behaviour and to pass laws to enforce them, not by reason, which is incapable of checking the affects (Sch.Pr.17,IV), but by threats. Now such a society, strengthened by law and by the capacity to preserve itself, is called a State (*civitas*): and those who are protected by its rights are called Citizens (*cives*).'[22]

Spinoza is not the type to beat around the bush – he tells it straight, even though we might not take kindly to it, especially when what he says appears to run contrary to our aspirations to 'freedom'. Inevitably, he raises the hackles of contemporary emancipationist thinkers, and it is not so much that they deny the obstacle but that they fail to see that there even is an obstacle. The fact nevertheless remains that, insofar as people are dominated by their passions, they are 'inconstant and variable' and thus will only 'live in harmony' in a society where there is the rule of law and obedience to it. We can well imagine the outcome of an experiment in which people were asked to indicate their spontaneous preference for either 'obedience' or 'emancipation'; but winning the popularity stakes does not equate to a triumph of clear thinking. Spinoza, by contrast, is perfectly clear on the constraints on our aspirations to emancipation, namely the servitude to the passions, inconstancy, the permanent possibility of divergence, the impossibility of horizontal stabilisation, the law and obedience.

And at this point, of course, the antinomy that tends to frame this debate rears its ugly head: either we have the great emancipation in which we are definitively liberated from the law and obedience, or else we have oppression beneath the iron rule of the state – please choose your camp, because there is no middle ground. Such a situation is no

---

22 *Ethics*, IV, 37, scholium 2, p. 175.

longer even a question of alternatives, it is an impasse. We can only extricate ourselves from it by adopting the perspective of critical realism: we need realism to avoid misrepresenting to ourselves the present state of affairs, and we need to be critical to avoid elevating that present state to the rank of an irredeemably fixed given and thereby implicitly endorsing it. Once again, we need to see people as they are *and* in terms of what they can become.

At the very least, we need to reflect both on how they are at the moment when we engage with them *and* on the conditions that would be required for them to become otherwise. The importance of taking people 'as they are' cannot be overemphasised, since this is the starting point from which everything else follows. The crux here is that people are by and large strangers to reason, whose full realisation is not yet a reality of our world: 'those who believe that ordinary people or those who are busily engaged in public business can be persuaded to live solely at reason's behest are dreaming of the poets' golden age or of a fairy tale.'[23] Emancipationist thinkers would do well to take this on board if they want to avoid spinning 'fairy tales', but they rarely seem inclined that way . . .

The objection is almost trivial in the case of the philosophy of Alain Badiou, which explicitly adopts an anti-positivist stance as a matter of principle. Badiou posits that what he calls the 'event' is a radical disruption of all causality and consequently exceeds all possible knowledge. Insofar as it is the *assertion* of a possibility that previously did not exist and thus a breach in the order of things, the event, though possible to conceptualise philosophically, is conceived of as empirically unknowable. This could hardly be more diametrically opposed to the philosophy of Spinoza, which posits that the real is fully intelligible in principle.[24]

'What is required of philosophy, instead of seeking to account for the structure of the world, its laws and its cohesiveness, is a capacity to accommodate or conceptualise the event itself and how the event, surprise, requisition and precarity can be conceptualised in a configuration that remains rational',[25] writes Badiou, indicating that the

---

23 *PT*, I, 4, p. 36.

24 This despite the fact that Badiou's philosophy sometimes displays genuine affinities with Spinoza's thought.

25 Alain Badiou, *Métaphysique du bonheur réel*, 'Métaphysiques', PUF, 2015, p. 31.

empirical is not a primary consideration in his philosophy. His belief that it is not the role of philosophy to conceptualise the structure of the world and its laws echoes the stance of Rancière, whose disdain for sociology, and for Bourdieu in particular,[26] is the correlate of a philosophy of performative assertion in which presuppositions are favoured over verification. It is a stance that has a certain intrinsic force, but its avowed aversion to the empirical leaves it in a strange relationship to the real world: it has a synthesising power and insists on the possibility of influencing the course of the world, but risks being vacuous in its ignorance of the actual preconditions for influencing it.

The Persistence of Self-Interest (Not Asking Too Much of People)

It is clear from this that the notion of 'self-interest', however susceptible to generalisations, finds no place in Badiou's philosophy because it is a concrete driving force and hence knowable – in other words, the very antithesis of the disruptive event. And, yet, in practical terms, what hope is there for the idea of communism if it forbids any form of self-interest in its militants? And, philosophically speaking, is it true that, since self-interest pertains only 'to the imperative to survive of living things',[27] it is not 'a distinctively human capacity'[28] – a status enjoyed only by thought and politics conceived of as thought? Yes, and no. Yes, insofar as self-interest is *first and foremost* the striving of living things to survive, among them the human finite mode, and subsequently to satisfy their material needs in all the utilitarian senses of self-interest. But no, insofar as thought is not antithetical to self-interest provided one does not constrain oneself to narrow utilitarian categories: in the expanded utilitarianism of power in Spinoza's philosophy, the conatus is fundamentally self-interest.[29] The striving to persevere in one's being *necessarily happens in the first person*, since 'nobody endeavours to

---

26 See Jacques Rancière, *The Philosopher and His Poor*, trans. John Drury, Corinne Oster and Andrew Parker, Duke University Press, 2004.

27 Badiou, *Abrégé de métapolitique*, p. 111.

28 Ibid.

29 See Lordon, *L'Intérêt souverain*.

preserve his being for the sake of some other thing.'[30] From this fundamental self-interest in perseverance derives all that the finite mode is capable of and all activity including that of thinking, which far from being antithetical to the self-interest and power of the conatus is one of its manifestations.

The conatus does not admit of a distinction between self-interest and thought, or indeed between self-interest and altruism. As a generic self-interest and therefore still intransitive, it is the source through affections, adequate or otherwise, of every specific self-interested goal whose pursuit we call human activity. In other words, every action is a specific expression of the generic self-interest of the conatus, even if it is perceived as the most altruistic or generous of deeds. Every action and every way of acting is a physical channelling, often modulated by external causes, of the fundamental impetus of the conatus from which they all derive: 'The conatus with which each thing endeavours to persist in its own being is nothing but the actual essence of the thing itself.'[31] This is why, though it may dismay the champions of altruism, everything ultimately stems from the striving *in the first person* of the conatus,[32] even the most ostensibly generous of acts. And given this fact, it is also why it would be as absurd to expect all self-interest to be overcome as to expect a thing to emancipate itself from its essence.[33] But it by no means follows from this, unless we insist on a very narrow definition of self-interest, that selfishness is an inevitable obstacle to any progress towards ethical truth. Spinoza is perfectly able to accommodate both. In the same way as virtue does not stand outside the regime of desire – how could it when desire is the very essence of man,[34] and, as an essence, inalienable? – but is an *adequate reorientation of its impetus*, so blessedness is not a relinquishing of all self-interest but an appropriately directed interest in intensifying one's participation in being. It would be a mistake to think that the striving to persevere in our being pertains only to the 'animal' part of our

---

30 *Ethics*, IV, 25, p. 167.

31 *Ethics*, III, 7, p. 108.

32 *Ethics*, IV, 25.

33 *Ethics*, III, 7.

34 For the purposes of the argument, the original has been truncated and was therefore incorrect: 'Now desire is the very essence, or nature, of each individual in so far as that is conceived as determined by some given state of its constitution to do something.' *Ethics*, III, 56, proof, p. 137.

nature and that virtue – that part of us that is 'really' human – represents a rupture with that striving. We need not abandon our striving to persevere (how could we, in any case?) to release ourselves from servitude to the passions and to access a regime of universality. Rather, it is a case of redirecting that striving appropriately: 'To act in absolute conformity with virtue is nothing else in us but to act, to live, to preserve one's own being (these three mean the same) under the guidance of reason, on the basis of seeking one's own advantage.'[35]

Why would the event, the originator of an emancipatory truth in Badiou, require self-interest to be sacrificed (while failing to take into account the extent of its registers)? As we have seen, the question does not really make sense in Badiou's philosophy, which rejects all attempts to apprehend the event as an empirically knowable phenomenon. This (erroneous) perception of a discontinuity between the 'animal' part of man and man as a being authentically capable of politics and truth – in other words, this failure to recognise the unity of the conatus, which is at work in both the highest realms of blessedness and the lowlands of the jostling passions – may ultimately be a consequence of conceptualising the event as an exceedance of the individual. Or perhaps it would be more pertinent to formulate the idea the other way around: to safeguard the exceptionality of the event as a radical exceedance, Badiou *has no choice* but to restrict the perseverance in one's being to simple biological self-preservation and to endow the conatus with a primarily 'animal' status so as to exclude the possibility of blessedness in it and to bar its route to the universal order of the *intelligere*. It is striking that in Badiou's own *Ethics*[36] (which is indeed very different to Spinoza's) he asserts that 'the ordinary behaviour of the human animal comes under what Spinoza calls "perseverance in one's being", which is nothing else but the pursuit of self-interest, in other words self-preservation.'[37] It is as if the whole of Part V of the

---

35 *Ethics*, IV, 24, pp. 166–7. The phrase 'preserve one's own being' should of course be understood as 'persevering in one's being'. In the context of this proposition, the substitution affords an a fortiori argument for not interpreting the 'preservation of one's being' as the simple (animal) preservation of our being.

36 Alain Badiou, *Ethics: An Essay on the Understanding of Evil*, trans. Peter Hallward, Verso Books, 2001.

37 Alain Badiou, *L'éthique. Essai sur la conscience du mal*, Nous, 1993, reprinted 2003, p. 74.

Ethics had been erased in one fell swoop . . . And it is in the scholium of *Ethics*, V, 4 that Spinoza reminds us that 'it is very important to note that it is *one and the same appetite* through which a man is said both to be active and to be passive.'[38] And this is what Badiou, in order to safeguard the exceedance of the event, chooses not to see – as is often the case with major thinkers, errors are not committed by mistake.

In any case, it is now easier to understand why the 'event' has so often run the risk of being understood as an act of grace.[39] By contrast, stressing that the conatus is the vehicle of blessedness (as well as the matrix of passive affects) reminds us that even the highest endeavours of man are in principle knowable, like everything else that occurs in the world, including the 'breach' of insurrection and emancipation. Everything that happens is *produced* – by the interplay of forces that can only be the forces of the conatus and its affective determinations, whatever their modalities may be. And as with 'self-interest', to dismiss the operation of the affects, even if they are passive, as an 'imperfection' would be a dubious move. Firstly, because this would be to overlook the essence of the conatus: any mode, finite or otherwise, is affectable. To seek to strip a thing of its affects is tantamount to trying to negate its existence. And, secondly, because it is through affects that people have ideas and become attached to their ideas. As Spinoza succinctly observes: 'Man thinks.'[40] He thinks under the influence of his affects in many different ways, from highly disordered thoughts – 'individual objects presented to us through the senses in a fragmentary and confused manner without any intellectual order', the 'casual' products of imagination taking precedence over understanding – to the clear thinking and adequate ideas of knowledge of the second and third kinds.[41] Even in this supreme register of reason and true ideas, affects are by no means disarmed. Without them, how could a desire to think even arise and how could the mind's power to think be activated and orientated? The possibility of an ethical evolution rests squarely on the affective benefits that we accrue from forming

---

38 *Ethics*, V, 4, scholium, p. 205, my emphasis.

39 See for example Daniel Bensaïd, *Alain Badiou and the Miracle of the Event*, marxists.org. This impression has not been completely dispelled in spite of the amendments to (or is it a decisive shift in?) the conceptualisation of the event in *Logiques des mondes* ('L'ordre philosophique', Seuil, 2006).

40 *Ethics*, II, axiom 2, p. 64.

41 *Ethics*, II, 40, scholium 2, p. 90.

adequate ideas and the taste we subsequently develop for forming more of them. Enjoying those affects is still an expression of the self-interest of the conatus, which is *not abolished but entering into a new regime*. It is still a regime of the affects, but of active affects.[42] The finite human mode cannot step outside the order of the affects but it can, through its evolving ethics, change the nature of that order or at least its composition by enriching its affective life with active affects and, to that extent, extricate itself (though only ever partially) from the servitude to the passions (passive affects). The stubborn old antinomy that we have already discussed does not apply: life guided by reason is not an emancipation from affects but the predominance of active over passive affects (the passions). Reason has its own characteristic affects and therefore its own affective forms of self-interest. To attain adequate knowledge of God and of things in their specific essence is to experience a special, immutable joy which Spinoza calls the 'intellectual love of God' – a joy that is immune to the affective fluctuations inflicted on us by constantly varying external things. The constant joy of the intellectual love of God is not the antithesis of self-interest but its highest form: that of partaking in the divine being of which we are ourselves a finite part.[43] It is, ultimately, the only motivation that can determine us to pursue the path of becoming active once we have embarked on it, and this is the only path along which we can experience a form of salvation. Attaining blessedness – which is to say knowledge of the world of the third kind – is not to breach the universal determinism of the natural order or to step outside the causal order of the conatus and the affects: it is to redeploy them in the direction of becoming an active being.[44]

Is Revolution within Man's Reach (or for Virtuosos Only)?

However powerful it is, a political event will not cleanse us of our self-interested essence – our conatus – for the simple reason that it *is* our essence. It will not even extricate us from the servitude to the passions, but by definition it will modify us. And, if there is a truth in the event, it

---

42 *Ethics*, III, definition 2, p. 103. See footnote 21 above.
43 *Ethics*, V, 33, p. 217.
44 Sévérac, *Le Devenir-actif chez Spinoza*.

will modify us in the right direction, increasing the deployment of reason and producing knowledge at least of the second kind (common notions of the properties of things) since militants of the Idea will find their minds modified by a universal and universalising truth. But moving in the right direction does not mean that we will arrive at the destination. Even the most affected of militants will not be able to claim to be living under the regime of active affects, *e pur si muove*! And under what driving forces, if not those of their affected conatus? There remain, of course, the opposing possibilities of convergence and divergence, although now, perhaps, they are not equally probable . . .

Whether it is communist in character or otherwise, political emancipation does not emancipate us from the laws of affective life or our servitude to the passions. It will only ever be emancipation in an exoteric sense, not in the esoteric sense of Spinozan blessedness. And there will be something missing – an additional element that needs to be conjured up, though with no guarantee that it will be available. Robespierre and Saint-Just called this additional element 'virtue', though not in Spinoza's sense of the word. For Badiou it is fidelity, the correlate of the subjective interpretation of the revolutionary event, that supplies this extra. But leaving aside leaps of faith, can we entirely count on that to ensure the political viability of emancipation? And should not historical experiences in this domain prompt us at the very least to reserve judgement? We can, of course, assert that the conservative majority has prevailed over the minority of faithful subjectivities, and such an assertion would not be entirely false. But it does not really answer the question satisfactorily, since it is likely that even in the camp of emancipation, not everyone has been transfigured by the event. Even in the heat of the event, there are limits to the powers of transfiguration. And, moreover, what happens when there are only embers of the fire left and it is time to return to normal? In the sense of Badiou's very strict definition of it, politics is no doubt a rare event, and Rancière agrees with him there. True politics is an intermittent, exceptional event – it is an unprecedented breach of the established state order. The rest of the time, as Rancière puts it, there is just the 'police'.[45] But, if political philosophy's sole concern

---

45 Rancière uses the term 'police' not to designate the forces of law and order but rather governmental management – an inferior form of politics. See Jacques Rancière, *Disagreement: Politics and Philosophy*, trans. Julie Rose, University of Minnesota Press, 2004.

is such a lofty realm of politics, who is going to take an interest in the 'rest of the time': that of the prosaic matters and routine everyday life to which even the most successful exercise in insurrection and emancipation will one day have to contemplate returning?

Communism cannot be a flash in the pan – it has to last, otherwise there is no sense to it. But what is communism? Badiou defines it as 'a freely entered into egalitarian society of multiskilled workers where activity is regulated not by categories of technical or social specialisations but by the collective mastery of necessities'.[46] All well and good, but unless we specify the concrete forms this 'collective mastery' will take, surely the problem remains unresolved? To paraphrase Camus and his rather grand declaration that 'there is but one truly serious philosophical problem, and that is suicide', we might say there is only one genuinely serious political problem (and thus but one genuinely serious problem of political philosophy) and that is knowing who is going to put the bins out – how the material necessities are going to be mastered collectively.[47] Badiou is perfectly alert to this question. Indeed, he addresses it explicitly, not in relation to the bins but in terms of the constraints of political discipline, which is formally the same question: namely, what are our motives for complying with the requirement to play a personal role in a collective undertaking?

The answer he gives is as follows: 'If you have to be on time to an early-morning appointment with two factory workers, you keep the appointment not because you have interiorised the superego of the organisation nor because the appeal of social and even convivial bonds means that you derive a certain perverse pleasure from acquitting yourself of onerous duties. It is because if you don't go, you are left out of the loop within which generic singularities share in your personal experience.'[48] One can identify in this eloquent formulation the three forms of obedience noted by Spinoza.[49] There is obedience in the strong sense: submission to an external authority (or one that is interiorised into the superego) and the fear of punishment – in other words the

---

46 Badiou, *Abrégé de métapolitique*, p. 91.

47 Albert Camus, *The Myth of Sisyphus*, trans. Justin O'Brien, Vintage International, 2018, p. 3.

48 Badiou, *Abrégé de métapolitique*, pp. 85–6.

49 In Alexandre Matheron's re-evaluation of Spinoza, *Le Christ et le salut des ignorants*, Aubier, 1971.

epitome of heteronomy, whereby the organisation commands and I obey out of fear. And then there is obedience in the weak sense: making the injunctions of the organisation into an object of one's desire and willingly complying – I have converted the 'onerous duties' into pleasurable occupations by associating them with desirable objects, thereby altering their affective valency. But obedience out of fear or out of pleasure – sad or joyful subjugation – remains a consequence of the servitude to the passions. And, finally, there is obedience under the guidance of reason,[50] which is no longer really obedience but rather an apperception of our understanding which prompts us to conform to a requirement – the subject no longer submits on account of the obscure interplay of the passions but in the clear 'consciousness of itself and of things', as Spinoza would put it. I do what I do because I know what I am doing and that *on its own* is sufficient to lead me to do it.

It therefore comes as no surprise that Badiou advocates an idea of politics as an unbinding.[51] In his view, the bond is the common affect that underpins affiliation to a collective identity, which is itself a specific identity – in short, everything that his philosophy rails against in the name of the universal. 'A genuinely political organisation . . . is the least bound place of all . . . On the ground, everyone is essentially on their own seeking direct solutions to problems, and the natural content of meetings or formal gatherings is methodology and research protocols, which are debated with no more conviviality or superego than discussions between two scientists discussing a highly complex question.'[52] Politics, in Badiou's view, should be an affair not of affectively bound groups but of monads guided and coordinated by reason. The only true bond between militants is that of the reason which they share – it is the reason of the truth (in Badiou's sense) under which they become subjectivised modes. But this is not really a bond, there being no common element that actually *binds* them. There is only the *simultaneous* operation of reason (truth) in each of them, synchronising them perfectly without binding them.

---

50 'However, the term "sin" is also commonly used of that which is contrary to the dictates of sound reason, and the term "obedience" of the constant will to control the appetites as prescribed by reason.' *PT*, 11, 20, p. 45.

51 Badiou, 'La déliaison politique' [Politics Unbound], Chapter IV, in *Abrégé de métapolitique*.

52 Badiou, *Abrégé de métapolitique*, p. 86.

However, this vision of politics is a pure 'ought to be' which is thoroughly contradicted by the reality of ordinary political processes. Badiou is clearly aware of this, too, and it is no coincidence that he refuses to qualify such ordinary processes as 'politics'. But one is entitled to wonder whether his redefined and elevated politics is not merely 'rare' but forever inaccessible. It is perhaps the tragedy of (theoretical) conceptualisations of revolution and revolutionary politics that they lead to such lofty ideals of politics that it requires virtuosos to live up to them. Virtuosos of disinterested reason in Badiou, virtuosos of a sort of ethical and visceral insurrectional joy in the case of the Invisible Committee.[53] And not an ordinary person in sight who will one day have to return to their ordinary occupations, which is to say to their ordinary passions (and one doubts whether even the virtuosic militants will have managed to liberate themselves entirely from those passions).

The Eternal Return of Institutions (the State Does Not Wither Away . . .)

To what extent can we count on the capacity of individuals to treat politics like scientists engaged in the solving of their complex problems? And if that is the only basis for an insurrection that can be stabilised over time, which is to say the only basis for a successful revolution and for communism to be established for the duration, what is the probability of those conditions arising? Equating revolution to the liberation from the servitude to the passions renders it a non-starter. But, by the same token, it is true that by acknowledging our continuing affective servitude we are constraining the ambitions of the revolution, including the ambition to break with all state forms of institutional and legal order. In that respect once again, it is the reality of affective forces that comes into play, since the necessity for institutions is to be understood not so much in functional terms but in a deterministic sense: in the non-synoptic condition of large groupings, institutions *are created*. A large grouping of affects secretes institutions, and power too. While one can agree with Badiou that 'the essence of politics, conceptualised . . . as the

---

53 For a critical analysis in the same vein, see Alberto Toscano, 'Burning, Dwelling, Thinking', metamute.org.

free operation of the thought of the collective under the effect of always singular events ... is not power at all [but] the emancipation of the collective',[54] there is reason to fear that if this form of politics does not pay attention to power, then power is likely to pay attention to it. This is because, for as long as we remain in servitude to the passions, the question of power and authority arises *of its own accord* and for the same reasons as institutions: there is an endogenous secretion. Like phoenixes, forms of authority and institutions regenerate themselves, so to speak. It is because they do not address the issue of power and authority, or because they suppose that the ethical conditions have been met for the issue to be resolved, that so many historical experiments in 'horizontality' end in failure. The large-scale ones tend to end in violent confrontation (and their survival would have called for some form of military organisation and thus coordinating institutions wielding some degree of authority). The smaller ones tend to discover, much to their bemusement, that they are re-engendering the monster of authority or else, in an effort to remain as horizontal as possible, they find themselves riven by affective instability.

And what are the ethical conditions that are supposed to exist and thus obviate the need to address the question of institutions and authority? The same ones as always: individuals who have been emancipated from their passions. But as Spinoza points out, 'if human nature were so constituted that men desired most of all what was most to their advantage, no special skill would be needed to secure harmony and trust. But since, admittedly, human nature is far otherwise constituted, the state must necessarily be so established that all men, both rulers and ruled, whether they will or no, will do what is in the interests of their common welfare'.[55] Only individuals who are authentically guided by reason could emancipate themselves from institutions and laws, since they would desire nothing other than reason itself and its universal prescriptions. In other words, reason alone is capable of defusing all conflicts of appropriation and recognition and, better still, of transforming them into their opposite: the desire for greater sharing without the slightest precondition or restriction. It is through reason that absolute convergence between people is possible, and its deployment renders all

---

54 Alain Badiou, *D'un désastre obscur. Droit, État, Politique*, pp. 53–4.
55 *PT*, VI, 3, p. 64.

institutions and forms of authority superfluous, as under the guidance of reason people regulate their desires and behaviours such that their actions cannot fail to produce concord: 'In so far as men live under the guidance of reason, *to that extent only* do they necessarily do the things which are necessarily good for human nature and consequently for every single man; that is, which agree with the nature of every single man. So men also are necessarily in agreement in so far as they live under the guidance of reason.'[56]

The Balance of Institutions and Reason (to Obey or to Understand?)

'To that extent only . . .' is the caveat missed by those who fail to see that, by aspiring to a world beyond laws, they are also asking us to move beyond the passions. It is possible to be guided by reason but only to a very limited extent, and that margin determines our capacity to dispense with institutions. We have direct experience of the fact that it is possible to dispense with them to a certain extent. The social order does not hold up solely on account of the constant influence of its institutions, for no state can closely control and coerce *all* of its subjects. They comply with the law 'of their own accord': it would only take a small minority of the population to deliberately flout the law for the police and judicial apparatus, whose resources are limited, to be completely overwhelmed and incapable of containing a seditious movement of this kind. This 'spontaneous' compliance of course rests primarily on affects (passive affects, it must be said) wherein state norms are interiorised (into the superego, if one will).

Primarily, but not solely – for there is sometimes in obedience the trace of a dictate of reason that apprehends the chaos that would ensue if transgressions from which one refrains oneself were to become commonplace. Spinoza, who, in this respect, anticipates Kant's categorical imperative, demonstrates that 'the free man never acts deceitfully, but always with good faith', since 'if reason urges this [deceit], it does so for all men', heralding a complete collapse of trust and harmonious dealings between people.[57] However, one cannot exclude the possibility

---

56 *Ethics*, IV, 35, proof, pp. 171–2. My emphasis.
57 *Ethics*, IV, 72, p. 194.

that even the ignorant (the word Spinoza uses for those who have not attained wisdom – in other words, all of us) will sometimes comply with certain common rules, on account not of a heteronomous dictate but rather of a clear understanding. An example would be an understanding of the requirements for the stability of a commune in which we live and which we are keen to see persevere. We apprehend through reason what this entails in terms of regulating our behaviour. I will perform such and such a duty in the collective life of the commune because I have a clear and distinct idea that shirking my duty is an attitude that, were it to be adopted by others, would destroy my commune, which I am keen to see survive. It would be mistaken to believe that commune life is a bed of roses. As with all collective living, onerous obligations must be carried out, since a collection of individual desires does not contain in itself the recipe for complete harmony – there will be concessions to make, which require effort. And it is precisely the affective costs of these obligations – the effort of having to make concessions and assuming one's responsibilities – which corrode the cohesiveness of the horizontal collective and threaten its viability. We only overcome this sense of an obligation to be endured under the guidance of reason which, by affording us an intimate conviction, removes any affective constraint in the regulation of our behaviours. There is no regret in renouncing a personal desire nor fear of external sanction (from the group) or internal sanction (the sense of guilt), but, instead, a perfect understanding of what is required by the situation, which reason leads us to desire exclusively.

The proportion of reason in our actions thus indicates the degree to which we, the ignorant, can do without institutions, and it is limited. There will, of necessity, be institutions, in both senses of necessity. There will necessarily be some institutions as we do not have the capacity to lead our lives *entirely* under the guidance of reason (if we could, that would induce in us all the *exclusive* desire to find common cause with our fellow human beings and *nothing else* would be required to ensure the indefinite prolongation of harmonious collective living). And so we will need *something else* in addition, and that something else is institutions which will hold us to their norms through the passions – in other words, through the various forms of obedience. Are we condemned to 'swap one form of policing for another', in the words of Benny Lévy, which Ivan Segré understandably worries would sound the death knell for any prospect of political revolution?[58] How do we chart a course between the opposing rocks of denying the servitude to the passions (and the concomitant necessity for institutions) and caving in meekly to the reactionary impulse ('things will always be like this')? Once again, we can only do so by invoking the possibility of modification. Bodies, both individual and collective, are modifiable. This is the crux of 'critical realism' (people are like this today but tomorrow they could be different), and this additional temporal dimension involving a possible future rescues us from the antinomy of emancipation as wishful thinking and conservation as an embalming of the current state of affairs. Emancipation rigorously understood, consistent with all the aspirations to a life beyond laws, is the esoteric emancipation of Spinozan blessedness. Any form of exoteric emancipation, that is, any finite attempt at emancipation here and now, will necessarily fall short of this promise and will always be a work in progress rather than an endpoint – a process of modification in which we become active.

The Universal through the Particular (Recomposing Our Particular Interests to Render Them Capable of Universal Self-Transcendence)

The goal of true emancipation is a long way off (and even unattainable), which is all the more reason to embark along that path without delay. We will remain caught to some degree in the servitude to the particular, but we can vary that degree. And the universal, in the historical reality of its expressions, is no sacred revelation. It is more like a water lily: the flower on the surface is beautiful but its roots are plunged into the mud. The universal does not fall from the sky – it is less a bolt from above than something torn out of the turf, another way of saying that its genesis is immanent. The universal, which cannot emerge *ex nihilo*, is necessarily born in a milieu that is antithetical to it: the particular and the self-interested (in the narrow sense of the term). Concerning ourselves with the universal does not therefore entail abandoning materialism. Bourdieu, for example, incorporates into his sociological history of the scientific field the influence of self-interested passions but demonstrates

---

58 Segré, *Judaïsme et révolution*.

that the scientific endeavour can nevertheless still objectively hold out the promise of universal truths.[59] It is because they are sufficiently beholden to this collective affective structure, which Bourdieu calls a field, that scientists hold themselves to norms of truth. Their doubtless genuine attachment to the idea of truth might not suffice on its own to hold them to these norms under all circumstances, as suggested by the frauds that are perpetrated when the institutional conditions for scientific research deteriorate (excessive internal rivalries, corruption by external interests, a weakening of validation procedures, etc.). Similarly, Bourdieu shows how the (limited) universalism of the law and the serving of the 'general interest' is bound up in the specific worldly interests of jurists as a particular group. As with science, this can be seen as a further illustration of the fact that the universal does not emerge in radical antithesis to particular interested parties but in a certain configuration that reflects those specific interests and, at the same time, transcends them.[60]

The bonds of the universal and the particular are decidedly intricate, and this is ultimately because the universal is not, and could not be, *causa sui*: there are *historical* emergences of the universal from a substrate that is necessarily particular since, until proof to the contrary, the human world and its history is not a stage on which the universal is universally realised. Instead, the universal necessarily expresses itself through particular vehicles. Examples of this are legion in our cultural history: great works which capture something generically human and appeal to us in their generic humanity may appear to transcend the particular, but they are nonetheless produced within a particular context and a particular time and place. While Japanese puppet theatre and ikebana (the Japanese art of flower arrangement) have the potential to enchant anybody, whether Japanese or not, they remain Japanese art forms – realisations of the universal produced in Japan, with Japan as the particular vehicle of the universal. The same can be said of any other historically and geographically situated culture, every one of which has

---

59 Pierre Bourdieu, *Science of Science and Reflexivity*, trans. Richard Nice, Polity, 2004.

60 We should not get waylaid by ideological quarrels on this matter. The point is simply that we can identify a certain category (however imaginary and however dubious the actions carried out in its name) that captures the idea of serving something as a good common, conceptualised as transcending particular interests.

produced works, tales, myths and cosmologies that have the power to resonate directly with all mankind.

Just as the universal is engendered from the particular, but a particular that is suitably arranged to produce the universal, emancipation as a work in progress requires us to rework our own particular arrangements. Detesting institutions *in general* because our institutions are detestable in the here and now is the surest means of failing to see that the question of institutions per se is not *primarily* a matter of love or hate. It is also a failure to see that the question necessarily arises under the servitude to the passions, but that this does not mean that we will inevitably be crushed beneath these institutions. Rather, it is up to us to configure them differently in such a way as to increase their universal content, which is to say the intensity of universal feeling they can induce in us. Do they accentuate our particular interests, or instead render them capable of self-transcendence? Do they give rise to an environment conducive to the development of our reason, or do they bind our powers of desiring and imagining to particular objects (and to particularly inappropriate objects, such as commodities)?

The Institutional Biotopes of Virtue
(the Politics of the Universal)

It was no accident that Spinoza wrote the *Political Treatise* after the *Ethics*. In his mind, these two domains of philosophy – conventionally regarded as distinct – were intimately connected, since the individual's path to blessedness depends crucially on the collective environment. Why the urgent need to analyse political institutions, having just elaborated a philosophy of ethical wisdom? Precisely because wisdom does not alight on individuals like an act of grace. They have to strive arduously towards it (knowing they can never possess it entirely) amid all the ordinary passions of individual and collective life. A myriad obstacles constantly threaten to divert us from this road to wisdom, as Spinoza warns us in the very final line of the *Ethics*: 'All excellent things are as difficult as they are rare.'[61] These obstacles are the many potential channels for our desire that come from society. Society occupies us with

---

61 *Ethics*, V, 42, scholium, p. 223.

the question of how we are going to survive, and thus first and foremost converts our desire into a base desire for material reproduction (though, of course, we do need to survive before we can think about developing our reason). And society also saturates our minds with ideas of inferior joys such as the pursuit of money and vain glories that become 'firmly fixed' affects and absorb all our power to act.[62] What remains to develop our souls depends on the particular nature of the institutions amid which we live. There is no ethics without politics, since there is no ethical path that can be divorced from the environmental conditions through which it winds – such a path would be stateless, so to speak, and hence outside politics. The environment of ethical trajectories is politics, and so there can be no ethics that is not complemented by politics – ethical development is dependent on the political institutions that either encourage or hinder it.

Bourdieu has perhaps stressed more firmly than anyone the materialist character of a politics of the universal. Virtue cannot be an affair of virtuous injunctions to be virtuous, and we can be sure that appeals for virtuous altruism launched into the void will never have any effect. Indeed, they are liable to come across as tiresome sermonising from on high by people who are blithely unaware of how their privileged situation gives them a slightly broader access to the universal. If we wish, we can claim Rosa Luxemburg as a poster girl for internationalism, though we would do well to take account of all the elements in her personal history that are likely to have inclined her to transcend the limitations of a national perspective and embrace the international. A Pole by nationality, she was born into a Jewish lower-middle-class family in the heart of the Russian Empire and ultimately settled in Germany – all other things being equal, this background was surely conducive to her moving beyond a narrowly national point of view. We could (and indeed should) conduct a similar survey of the backgrounds of the champions of abstract internationalism, who generally possess a high level of education and cultural capital; will, at some point in their lives, have had a decisive experience of internationalisation; and are often fond of lecturing lesser (obtusely nationalist) people while remaining entirely oblivious to their own sociological privilege, which is to say all the particular conditions that have made it possible for them to move

---

62 *Ethics*, IV, 6, p. 158.

beyond the national perspective. Do those particular social circumstances continue to be the precondition for that perspective, and might an analysis of those circumstances detract from the virtue that is sometimes associated with self-serving internationalist postures? That would be to miss the point, since this is not a blame game. The purpose of analysing the context is to do away with moral judgements and to re-politicise the question: what are the social conditions for access to the universal, or, as Bourdieu puts it, how do we universalise the conditions of access to the universal? This is an entirely political affair since it involves conceiving of, and above all setting up, concrete biotopes of virtue (of the true type), whose chances of success will be better boosted by the quite demanding task of establishing appropriate institutions than by placing our faith in the miracle of intermittent 'events'.

When the common affect of the insurrectional moment, which is typically one of those extrinsic forces that induce intrinsic virtue, has abated, virtue becomes a political business of well-conceived institutions that prompt individuals to take the path of virtue. As we have seen, the institutions of science constrain scientists to scientific virtue just as much as their own desire for scientific truth (which undoubtedly exists but is fallible). Spinoza tells us that it is possible to 'have a true idea' (perhaps that *is* an act of grace . . .), for example the true mathematical idea that the sum of the angles of a triangle equals two right angles, and adds that, since true ideas follow from true ideas, we can formulate other true ideas using the one we were initially given and thus constantly increase the number of true ideas in our mind.[63] In the same way, we can say that a good institution has been given to us (we could take the scientific institution as an example) and that based on this model we can conceive of other good institutions, which is to say institutions that prompt us towards virtue in the sense of developing reason within us. This endeavour would take place under the guidance of knowledge of the second kind, that is, of common notions.[64] For these common

---

63 Baruch Spinoza, *Treatise on the Emendation of the Intellect*, 33, in *Ethics*, p. 240.

64 To speak merely of 'common notions' is insufficiently precise. We need to distinguish between notions that are 'common to all things' and (ideas of) 'that which is common and proper to the human body and to some external bodies' (see respectively *Ethics*, II, 38 and 39). The former generally possess a common attribute of substance. It is the latter which fall within the purview of a political philosophy of universality which seeks to identify 'that which is common' to human beings.

notions occupy, by definition, a realm beyond the imagined and ill-conceived particulars formed not by reason but by the 'fragmentary and confused' ideas of our particular complexions and our particular ways of feeling and judging.[65] In taking us beyond the realm of the particular, common notions are the cognitive vehicle of the universal and therefore, in political terms, the expression of what we *agree on*. If a 'good institution is given to us', we should create other good institutions based on the same template. Unless we are interested in the universalism of the pulpit, the true politics of the universal lies not in the self-serving discourse of the universal but in the construction of institutions that universally broaden access to the universal.

Historical Reflexivity as a Duty of Reason (Not an Exercise in Repentance)

There are, therefore, institutions that set us on the path towards that which Spinoza calls 'useful to us', namely 'that which we certainly know to be the means for our approaching nearer to the model of human nature that we set before ourselves'.[66] By contrast, we also know that there are institutions that distance us from it, such as mercantile institutions or, at another level, those that peddle the essentialist notion of the nation – they are the crystallisations of fragmentary and confused ideas of collective identity which root that identity in the particular and render its self-transcendence even less probable. The question of a particular identity is always couched in terms of the group's imaginary self-image, and moving beyond that particular identity, even partially, relies on converting those imaginary schemas into ideas of reason. And the group's relationship to its own past is especially revealing in terms of its universalising powers. Whereas the unconditional endorsement of a nation's entire history (crimes included!) is the very essence of the collective servitude to the passions, blindly dictated by the refusal of any restriction on the national *acquiescentia in se ipso* (the desire that nothing be allowed to impugn the group's self-esteem), repentance, although it involves at least some scales falling from our eyes, is still an affair of

---

65 *Ethics*, II, 40, scholium 2, p. 90.
66 *Ethics*, IV, preface, p. 154.

the passions (in this case, sad ones). As Spinoza reminds us, 'repentance is not a virtue, i.e. it does not arise from reason; he who repents of his action is doubly unhappy or weak.'[67] In contrast to the fierce refusal to engage in any kind of self-examination, which amounts to a virtually psychotic form of nationalism apt to proclaim that colonisation was a civilising influence and collaboration a reasonable form of resistance, the appropriate response is not the affective reflexivity of contrition but a historiographical engagement with a past reconstructed by reason.[68]

Why does the question of the past need to be posed? Because it is part of the effort of the mind to be 'highly conscious of itself and of God and of things', which is the very essence of our striving under the guidance of reason.[69] And how should the question of the past be posed? The answer is exactly the same as the answer to the 'why' question: if it is indisputably an advance on blind celebration and brute denial, the reflexivity of commemoration and repentance is no more than an internal correction to the regime of the servitude to the passions. Looking back at the past to repent of it serves no purpose except to 'correct' the joyful passions of an obtuse nationalism with sad and slightly more enlightened passions. But there is every point in looking back at the past through the eyes of reason in order to become more conscious of oneself, of what one has done and of what one will do – in other words, to enrich through rational reflexivity one's stock of adequate ideas. Though it is a necessity, examining history should not be motivated by the affects of contrition – it is something that should be dictated by reason.

Failing Better

By extension, it is also a necessity of the collective process of becoming active. Everyone should contribute to appropriate collective modifications, which would include: the conscious reappropriation of the past, the elimination of essentialist notions of identity, and the rational apperception of the requirements of collective living such that there is a reduction in the 'institutional content', legal burden and affective group

---

67 *Ethics*, IV, 54, p. 184.
68 Although it is probably necessary to pass first through a phase of sad repentance.
69 *Ethics*, V, 39, scholium, p. 221.

affiliations of collective life. These would be the first steps in forming the universal community of reason and reducing the national *acquiescentia in se ipso*, that manifestation of the individual ego writ large which arises from a perceived participation in the achievements of 'our country'. Rousseau did not have quite the same considerations in mind when he drafted a constitution for Corsica, but his advice to relinquish aspirations to national glory has a striking pertinence: 'The nation will not be illustrious but it will be content.'[70] Is weaning ourselves off toxic notions of national grandeur not an example par excellence of the tasks we face in converting political passions into conducts guided by reason? And is it not just what the doctor ordered, too, for even our most prominent internationalist intellectuals, in whom more than a trace of the national *acquiescentia in se ipso* affect shows through as they contemplate with affective pride 'what [their] country is sometimes capable of'? The fact that the 'French Revolution' was French is, or ought to be, of no consequence at all (other than for historiographical knowledge). But the urge, as always with passions, is stronger than we are, and irrelevant affective considerations can interfere with knowledge attained by the light of reason.[71] That thinkers who can hardly be accused of nationalism still fall into this trap supplies a strong a fortiori argument for the fact that we still have a long road ahead. The error consists in supposing ourselves already liberated from the servitude to the passions (which would be the only way of liberating ourselves from the need for institutions and the law). The only possible communism is a communism of reason. It is only when people are guided by reason that laws and institutions will, like useless religious relics, cease to matter.

But that is all a long way off (and, in truth, will never be entirely within our reach), so where does that leave us in the meantime? With a continuing need for laws and institutions, and the hope that we are setting off down a path that will lead to us needing them less and less. The question is whether emancipation is doomed to forever recreate that which it is seeking to emancipate us from. Indeed, we can state it more bluntly: is emancipation always doomed to fail? Yes and no. Yes, because the interplay of the passions makes it necessary (in both senses

70 Jean-Jacques Rousseau, 'Projet de constitution pour la Corse', in *Discours sur l'économie politique et autres textes*, GF Flammarion, 1990, p. 156.

71 *Ethics*, IV, 14, p. 161.

of necessity) for institutions, and consequently for authority, to be re-established. And no, because there is a trajectory of hope for emancipation. A trajectory of modification that reaches for the omega point of individuals becoming active; a trajectory characterised by a reduction in the authority-wielding institutions populating the landscape, and by the asymptotic extinction of the law. It was Beckett who furnished the maxim for this asymptotic trajectory: try again. Fail again. Fail better.

Conclusion
The Unresolved and Unending

Politics also has its elementary structures: the self-affecting of the multitude, which underpins the coherence of political bodies, and the *certa ratio*, the relationship between the parts that determines their particular character. Distinct finite groupings necessarily form into totalities which also have a distinct *form*. In the most general sense of the term, that is what a state is. These distinct finite ensembles are not essentialist communities but modifiable bodies. Their composition is determined by the *imperium*, the necessary exercising of the power of the multitude, which both underpins the coherence of social totalities and creates the conditions for capture. It is the resource for every form of authority, and that authority is always borrowed.

And What of Capital, Incidentally?

The reader may have been surprised to see so little mention of capital as a capturing agent. However, our focus has been on the general nature of capture rather than the diverse historical forms that it has assumed. Capital is a second-string capturing agent operating in the shadows (though not exactly unobtrusively) of the modern bourgeois state. Their destinies are closely interlinked but they are not one and the same thing. To the question 'How can we talk about the state without talking about capital?', the answer is that the 'state' implied is only a very particular type of state which does not encompass the general problem raised by the state, and still less the problem of what we have called the 'general state'. The latter has been the subject of this book, not the modern bourgeois state – the capitalist state par excellence. Had that state been our subject, it would indeed have made little sense not to talk of capital.

A social group only achieves the crushing dominance of capital by sticking as closely as possible to the state, which is the agent that captures 'this right which is defined by the power of the multitude' and ultimately holds all the levers of domination. Capital first established the foundations for its domination within the framework of the modern state, which furnished it with resources such as property law, free labour power (the insecure employee defined as a 'free worker'), and all the conditions for primitive accumulation. An establishment as brutal as capital's would have been inconceivable had it not piggybacked on the historical form of the state, which alone could endow it with the conditions for its enforcement and domination.

Nevertheless, capital could not anticipate the later developments of the class struggle which resulted, *within the political framework of the modern nation state*, in the creation of state welfare institutions that have regulated its domination. This is why we can *almost* equate the modern bourgeois state with the state of capital, but not entirely. On account of its relative autonomy, the state is not an entirely subservient handmaiden. And its internal organisation, especially but not solely its political institutions, always leaves open the possibility that its policies will lean in a direction that does not immediately align with the desiderata of capital. As the ultimate holder of the power of enforcement, the state is the condition of possibility of all institutional constructions and it exercises this capacity in one direction or another depending on the current balance of power, public policies being subject to the influence of various social groupings. This is why capitalism could only be regulated within the framework of an authentic political community, and that framework happens initially to have been the nation state. Regulated means institutionalised, and the building of institutions is only possible on the back of an existing *imperium*.

This is also why capital – which historically had a vested interest in the modern state in order to establish its *own* institutions (property law, the legal category of the 'free worker', etc.) but then appreciated that nation-state institutions could also act to thwart it – embarked on the vast shift known as 'globalisation'.[1] This involved redeploying itself in an international space characterised by the void of political sovereignty – in other words, the absence of constraining forces. The ends of capital and the modern bourgeois state do not perfectly coincide and so, having secured the institutional bedrock for its domination from the nation state, capital has had no hesitation in circumventing the state when it has ceased to meet its needs in full.

The relationship between the state and capital is fluid, as attested to by its ambivalent reconfiguration under neoliberalism. For, alongside the process of systematically moving beyond the reach of political sover-eignties, the contemporary domination of capital is also based on a new deployment of the powers of the state – the state is the general supervi-sor of the competitive order of the market, but it is also a vehicle for the value norms of capital to penetrate into every level of the social body.[2] In this new age of liberalism, the inclination has been to resist attaching the prefix 'ultra', since 'neo' better encapsulates its paradoxical nature: a liberalism with and even *through* the state rather than *against* the state. And yet, one should also have reservations over 'neo', as it suggests that the relationship between state and capital is merely a new form of alli-ance. But this new alliance contains its contradictions, and specifically the element of ultra-liberalism in neoliberalism. This can be seen in the strategic movement of capital interests beyond the spheres of sover-eignty and their redeployment in an international space where the void of public power guarantees the predominance of private powers, which are able to mass their forces in that void and in turn influence public powers.

To overlook this 'ultra' element in neoliberalism is to also overlook the fact that institutionalisation, and the creation of regulatory institu-tions in particular, is made possible by the power of enforcement of an established political sovereignty – an *imperium*. Capital's interests have not overlooked this fact, however, and are methodically engaged in neutralising such political authority. One example is the misguided European project to redeploy sovereignty on a continental scale, which

---

1 It is worth, however, highlighting a remarkable paradox: it was originally governments themselves which spearheaded the international deregulation (of markets for goods, services and capital) that characterises globalisation.

2 See Pierre Dardot and Christian Laval, *The New Way of the World: On Neoliberal Society*, Verso, 2014.

was happily (from the point of view of capital) stopped in its tracks once national sovereignties had been undermined.

'Historical logic' suggests that we should seek to reproduce at the international (European) scale the process which led capitalist nation states, under the pressure of the class struggle, to create regulatory institutions. But this, in turn, is to overlook the fact that it took a century and a half for this to come about *within politically established national frameworks* where the power of an established *imperium* was already available, whereas an international political community, which alone would be in a position to furnish the power to historically replicate this process, is still at the drawing board stage. And that is no coincidence: the 'ultra' component of neoliberalism is methodically working to prevent the emergence at this scale of any political framework with institutional power . . .

It also remains the case that we cannot expect much more from the institutions of the modern bourgeois state (even if they tried to counter the hollowing out of their power by neoliberal globalisation) than a simple attenuation or regulation of capitalist tendencies. And, indeed, regulation implies that the thing being regulated continues to exist, and there is no doubt that within this framework capitalism will continue to exist. Every political formation has its non-negotiable component since a political formation is also a way of living, and, by definition, a way of living will not tolerate a calling into question of the principles underlying it – in other words, we should not expect it to negate itself. There is therefore a certain logic in defining a political formation in terms of its non-negotiable component, and that is why 'capitalist' is an appropriate label for the modern bourgeois state: its non-negotiable component is the very bedrock of the capitalist order, namely the private ownership of the means of production (and all the social relations which accompany it). The 'democracy' in which political capitalism ostensibly cloaks itself is a lie when it proudly claims that it allows everything to be discussed and negotiated 'democratically'. The limits of its tolerance have been tested on several occasions in history and the procedures for peaceful deliberation have evaporated when that non-negotiable capitalist component is put on the table – violent military repression ensues. So, bearing in mind the caveats already mentioned, one may well conclude that the modern bourgeois state is indeed the state of capital and that to free ourselves of the domination of capital, we need to rid ourselves of the capitalist state.

But this cannot mean the state in general, since the presence or absence of the state in general is not an option at our disposal.

Horizontal? Really . . .?

People sometimes think that they can escape from subservience to a central government and from the rule of institutions and the law by returning to life in a local community, but it is an uncertain prospect. If returning to small community scales is a solution, it is only a partial one. And it may also be a selfish solution if it involves the illusion of a radical secession and if, incapable of seeing its autarchic project through to fruition, the community *also* survives as part of a larger ensemble in which it retains a vested interest and at the scale of which those same questions arise that it does not want to confront on the community scale. And if the community does address these questions at its own scale, having seemingly managed to relinquish its vested interest in the larger ensemble, a second potential error looms: the belief that, in its horizontality, the local community affords a small-scale model of a collective political form.

We would certainly need to take a closer look before accepting that this kind of community is as horizontal as it claims to be. If it is *genuinely* horizontal, it will be perpetually at the mercy of its internal affective instability and its life expectancy will be low. How many such communities have we witnessed breaking apart in chaos? If it lasts, on the other hand, that must be down to a hidden or unacknowledged verticality, such as a charismatic leader or a domineering guru, or alternatively the force of a common affect that induces an attachment to a certain way of living (which is also a vertical effect). Exceptional situations, states of war and insurrectional flare-ups have a mobilising power which seems to dispense collective life from any institutional regulation, with the collective united in its pursuit of a common goal. In the middle of its struggle, the Commune barely needed the police and 'Paris [was] running smoothly all by itself'. These exceptional situations are, by definition, states of intense affective polarisation. But the common affect can display its proto-institutional cohesive power outside these states, albeit at a lower level of intensity. This can be the case, for example, when it is the emanation of a way of living that is tightly defined, which is to say, selective: group cohesion is immediately produced by the new arrivals being predisposed to, and determined to adhere to, the explicitly and firmly stated principles of this particular way of living. A report on the Longo Maï community[3] contains a highly revealing, and indeed typical, remark in this respect: 'This place is not for everybody', declares one of the community members in no uncertain terms. And no doubt he is right, though those who champion tolerance and openness might nevertheless be somewhat shocked by a declaration that is difficult to interpret as anything other than a statement of exclusion. However, it has a certain legitimacy relative to *that* way of living, and it is practical, in that it makes clear that membership of the group is selective, which should guarantee the stability of the community without the need for a heavy institutional apparatus. In other words, we need to appreciate that these communities only survive by ensuring that they remain very homogeneous, and that they will struggle to tolerate diversity (which they are better placed to defend in words than in acts). So something additional is always needed: either institutions that enable the community to keep to a tolerable level the centrifugal forces of the conatus, or a much more rigorous and selective process of homogenising membership in advance so that the community can do without institutions. One may indeed take the path of living outside institutions, but only if desires are duly pre-vetted and pre-selected to conform to the norms of a way of living that aims to do without institutions. Whether under the auspices of formal institutions or not, there is no collective way of living beyond norms, which is to say outside the vertical.

Federal Verticality (a Pyramid Is Not Flat)

Local horizontal communities tend to deceive themselves as to the real reasons why they manage to endure (if they endure). But they are still more mistaken if they believe that their 'model' can be extrapolated and rolled out on a wider social scale. If verticality can arise even in small groups, what is a fortiori likely to happen with larger ensembles? The exceedance of the social and its immanent elevation is bound to manifest itself more clearly still. The promise of radical horizontality, already

---

3 Jade Lindgaard, 'La ferme des radicaux', *Mediapart*, 26 February 2015.

dubious at the local level, definitively goes up in smoke at this larger scale. We may grant that anti-state intellectuals do not on the whole make the mistake of striving for a society that is a very large horizontal community – their model tends to be a community of communities, or an association of associations. But, for a start, an association of associations has to stop somewhere – it will never encompass mankind as a whole. And, secondly, such an ensemble cannot be flat: by definition, a federal system of communes is a hierarchical pyramid structure. It is trivially true that the association that encompasses the other associations is of a higher rank, and thus verticality once again enters into the equation. Such an association is a state in every respect. The very fact that it is a totality means that it is an instance of the *imperium* – it is only through its self-affecting power that *this* multitude has assembled itself into *this* federal meta-association, which is to say into a certain political *form* as opposed to being a scattered collection of parts. Indeed, the very mention of the word 'federation' should be enough to dispel any horizontalist illusions, since a 'federation' is the name for an institutional structure, and an institution embodies the capture of the *potentia multitudinis* – it is the crystallised form of the *imperium*, which is to say a state. Even the Commune, which would hardly qualify as a monument to state centralism, saw itself as a state: when Édouard Vaillant addressed the Commune in 1871, he began by saying: 'When the state goes by the name of the Commune . . .'[4] Philosophies centred on the notion of moving beyond the state, or of the state withering away, will forever falter in the face of this brute fact: political forms (as opposed to scattered collections) only ever emerge through the morphogenetic effect of the power of the multitude, which produces a totality within a finite jurisdiction that is a particular realisation of the general state and is unavoidably prey, to a certain degree, to institutional capture.

There will necessarily always be something called a 'state', for that is the generic name we can give to any institutional apparatus emerging out of the *imperium*. The discussion only becomes interesting and relevant when we ask what form it will take (rather than wasting time on the forlorn chimera of the state first 'withering away'). Those with radical horizontalist aspirations will not be pleased to learn that the state will continue to exist and are likely to be ill-disposed to addressing the

---

4 Paris Commune, Session of 19 May 1871, *Mediapart*, 9 May 2017.

question of its form, but the question has the virtue of indicating certain practical and significant consequences of this state of affairs. Although capture, which is to say the existence of institutionalised political communities, is inevitable, the degree, intensity and form of this capture can vary. Although direct self-government, strictly defined, is impossible, it should nevertheless remain a legitimate concept in our mental landscape, not as an imagined configuration which we believe can be concretely achieved but rather as a guiding ideal. If our only choice in relation to institutionalisation is the form that it takes, the impossible ideal of self-government affords us a signpost to the direction in which we should be heading, and it also alerts us to the extent to which institutional capture is diverting us from that path.

Beware the Golem

One thing is certain, however: our productions slip from our grasp, at least partially. The products of our own collective power dominate us and are sometimes turned against us – we find the Hokusai wave crashing down on our heads. The category of commodity fetishism was developed by Marx specifically to analyse this scourge. Commodity fetishism is the central concept in a theory of generalised depersonalisation. The truth of the social is that the power of the multitude is forever engendering Golems, such as the state, currency, commodities and capital. These sometimes monstrous things are made in our own factories, or rather the factory of the social (since the social is more than just the sum of all our individualities), and as Marx observed, they can take on lives of their own and come to haunt us. Some end up dying out, but their death like their life is a process that eludes our control, most often taking the form of a new Golem emerging and killing off its predecessor, as, for example, capitalism did with feudalism.

We need to step back and view the phenomenon as a whole if we are to avoid being overcome by a fatalist sense of impotence, for, in spite of everything, the situation is not 'our' fault. Admittedly, the multitude is always busy self-affecting itself, but we are in the multitude. And, as the multitude is always already socialised and riven, it is different versions of 'us' operating within it and often in opposing directions, pursuing antagonistic desires and seeking to assert opposing values. As always, history will decide the outcome according to the law of the strongest powers, and some of these resolute movements will be crowned with success. But the concept of commodity fetishism should not lead us to suppose that the social world is a puppet show orchestrated entirely from the outside (by whom? God?), or that *nobody* has *any* role to play and that everything is *entirely* beyond our control. It has transpired that capitalism has ended up dominating even those who had historically contributed to its advent, imposing its systemic logic and weighing heavily on them and their successors, like a foreign power. But the same will be true of the next Golem. Let us suppose that the next one is 'ours', the post-capitalist Golem ('ours' being limited in this case to just one of the movements struggling within the multitude). Even if it is ours, it will be a big beast that is no more docile than the previous one and there is every chance that it will break loose and come back to haunt us.

The *Theses on Feuerbach* are a programme of thought and action for understanding why our Golems escape from our control and how to rein them in. That is the meaning of the injunction in the eleventh thesis to 'change the world'. Marx sees society as sunk in the abyss of religious alienation and begins by noting that this alienation is a form of self-alienation: society has done this to itself. He perceives the bigger picture of society becoming addicted to successive fetishes, with capital following on from religion. His aim is to understand the mechanism of fetishism so that we can definitively break its spell – that is what changing the world consists of. From this perspective, Marx, who is often and with good reason associated with the heretical tradition that begins with Democritus and is carried forward by Machiavelli and Spinoza, is *also* an heir of mainstream Enlightenment and its aspiration to a rational mastery of the world. He never doubts for a moment that we can reason with our Golems and bring them to heel, and one might even say that this is the ultimate point of his whole philosophy.

But can we ever entirely succeed in that enterprise? Not if we take seriously the notion of the exceedance of the social. Transposing the individual ideal of self-transparency onto society as a whole turns out be a doubly perilous operation. Firstly, because we have known at least since Freud that such transparency is a chimera, even at the level of the individual. Secondly, and more importantly, even if we granted this (false) premise as far as individuals are concerned, the formation of a group will necessarily entail the opacity of exceedance. Expressed in more direct language, if individuals do not have a very sound grasp of what they themselves are doing, what chance have they of knowing what they are doing as a group?

To Reappropriate Power or to Seek Happiness (Hilaritas)?

Despite this, we can detect the ideal of transparency when we hear claims that the object of politics should be for the multitude to 'reappropriate its own power' from which 'it has been separated' under the nation state. But do these statements really make sense, conceptually speaking? Is it conceptually possible for a political body to be separated from its own power?[5] If the power of a mode is the essence of that mode, existing 'separately' from its essence is logically absurd. Even in the most tyrannical of regimes, the multitude (of which the tyrant is a part) is always coextensive with its own power and, in accordance with the principle of integral immanence, always does what it can, no more, no less. With immanence, there is nothing kept in reserve and no unrealised additional potential. In other words, there is no sense in which it is *at fault*. The power of a body is measured strictly by what it has done and is doing at each instant, and the idea that it 'could have' done better means nothing: the past conditional, the tense of regret, does not exist in Spinozan grammar.

The fact that the multitude may arrange its body in such a way as to place the vast majority of its parts under the domination of the tiniest minority of its parts in no way implies that it has lost contact with its own power. Rather, it indicates that its power has been exercised to unbalanced and disharmonious effect, since only the ruling (or tyrannical) part of the body derives pleasure from it. For the political body as for the human body, *titillatio*, which only affects certain parts, is a regime of pleasurable affects that is much less powerful than *hilaritas*, which affects all of the parts; the human equivalent of political tyranny would thus be the inveterate womaniser who is completely at the mercy of his penis (the pop-psychology analogy with the 'tyrannical individual' is

---

5 As I have myself unwisely implied in the past (for example in certain passages of *La Société des affects*). I am grateful to Ariel Suhamy for drawing my attention to this point.

too anthropomorphic to be viable). Contrary to these notions of an authority that is separate from us, which only really make sense from the point of view of individuals who are excluded from that authority, the multitude cannot, by definition, be separated from its own power for that is its essence. Unfortunately, it can deploy that power, which is to say it can structure its body, such that its power is diminished, as is the case when it abandons itself to the institutional *titillatio*. This deprives many parts of the opportunity to exercise their own powers and to contribute better to the power of the whole. The multitude is not separated from its power but, amid the diversity of the institutional *configurations* of the political body, there are regimes of unequal power. And certain political bodies fix themselves durably into arrangements in which they can do very little, and their diminished power is reflected in the fact that they give themselves up, for example, to absolutist monarchy. They are capable of slightly more (though not much more) when they succeed in endowing themselves with parliamentary institutions, and they move to a regime of much greater power (or at least to a much more hands-on approach) when they embark on a project of self-government. The political body has no need to dream of 'reappropriating' its power (which conceptually makes no sense) – rather, it should be striving for happiness (*hilaritas*).

Disintermediation and Shifts in Habit

Striving towards political *hilaritas* therefore depends on the capacity of a body to disintermediate the expressions of its collective power. Institutions, which capture and crystallise the *potentia multitudinis*, constrain its field of expression: the power of the multitude no longer expresses itself dynamically and creatively in society but is mainly content to conform to the law and the rules. It no longer strives to express its power in new ways but rather acts to reproduce and sustain the (institutional) instruments which enforce its own conformity to social norms. Disintermediation can thus serve as an antidote to capture and above all to the diminishment of the power of the collective body, enabling it to invest its energies less in obeying and more in creating. That is precisely what the Communards had in mind: sustaining the highest possible degree of dynamism within their political body through disintermediation. 'People, govern yourselves through your public meetings and your press. Bring your influence to bear on those who represent you, who will baulk at nothing on the revolutionary path.'[6] And yet, even here, 'those who represent you' constitute an intermediate, and the aim is to reduce such intermediates to a minimum. Since it would not have been viable for the people to hold a permanent assembly, some form of delegation was clearly inevitable, but of what kind? The Commune's answer was very clear: it rejected both 'député'[7] (which as Rougerie points out was a 'word of the Empire'[8]) and 'représentant' (a parliamentary intermediate) and opted for the word *mandataire*.[9] Bestowing an imperative mandate that can be revoked is an example of how some degree of disintermediation can be achieved. And here is what the newspaper *Le Prolétaire* had to say about the captures of the Commune (for there were bound to be some), which it felt had already gone too far: 'Do not be hasty in judging and deciding in the name of the people and in its stead. Remain in your role of *simple delegates.*[10] Servants of the people, do not adopt the false airs of sovereigns. They do not become you any better than the despots whom you have dispossessed.'[11]

An imperative mandate is not merely a concrete institutional tool: it underlies a more general recalibration of the political ethos of subjects. But why the word 'subjects'? The reason is that they are no longer quite the same as simple voters, which is to say a subservient subject (*subditum*) most of the time and a political subject (*subjectus*) intermittently, when voting or mandating. An imperative mandate is a recalibration that produces political subjectivity – it is an institutional transformation that decreases the extent to which people are subservient subjects and increases the extent to which they are active subjects. Rougerie reports the terms in which a delegation of bakers responded to the Commune assembly after it abolished their night shifts: 'The people do not have to

---

6 Programme of the Nicolas-des-Champs Club, in Jacques Rougerie, *Paris libre 1871*, Seuil, 1971, p. 221.

7 [TN] The French equivalent of a member of parliament (MP).

8 Rougerie, *Paris libre*, p. 221.

9 [TN] Possible translations in this context are 'proxy' or 'delegate', but the important point is that the word conveys the notion of a person who holds a *mandate* (which can be bestowed and also revoked).

10 The editor's emphasis.

11 Cited in Rougerie, *Paris libre*, p. 221.

thank its *mandataires* for doing their duty; they would be derelict in not doing it. It is an irksome habit to express gratitude to them for taking a measure that it would have been remiss of them not to enact.'[12] One word here goes to the heart of what is at stake when it comes to the power of the collective body: 'habit'. It is through altering its habits that a political body can access a higher order of power. And those 'irksome' habits of deference and gratitude for what is merely our basic political due are the ones we need to break. These habits of servitude, perceived as 'normal', are the embodied fold of our dispossession, and the modifying power of the insurrectional event will be judged by the speed with which this inveterate fold is smoothed out. Adopting a different habit, that of the majority, and creating another fold, that of equality, is the key to the transition of the political body to a regime of increased power. Becoming a majority is the trajectory of a new and empowering habit. For, although conceptually speaking the multitude cannot be separated from its power, practically speaking, individuals (most of them) can indeed be divorced from authority through institutional capture. Dispossession is the miserable fate of being reduced to a minority. It is a fate that must be overcome.

The State That Refuses to Wither Away

Capture is a necessity that can be accommodated, since the servitude to the passions is not a uniform black hole. Who could deny that the Communards were caught up in it again? But equally, who could deny that they made some headway, even though they didn't see it through to the end? If truth be told, the Commune was a joyous ragbag of passions of the most varied and conflicting kinds. Jacques Rougerie paints a sympathetic picture of it but never allows his empathy to cloud his lucidity, describing the persistent patriotic fervour among the people of Paris, the excessive and somewhat puerile taste that officers in the National Guard developed for spurs and decorations on their uniforms, and the insurgents' hatred of their oppressors – the clergy, the landlords, the speculators, and the 'Auvergnats' who monopolised the coal supply. It would probably be safe to say that we are not in the presence here of the

---

12 Ibid., p. 222.

perfect realisation of the universal, but Rougerie also highlights their 'devotion to the Idea' (one could be forgiven for thinking one was reading Badiou).[13] This confirms once again that the universal is born of the passions and not of an immaculate conception . . . *E pur sorge*, one could imagine a modern political Galileo exclaiming: and yet it emerges! It emerges as best it can in a milieu that persists in thwarting it.

It is perhaps time to temper our grandiose dreams of horizontality, of universalism achieved and of a miraculous leap beyond the human condition and arrive at a more sober assessment of what a multitude is capable of *hic et nunc*. But we should not fall into the logical error of thinking that this more sober assessment is merely an endorsement of the current state of affairs. Rather, we should be aware that our project implies working to reduce the gap between the current state of affairs and our aspirations – a project involving collective empowerment and an increased majority, both of which remain entirely viable propositions.

Provided that it abandons its deluded pretensions to doing away with the state, the federalist-associative model can make a compelling case for itself and its central argument: that disintermediation and overcoming the separation from authority depend on subsidiarity. Subsidiarity is the precondition for maintaining small numbers, which in turn is the precondition for arriving at a close approximation of the synoptic condition, wherein the largest number of people are able to perceive the largest number of objects of common interest. It also obviates the need for an ever-increasing division of labour and hence avoids the excessive institutionalisation to which that inevitably gives rise. These are ways of neutralising the principal forces that lead to us losing control of our own productions. At the same time, we should be under no illusions: the complexity of social life on a large scale, the problem of goods that are not only common but also public, and the existing divisions of labour that we inherit are all obstacles to greater subsidiarity. Nor should we get carried away with the beautiful idea of the immanent and ascending process of delegation in associations of associations: this will inevitably create a (federal) pyramid, and that ascending movement will reverse itself and come back down on the delegates. But leaving unrealistic aspirations aside, the essential point remains: the more we succeed in

---

13 Ibid., p. 232.

organising ourselves locally, the less we will need to delegate organisation to higher rungs of the ladder.

And Affiliation, Too, Is Here to Stay

Just as we can never entirely do away with the state, affiliation too is here to stay, even though it is seen as a parochial scourge by universalists who rather overestimate the chances of achieving genuine universalism. The common affect produces affiliation *by its very nature*. Regardless of its form, a social totality – commune, federation, central state or other – which is only held together by a common affect necessarily produces affiliation. Only a grouping of people guided by reason, synchronised and brought into agreement by reason, could aspire to 'unbinding' and to a genuine release from community imperatives, which are, by definition, founded on affective bonds. There is a significant tautology here: to form a collective without affiliation, which is to say outside of affective bonds, one needs to have emancipated oneself from the servitude to the passions. But does reason not lead us to conclude that the universal application of reason is itself an unreasonable proposition? And there is also an attendant tautology: if political forms and enduring collectives do exist that have been stabilised in a certain configuration, rather than remaining an amorphous soup of individuals, this is because common affects have bound them *into a certain affiliation*. The shrinking of scales, subsidiarity and a privileging of the local do not alter this fact – Longo Maï is not for everybody and the Commune was not for the Versaillais (unless they agreed to become Communards, in which case they would of course have been welcome). And, indeed, the very notion of converting to a community surely implies affiliation – an affiliation to be espoused.

Some emancipatory thinkers believe they have left affiliation behind by rejecting the dominant and *current* fault lines of affiliation, namely national affiliation. But merely tracing new lines does not amount to eradicating fault lines. A fault line that differs from the current fault lines nevertheless remains a fault line. Even if we redefine the community by admitting individuals previously excluded on the basis of the former criteria of (national) affiliation, we are simply modifying the constituency, rather than emancipating ourselves from the principle of a constituency. In other words, we are merely producing a new type of affiliation. The 'Universal Republic' was an affiliation intensely felt by its French, Polish and Russian members in opposition to the Versaillais. The Paris Commune saw itself as an enduring political entity and specified its own constituency so clearly that it explicitly rendered problematic its potential future relations with its counterparts (the other Communes) and with the country as a whole, from which it had no intention of separating itself. In other words, it was acutely aware of questions of distinct identity and inclusion, which is to say the dynamics of affiliation; a very long way from claiming emancipation from affiliation or subscribing to illusions of a universalism encompassing all of mankind.

'How Anarchists Abuse the Word Sovereignty'

It comes as no surprise – though, as we will see, it gives rise to some remarkable historical paradoxes – that contemporary debate on emancipation descends into aporia by framing the question in terms of sovereignty, which is unequivocally equated with state rule and the traditional nation. By implying that sovereignty is an apology for the nation state, certain thinkers on the left have lost sight of the fact that sovereignty is not only their historical inheritance but also their actual object of desire, lexical niceties notwithstanding. Conceived in its purest form, sovereignty is nothing other than the process of *deciding jointly*, and is thus the very essence of reappropriation. To declare that we intend to decide jointly is to declare that our collective is sovereign – it is a realisation of the principle of sovereignty.

Conceptually speaking, sovereignty is not synonymous with the nation state, even if at present the nation state is the dominant historical expression of sovereignty; what we can do is to redefine the nation as a sovereign community. This is a tautological definition, but it is productive in that it captures the contributory nature of the nation. A nation conceived in these terms is a collective that is regulated not by a principle of essentialist affiliation but by a principle of *participation* – participation in a way of living. From this perspective, sovereignty is defined not by a pre-existing collective identity but by the common affirmation of political objectives. It is this affirmation of principles, in itself the affirmation of a way of living, that *creates* a community by inviting all who identify with those principles to join the community and to contribute to it: to belong to it by contributing to it.

In its own way, Chiapas affords perhaps one of the best contemporary illustrations of this logic. Chiapas is a nation. But it is a nation that has gone beyond its indigenous origins to reach the stage of a nation 'for itself': a nation that has achieved national consciousness by the explicit (sovereign) affirmation of its political principles, which, *in themselves*, transcend former nations (the nation 'in itself') whose coherence depends on an essentialist perception of their origins. None of this involves abolishing the nation or affiliation, but it does profoundly reconfigure them. It is a reconfiguration that represents an advance of reason since it expresses a greater consciousness as well as a liberation from the affective illusions of mythical (and mythically reconstructed) pasts, replacing them with a more self-aware affirmation of the community's principles. It is not an essentialist nation but a political nation.

And, when one reflects on it, that is precisely what sovereignty is. Needless to say, actual historical situations never let us see these concepts in their purest form – we only glimpse them when there is an alteration in their concrete historical realisations. In reality, the landscape of sovereignty, which tends to be reduced to a single notion of *the* sovereign, is more complex, fragmented and can operate on multiple scales. There is partial sovereignty at every scale, though to varying degrees depending on what is tolerated by the upper level of the overall sovereign structure. There is not so much a sole locus but something more like an architectonic of sovereignty, composed of partial local sovereignties configured hierarchically (a federation or association of associations is founded on a hierarchical principle), with the tip of the pyramid enjoying relative pre-eminence. Just as the question is not the disappearance of the state but the nature of its forms, so (and this is in fact the same thing) the debate on sovereignty should be about the forms it takes, which is to say the relationship between its various levels: to what extent does the upper level appropriate the governance of social life, what arrangements for subsidiarity does it make, what forms of delegation does it entail, etc.? In other words, how is the responsibility for joint decision-making shared out? It may be a multi-level and fragmented landscape, but it forms a finite and distinct totality. This is why, although conceptualising the 'commons' affords the possibility of the renewal of political configurations, it is a mistake to believe it will 'solve' the problem of sovereignty. And it would be a still greater mistake to suppose that we have thereby done away with the state – it is that same old error of refusing to acknowledge its necessity (and the contingent variety of its forms). Whether we call them *consociationes*, associations, going concerns or commons, these local entities will not survive if they do no more than establish unstable and reversible contractual relations among themselves. They need to form a coherent entity on a higher level which, by bringing them all together, caters to the social life of the ensemble.

If, as Freud said, 'to give ground on words is to give ground on one's desire', it would be injudicious to repudiate the vocabulary of sovereignty – especially if we take the trouble to rediscover the fundamental meaning of the word, which has nothing to do with a state prerogative but rather is the very principle of democracy in the highest sense. The Communards, whose historic insurrection has been attracting ever more intellectual and political attention of late, had no such qualms: the word sovereignty is an integral part of their discourse and indeed the most explicit statement of their rejection of servitude to the state. It is a remarkable paradox to see an uprising in which one has rightly identified anarchist aspirations constantly cloaking itself in the language of sovereignty. 'I've been as active as possible in associations . . . In politics, I want the widest possible sovereignty of the people,' declares a carpenter named Brousse.[14] It is 'the sovereign power [of the people of Paris], of whom the Commune is only the executive agent' which Lefrançais invokes in opposing the Committee of Public Salvation, seeing in it the threat of alienation.[15] The programme of the Nicolas-des-Champs Club 'asserts the sovereignty of the people, who must never abandon their right to oversee the acts of the *mandataires*'. The people of the Commune deeply identified with the French Revolution, were conscious of being its direct heirs and determined to perpetuate its legacy. For all that Rougerie warns us of the dangers of anachronism, he himself concedes the similarities ('albeit inexact, deformed and distant, but present nevertheless') between 'that old well of sans-culotte anarchism' and the

14 Rougerie, *Paris libre*, p. 234.
15 Ibid., p. 223.

spirit of the Commune, noting that the Girondist Vergniaud 'complained about how the *anarchists* abused the word sovereignty'.[16] Anarchists abusing the word 'sovereignty' . . . The phrase strikes a chord today, and one can only hope that the true sense of the word will finally be rediscovered.

Irresolution

To employ the word sovereignty is not to endorse the confiscated form that we are used to seeing in the modern state, which is a disfigured form since its capture by such an apparatus is the very negation of sovereignty. However, given the necessity of captures of the *imperium*, this negation is our condition. And it is a condition that we reject. This is where the battleground of a lucid politics of emancipation lies: between necessity and the rejection of necessity.

In other words, it fundamentally involves a *tension*, which is the condition of any politics that does not hold out the illusory promise of definitive resolution. Were it to aim for such a resolution, there would in all likelihood come a moment when it decisively fails, since conflict is one of the necessary properties of the social under the regime of the servitude to the passions – 'in so far as men are assailed by affects that are passive, they can be contrary to one another.' People can of course be otherwise and agree with one another, but the fact remains that they can also be contrary. Above and beyond merely interpersonal disputes, this divergence can arise along collective lines and assume varying forms, such as class, religious or identity-based conflicts. Though probably never predominant (otherwise there would be only chaos), divergence can never be completely eradicated either, and is forever poised to erupt again in other forms. Unless we are living under the guidance of reason, nothing can ever pacify definitively this conflict which is inherent to the servitude to the passions – indeed, conflict could be characterised as the perpetual motion of history.

We must contend, then, with a conflict that we will forever fail to resolve, the project of emancipation consisting therefore of 'failing better'. For at the end of the anti-institutional line of flight lie new

---

16 Ibid., p. 224. Rougerie's italics.

institutions. After existing authorities have been deposed, new
authorities emerge, sometimes in the perverse form of tinpot identity-
based dictatorships loudly claiming to have superseded the state. Such
entities need only look in the mirror to appreciate that *they* are the state.
On other occasions these new authorities assume the familiar traditional
form of before, and can be a source of particular despair – a case of
failing again, rather than failing better. And sometimes our efforts are
rewarded by improved forms consisting of less capture, a greater
autonomy at grassroots level and a broader distribution of sovereignty,
but equally consisting of the state, the law and the police (the mere
mention of which will doubtless be interpreted as an endorsement of the
status quo by those too intellectually lazy to think this crucial question
through). However, there will perhaps be less law, fewer police and fewer
institutions. As ever, it will still be the state but in a different, better form
that represents a genuine milestone along the interminable path towards
a more harmonious way of living guided by a greater degree of reason.

The striving towards the universal remains a dialectical process.
Neither sacred revelation nor *causa sui*, it only ever emerges from the
particular, though admittedly a particular arrangement that is structured such that it has the potential to transcend itself. But the universal
is of necessarily impure extraction, for there is an inherent paradox in
the transition from the particular to the universal. A community that
achieves a degree of universalism necessarily does so by distinguishing
itself from the particular, its very distinctness endowing it by definition
with a particular character ... The paradox of the transition to the
universal is that it emerges from the particular, and, like all particular
entities, the community aspiring to the universal first *sets itself apart as
distinct* and may then enter into a struggle with other entities. The struggle for universal equality, for example, will first have to battle the particular entity of inegalitarian capitalism. And the universalism of reason
necessarily comes into conflict with particular religious entities, and in
so doing will behave like a particular entity itself. In the transitional
phase before it comes to reign universally, the universal is thus another
particular entity that sets itself apart in a landscape of other particular
entities. Developed by Étienne Balibar, the idea that democracy has
historically been enacted through the institution of the border is the
classic illustration of this paradox in the transition to the universal. In
order to establish its reign of equality (in principle, if not in practice),

democracy required the border, which institutionalises inequality. Equality as a universal aspiration thus emerges out of its exact opposite, which is to say discrimination.

Attempts to supersede the state lead to the reconstitution of the state, and equality is founded upon inequality: under the regime of the servitude to the passions, the politics of emancipation is doomed to experience these terrible ironies. Such contradictions are necessarily the natural element through which it must navigate, and it must acknowledge these contradictions since they do not admit of any Hegelian *Aufhebung*. One is reminded of Lacan's celebrated rejoinder in 1969, seemingly intended to raise the hackles of the students of Vincennes: 'As revolutionaries, what you are aspiring to is a master, and that is what you will get.' But, as Ivan Segré points out, it is one of those quotes that has passed into posterity only in truncated form. Lacan in fact went on to add: 'I'm with you.'[17] We need to be in possession of the complete message in order to attain a measure of lucidity regarding the possibilities of emancipation: you are trying to rid yourself of the master, but you will create a new form of control – *and yet it is worth fighting for*. That is the decisive clause, which eschews the stance of resigned conservatism that is all too ready to endorse the current state of affairs. It is an injunction to continue pushing forward in the confident hope that the new forms of control will not be identical to those that preceded them. The master will rise again, but the extent of their mastery will have been altered and perhaps diminished. Admittedly, this is progress of a less exhilarating kind than dreams of the dawn of the social revolution or of the enlightened individual guided solely by reason. But, perhaps, such progress is more durable, as we will not have to experience the ardent fire burning itself out and the return to the embers of the everyday.

Lacan's remark in full tells us something else, too, or at least we can interpret it as such: that there is a stubbornness in our desire to struggle and to emancipate ourselves from everything that contradicts that desire, even if we may sometimes despair of the task. And, of course, we will also see what people actually do when it comes to the crunch. Who will stay at home, and who will take to the streets if history affords us a new opportunity? Who has come to terms with the capitalist nation

---

17 Jacques Lacan, *Le Séminaire XVII. L'envers de la psychanalyse*, Seuil, 1991, p. 234, cited in Segré, *Judaïsme et révolution*.

state and derives comfort from it, and who has declared it to be an irreconcilable enemy? Who resigns themselves out of contentment with the way things are, and who resolutely keeps on trying?

There exists a middle ground between the anarchist's waking dream and the simple abdication of the struggle, and that middle ground arises from the possibility of modification. Modification is emancipation operating within a context of tension. It requires perseverance, since we cannot hope to triumph *completely*. And that is the nature of the tension: keeping our revolutionary desire alive while eschewing revolutionary illusions, and seeing things as they are without surrendering to the current order. The tensions of emancipation will always remain unresolved, and the task of coming to terms with them is literally unending. There is no refuge or consolation to be found in the hope of a dialectical resolution, and no green and sunlit upland of definitive emancipation where, after an arduous uphill climb, we will finally be able to rest in peace. Politics is an ever-recurring confrontation with irresolution, since the only genuine resolution would be the communism of reason, and that is out of our reach. It is an eternal struggle against a state that is forever re-emerging. Like all politics, the politics of emancipation will never end.

Index